Acts and Shadows

The Vietnam War
in American Literary Culture

Philip K. Jason

ROWMAN & LITTLEFIELD PUBLISHERS, INC.
Lanham • Boulder • New York • Oxford

ROWMAN & LITTLEFIELD PUBLISHERS, INC.

Published in the United States of America
by Rowman & Littlefield Publishers, Inc.
4720 Boston Way, Lanham, Maryland 20706
http://www.rowmanlittlefield.com

12 Hid's Copse Road
Cumnor Hill, Oxford OX2 9JJ, England

Copyright © 2000 by Rowman & Littlefield Publishers, Inc.

British Library Cataloguing in Publication Information Available

Library of Congress Cataloging-in-Publication Data

Jason, Philip K., 1941–
    Acts and shadows : the Vietnam War in American Literary culture / Philip K. Jason.
        p. cm.
    Includes bibliographical references and index.
    ISBN 0-8476-9956-0 (alk. paper) — ISBN 0-8476-9957-9 (pbk. alk. paper)
    1.   American literature—20th century—History and criticism. 2. Vietnamese Conflict,
    1961–1975—United States—Influence. 3. Vietnamese Conflict, 1961–1975—Literature
    and the war. 4. Soldiers' writings, American—History and criticism. 5. War stories
    American—History and criticism. 6. War poetry, American—History and criticism. 7.
    Vietnam—In literature. I. Title

    PS228.V5 J37 2000
    810.9'358—dc21
                                                                99-051308

Printed in the United States of America

♾™ The paper used in this publication meets the minimum requirements of American
National Standard for Information Sciences—Permanence of Paper for Printed Library
Materials, ANSI/NISO Z.39.48–1992.

Contents

Acknowledgments and Credits

I am grateful to the editors and publishers of the following publications in which portions of this work, in somewhat different form, originally appeared:

Sections of the introduction to this volume are adapted from my introduction to *Fourteen Landing Zones: Approaches to Vietnam War Literature*, published by the University of Iowa Press, © 1991 University of Iowa Press, and are used with permission.

Sections of the introduction and chapter 10 are derived from materials under copyright to Salem Press, Inc., and are used by permission. These are: introduction to *The Vietnam War in Literature: An Annotated Bibliography of Criticism* (Pasadena, Calif.: Salem Press, 1992); essay-review on Bruce Weigl's *Song of Napalm. Magill's Literary Annual 1989* (Pasadena, Calif.: Salem Press, 1989); essay-review on John Balaban's *Remembering Heaven's Face: A Moral Witness in Vietnam. Magill's Literary Annual 1992.* (Pasadena, Calif.: Salem Press, 1992). © 1992, 1989, 1992 respectively by Salem Press, Inc.

The following publications will be recognized as early versions of chapters in the present study. I am thankful to the respective editors for giving these arguments their original homes:

"Sexism and Racism in Vietnam War Fiction." *Mosaic* 23.3 (Summer 1990).

"Vision and Tradition in Vietnam War Fiction." *America Rediscovered: Critical Essays on Literature and Film of the Vietnam War*, ed. Lorrie Smith and Owen W. Gilman, Jr., New York: Garland Publications, 1990.

"'How Dare She?' Susan Fromberg Schaeffer's *Buffalo Afternoon* and the Issue of Authenticity." *Critique: Studies in Contemporary Fiction* 34.3 (Spring 1993).

"Becoming the Other." *Viet Nam Generation* 6.3-4 (1995).

"Vietnam War Themes in Korean War Literature." *South Atlantic Review* 61.1 (Winter 1996).

"'The Noise Is Always in My Head': Auditory Images in the Literature of the Vietnam War." *The Midwest Quarterly* 37.3 (Spring 1996).

"Representations of War in Ethics Education." *JGE: The Journal of General Education* 46.2 (1997).

"Vietnamese in America: Literary Representations." *Journal of American Culture* 20.3 (Fall 1997).

Grateful acknowledgment is also made to the following poets and publishers for permission to quote from materials held in copyright:

Douglas Anderson: "Infantry Assault" from *The Moon Reflected Fire,* published by Alice James Books, © 1994 by Douglas Anderson. Reprinted by permission of the author.

John Balaban: Excerpt from "Mr. Giai's Poem" from *Locusts at the Edge of Summer* published by Copper Canyon Press, © 1997 by John Balaban. Reprinted by permission of the author.

W. D. Ehrhart: Excerpts from "Night Patrol" from *To Those Who Have Gone Home Tired: New and Selected Poems*, published by Thunder's Mouth Press, © 1984 W. D. Ehrhart; "Second Thoughts" from *Just for Laughs,* published by Vietnam Generation, Inc., © 1990 W. D. Ehrhart; *Vietnam-Perkasie* published by Zebra Books (by special arrangement with McFarland & Company), © 1983 W. D. Ehrhart; *Going Back: An Ex-Marine Returns to Vietnam*, published by McFarland & Company, © 1987 W. D. Ehrhart. All reprinted by permission of the author.

Robert Graves: "Hate Not, Fear Not" from *Poems About War*, published by Moyer Bell, Kymbolde Way, Wakefield, RI 02879. Reprinted by permission of Moyer Bell.

Wayne Karlin: Excerpt from *Lost Armies*, published by Henry Holt, © 1988 by Wayne Karlin; "Meeting," originally published in *Poet Lore* (Spring 1994), © 1994 by Wayne Karlin; from *Rumors and Stones: A Journey*, published by Curbstone Press, © 1996 by Wayne Karlin. All reprinted by permission of the author.

Gerald McCarthy: Excerpt from "The Sound of Guns" from *War Story*, published by The Crossing Press, © 1977 by Gerald McCarthy. Reprinted by permission of the author.

Walter McDonald: Excerpt from "After the Noise of Saigon," reprinted from *After the Noise of Saigon* (Amherst: University of Massachusetts Press, 1988), © 1988 by Walter McDonald. Reprinted by permission of the publisher.

Perry Oldham: "War Stories" first appeared in *Nexus* (Winter 1976) and was reprinted in W. D. Ehrhart. ed., *Carrying the Darkness: American Indochina—The Poetry of the Vietnam War,* published by Avon Books (1985), © 1976 Perry Oldham. Reprinted by permission of the author.

Basil T. Paquet: "Night Dust-Off" first appeared in *Winning Hearts and Minds*, ed. Jan Barry, Basil T. Paquet, and Larry Rottman, published by 1st Casualty Press (1972), © 1972 Basil T. Paquet. Reprinted by permission of the author.

Bruce Weigl: Excerpts from "Song of Napalm," "Girl at the Chu Lai Laundry," "Surrounding Blues on the Way Down," "Snowy Egret," "The Way of Tet," "Song for the Lost Private," "The Soldier's Brief Epistle," "Him, On the Bicycle," "LZ Nowhere," "Temple Near Quang Tri, Not on the Map," "Burning Shit at An Khe," and the last seventeen lines of "Dialectical Materialism" from *Song of Napalm,* published by the Atlantic Monthly Press, © 1988 by Bruce Weigl. Excerpt from "Noise" from *The Monkey Wars,* published by University of Georgia Press, © 1985 by Bruce Weigl. All reprinted by permission of the author.

Bruce Weigl and Thanh T. Nguyen, trans.: "Remembering Past Love" and "Tenth Night of the Moon" reprinted from *Poems from Captured Documents*, selected and translated by Thanh T. Nguyen and Bruce Weigl (Amherst: University of Massachusetts Press, 1994), © 1994 by University of Massachusetts Press. Reprinted by permission of the publisher.

Billy Joel: Excerpts from "Goodnight Saigon," © 1981 by JoelSongs. All rights reserved. Used by permission.

I am most thankful to the United States Naval Academy, the Naval Academy Research Council, and the members of the Nimitz Library staff for many acts of assistance over the years. Without such support, this book would have not been possible.

Introduction

In 1966, as the United States built up its forces in Vietnam, I took my first full-time college teaching position. This was at Georgetown University, in the nation's capital, where a year earlier I had completed a master's degree in English and American literature. In the intervening year, I had finished most of my Ph.D. course work and become a father. Safely removed from any risk of being drafted, both as a household head and an educator, I maintained the most low-level awareness of the war raging in Vietnam. I opposed it on convenient principles, as did my colleagues and students.

Though we held classes minutes from the White House, the State Department, and the Pentagon, very little about the war contaminated our classes. Sure, we would see posters on the front of the S.D.S. chapter headquarters. Sure, the Reverend McSorley was a high-profile antiwar activist. But these were fringe characters in our play of education and professional advancement.

For seven years, through the heart of the war, students passed through my classes and out into graduate schools—only a small handful ever seeming to be headed for Vietnam. In 1971, I finally had a dissertation approved and earned my doctorate from the University of Maryland. Two years later, having battled a much tougher job market than existed in the mid-sixties, I moved on to a very different type of school. As a faculty member at the United States Naval Academy, the all-but-ended war in Vietnam now had my attention, as it held that of my students and their military instructors, many of whom had served there. I wondered how I had managed to be so oblivious. I still wonder. By 1975, with Saigon evacuated and American troops safely removed from Vietnam for the better part of two years, I joined others in letting go of my slim connection to the war's reality. It took another ten years for me to find myself being drawn into the war in its literary, cultural, and historical dimensions.

There were intermediate steps, such as witnessing James Webb's brief and somewhat notorious sojourn on our faculty. Webb's presence and authority, both as a writer and a decorated veteran, set something stirring inside of me. I exchanged few words with the man, but he seemed a shadowy exemplar of experiences I had not known and knowledge I could only gain secondhand. Moreover, working in a military environment, I found that the war—even as its chronological boundaries receded—was never far from the kind of awareness that casual conversation gives to contemporary historical events.

But it was a book of poems that changed my professional life, initiating a rearrangement within that system of values, goals, actions, and even memories that define my stance as an educator, a critic, and a citizen. Bruce Weigl's second full-length collection, *The Monkey Wars*, published in 1985, hit me with the force of an explosion. I came upon Weigl's work as a reader and lover of poetry, not as a student of the literature of the Vietnam War. Within a few months, the need to come to terms with the war and its representations—perhaps to come to terms with the war *through* its representations—became a thirst that has never been slaked.

Though much important literature of the Vietnam War—including some of Webb's—preceded Weigl's, neither I nor my colleagues knew or cared much about it. Trailblazing books on the war's literature had already appeared, but I had paid no attention to them. My colleagues thought it odd when, in the fall of 1986, I requested travel money to give a paper on Vietnam War poetry at the Popular Culture Association meeting in Toronto the following spring. But what I discovered at that meeting was a large number of scholars hard at work exploring the war's impact on American culture—and American culture's shaping of the war. I was, in 1987, a latecomer to a field that a year or two earlier I didn't even know existed. The PCA had several sessions each day on matters relating to the war, mostly literary representation. The participants were older professionals for whom war literature was an established interest, Vietnam veterans who had entered academic life, and younger scholars who in many cases were drawn to their father's or older brother's war. Unexpectedly, many of the participants were (and are) women. My first paper was a poor one, so naive was I about the subject, but it was a beginning.

Since that 1987 PCA meeting, I've been a steady worker in this dynamic field of inquiry. My courses regularly offer Vietnam War texts, and on occasion I've taught special offerings on the literature of the Vietnam War. By contributing articles to journals and essay collections, I have engaged with other scholars in building a critical discussion of the war's literary representation. The present effort attempts a synthesis of my older and newer observations on the literature of the Vietnam War and of the war's aftermath. The unity I seek is the unity of the process itself, which I hope has not been revised away.

II

Because the Vietnam War is a living memory for thousands of men and women who participated in it, who witnessed it from near or far, or who otherwise felt its impact on their lives and on their cultural environment, the imaginative responses to the war are still being written. Even as the critical enterprise has traveled a long way toward giving the large body of creative works already in print an initial winnowing and judgment, new novels, stories, poems, plays, and memoirs alter the literary landscape. Thus, while the creative "field" is not fully sown, the critical harvest is already abundant and rich. The present work follows on the heels of many distinguished predecessors.

Like its predecessors, this exploration is immediately limited by the changing shape of the field, though enough years have now passed that the shape changes more and more slowly even as new texts interact with those that have come before and with the solidifying critical positions. Present cultural considerations include the positing of a post-Vietnam era, an era defined in part by a reevaluation of the cultural certainties of pre-Vietnam myth. That is, the business of "lessons learned" is still unfolding: lessons learned about nationalism, Communism, democracy, technology, purpose, moral principle, warfare, heroism, masculinity. As a label for cultural historians, "post-Vietnam" is likely to have a life beyond the twenty-five years from war's end to century's end.

The imaginative literature of the Vietnam War, broadly defined, participates — whether overtly or covertly, consciously or unconsciously — in a struggle for the national memory. Through interaction with these imaginative works, readers individually and the society as a whole will most likely come to an understanding — a gradually built and deeply ingrained consensus — of the place and meaning of the Vietnam War in the American experience. Critics, as they raise the banner of one or another work and offer responses to artistic endeavor, participate in this struggle as well. Debate over how the war should be taught, which works should be canonical in Vietnam studies, and which works will find a place in the canon of American literature is obviously connected to that struggle for the national memory.

Even esthetic discussion can have a political bias. Genre, structure, and style make a difference not just in our pleasure or appreciation but in the ways we absorb the issues that literature addresses. Literature makes things happen inside readers. What lasts — what becomes part of future generations' required reading lists — is accommodated to an ongoing definition of American values and American myth. At the same time, what is newly absorbed becomes a new factor in the mythic equation.

One of the more notable characteristics of post-Vietnam fiction is the lodging of the veteran's story and psyche within the evolving genre of the hard-boiled detective novel. As we shall see, representative texts provide material for exploring the nexus of pre- and post-Vietnam genre conventions and the cultural burdens that they bear. A more recent motif is that of the veteran's return to the land that was the crucible of his youth.

Critics have raised a wide range of questions about particular works and about the growing body of Vietnam War literature. Some have searched for the distinctive features, both in vision and technique, that separate this literature from other contemporary writing or from the literature of other wars. This inquiry has been conducted on the most general level and also within the various genres. Students of fiction, nonfiction, poetry, and drama have examined how the major themes, experiences, and understandings regarding United States involvement in Vietnam extend or reshape genre boundaries. They have also argued the relative success of each genre in expressing the essential truths of what is too tritely labeled the "Vietnam experience."

Among the genre issues is a concern among critics with erasing the conventional distinction between fiction and nonfiction, especially autobiography. Indeed, the concern goes back to authors like Michael Herr, John Sack, W. D. Ehrhart—and to their publishers. Each of these writers (but not only these) has created autobiographical works that have come very close to being offered as novels. More recently, Albert French's *Patches of Fire: A Story of War and Redemption* (1997) has come to us, according to the book jacket, as "the very personal story of French's trials and triumphs." Oddly, *Patches of Fire* is officially categorized, in the Library of Congress Cataloging-in-Publication Data, as a work of fiction.

While this issue of an encompassing genre of narrative has a life outside of interest in Vietnam War fiction, the literature of the war and the commentaries on it have focused and amplified the problem. The suggestion is often implicit, and sometimes explicit, that when it comes to war stories—at least those written by participants or witnesses—the distinction is not serviceable and perhaps not even real. In his landmark study *The Great War and Modern Memory* (1975), Paul Fussell argues that "the memoir is a kind of fiction, differing from the 'first novel' only by the continuous implicit attestations of veracity or appeals to documented historical fact" (310). Critics like Thomas Myers and Lloyd Lewis have chosen to examine Vietnam "narratives"; for their purposes, the old distinction is not particularly relevant. Although Myers usually pairs titles that have generic identity, he examines Herr's *Dispatches* and O'Brien's *Going after Cacciato* together as examples of "a revised American romanticism." In her provocative essay, "Disarming the War Story," Lorrie Smith is more concerned with the power of "mimetic stories" than with whether they present themselves as fiction or fact.

The history of criticism on the Vietnam War is, of course, not a very long one. The key early titles are James C. Wilson's *Vietnam in Prose and Film* (1982), Philip Beidler's *American Literature and the Experience of Vietnam* (1982), Lloyd B. Lewis's *The Tainted War: Culture and Identity in Vietnam War Narratives* (1985), John Hellmann's *American Myth and the Legacy of Vietnam* (1986), Timothy J. Lomperis and John Clark Pratt's *"Reading the Wind": The Literature of the Vietnam War* (1987), and Thomas Myers' *Walking Point: American Narratives of Vietnam* (1988). Incidentally, the first general anthology of imaginative literature designed for classroom use, Nancy Anisfield's *Vietnam Anthology: American War Literature*, appeared in 1987. The first edition of John Newman's annotated bibliography, *Vietnam War Literature*, appeared in 1982 (the second edition in 1988, the third in 1996).

As suggested above, one set of questions is concerned with the ways in which the literature of the war challenges and adjusts American myths. The trailblazing works of Philip D. Beidler and John Hellmann have been influential here, while issues that these critics raise are placed in a larger context by Richard Slotkin. Much has been made in the criticism (and in the literature itself) of Vietnam as an extension of the powerful frontier myth, and Slotkin has given us a rich understanding of that myth and its many ramifications in three major studies: *Regeneration Through Violence: The Mythology of the American Frontier, 1600-1860* (1973); *The Fatal Environment: The Myth at the Frontier in the Age of Industrialization, 1800-1890* (1985); and *Gunfighter Nation: The Myth of the Frontier in Twentieth-Century America* (1992). This last work draws upon some representations of the Vietnam War.

Other critics, like Philip H. Melling (*Vietnam in American Literature*, 1990), write of the way the literature reveals the continued unfolding of our Puritan past. In his *Vietnam and the Southern Imagination* (1992), Owen W. Gilman, Jr. shows the peculiar adaptability of Slotkin's "regenerative violence" concept to the Southern ethos. Myths of innocence and invincibility, myths of home and homecoming, and myths of race and gender all have powerful representation and—more often—counterrepresentation in the literature and in the criticism. The title of Tobey C. Herzog's *Vietnam War Stories: Innocence Lost* (1992) addresses one of these loci. This concern with mythmaking in literary production owes a debt to the more broad-based analysis of mythmaking that is part of the culture process in which we all share. Loren Baritz's *Backfire* (1985) is a prime exploration of that process. On the other side of the critical timeline, James William Gibson's *Warrior Dreams: Violence and Manhood in Post-Vietnam America* (1994) follows the mythmaking (and remaking) process through the Reagan-Bush years and into the closing decade of the twentieth century. Also appearing in 1994, Don Ringnalda's *Fighting and Writing the Vietnam War* turns the program of myth analysis on its head by exploring the absurd element both in the nature of the war and those texts that best capture this absurdity.

Genre-specific studies include several remarkable works on poetry: James F. Mersmann's *Out of the Vietnam Vortex: A Study of Poets and Poetry against the War* (1974), Vince Gotera's *Radical Visions: Poetry by Vietnam Veterans* (1994), and Michael Bibby's *Hearts and Minds: Bodies, Poetry, and Resistance in the Vietnam Era* (1996). Complementing the studies by Mersmann and Bibby is Nora M. Alter's *Vietnam Protest Theatre: The Television War on the Stage* (1996).

It is a high but productive irony that the Vietnam War and the woman's rights movement gained momentum at the same time. One consequence of this dichotomous parallel is that the literature of the Vietnam War and feminist criticism have matured together, and some sort of symbiotic relationship has developed. Perhaps no other contemporary body of literature has found itself as susceptible to the perceptions and methods of feminist criticism—and, more broadly, gender criticism. Much attention in the criticism has been drawn to representations of and by women in what, at first sight, would seem an unlikely arena. More importantly, the range of Vietnam War representation has been a fertile ground (no sexist metaphor here) on which to dramatize the central issues in the feminist cultural critique of patriarchal society. No critic has been more constructive in this endeavor than Susan Jeffords, whose *The Remasculinization of America: Gender and the Vietnam War* (1989) has already influenced a generation of scholars. One major adjustment in vision between Philip Beidler's trailblazing study of 1982 and his broader and richer study of 1991 — *Re-Writing America: Vietnam Authors in Their Generation* — derives, I believe, from the influence of feminist thinking on Beidler's own understanding.

Jeffords prepares the way for writers like Lynne Hanley, whose *Writing War: Fiction, Gender & Memory* (1991) extends the boundaries of how we define war writing. Critics whose concerns and approaches are as different as Renny Christopher (in *The Vietnam War/The American War: Images and Representations of Euro-American and Vietnamese Exile Narratives*, 1995) and Milton J. Bates (*The Wars We Took to Vietnam: Cultural Conflict and Storytelling*, 1996) have seen the war and its literary representations as a lens through which the pathologies in American culture are magnified. Each owes a debt to Jeffords, but not only to Jeffords. And each makes a new contribution to this seemingly inexhaustible area of study.

Aside from Newman's bibliography, several other reference works help the student/scholar contend with the literature, its context, and the critical responses. These include Sandra M. Wittman's *Writing About Vietnam*: *A Bibliography of the Literature of the Vietnam Conflict* (1989), Deborah A. Butler's *American Women Writers on Vietnam*: *Unheard Voices — A Selected Annotated Bibliography* (1989), my own *The Vietnam War in Literature*: *An Annotated Bibliography of Criticism* (1992), Kevin and Laurie Collier Hillstrom's *The Vietnam Experience* (1998), and Jim Neilson's *Warring Fictions: American Literary Culture and the Vietnam War Narrative* (1998).

Collections of critical essays edited by William J. Searle (*Search and Clear*, 1988), Jeffrey Walsh and Alf Louvre (*Tell Me Lies About Vietnam*, 1988), Jeffrey Walsh and James Aulich (*Vietnam Images: War and Representation*, 1989), Owen W. Gilman, Jr. and Lorrie Smith (*America Rediscovered*, 1990) precede my own *Fourteen Landing Zones* (1991). Also in 1991 came *The Vietnam War and American Culture*, edited by John Carlos Rowe and Rick Berg, which grew out of a special issue of *Cultural Critique*.

Like *Cultural Critique*, several journals have published special numbers given over entirely or partially to the study of Vietnam War representations. These include the Summer 1981 and Fall 1993 issues of the *Journal of American Culture*; the Winter 1988 issue of *Genre*, titled *The Vietnam War and Postmodern Memory*, edited by Gordon O. Taylor; and *Critique* (Winter 1983). The Spring 1984 *Modern Fiction Studies*, a special issue on modern war fiction, contains several pieces on Vietnam War novels.

Viet Nam Generation, a journal begun in 1988 and in recent years published intermittently, is a major resource for interdisciplinary studies on the war's centrality to contemporary American culture. Many issues are titled separately and sold as books, including *A White Man's War: Race Issues and Vietnam* and *Gender and the War: Men, Women, and Vietnam* (both 1989).

Items of special interest are Eric James Schroeder's *Vietnam, We've All Been There: Interviews with American Writers* (1992) and Andrew Martin's *Receptions of War: Vietnam in American Culture* (1993), which assesses ideological strains not only in writings on the war but also in film and television treatments. In one way or another, all of the works listed above, and many others besides, have influenced *Acts and Shadows*. Noteworthy as well is H. Bruce Franklin's splendid classroom anthology, *The Vietnam War in American Stories, Songs, and Poems* (1996), a text in which Franklin's section introductions add up to a powerful critical statement.

III

The chapters in this book are linked, to some degree, by the cultural concerns with gender that the literature reveals. After the consideration of genre issues in chapter 1, chapter 2 focuses directly on the manifestations of masculinist sexism in the literature. Several of the chapters that follow, most notably chapter 3 on authenticity and chapter 4 on wounds in the writings of Joe Haldeman and others, amplify this discussion of sexism. Some of its constant and changing terms are elucidated by reference to professional and personal partnering with women in the texts of thriller and detective fiction in chapters 6, 7, and 8.

The title *Acts and Shadows* asserts, metaphorically, an inclusive and possibly expansive stance in terms of what may be defined as Vietnam War literature. "Acts" embraces the kind of works listed in John Newman's excellent *Vietnam War Literature: An Annotated Bibliography of Imaginative Works about Americans Fighting in Vietnam*, now in its third edition. Newman does not choose to include personal narratives or nonfiction novels. Moreover, to be included by Newman, a work must have a substantial segment set in Vietnam during the war years.

Though battlefield stories still dominate the body of Vietnam War literature and thus the attention of critics, it is clear that the focus of Vietnam War criticism has shifted just as that of the literature itself has shifted. The shift, among writers who were veterans of the war, follows their own experience from the war they fought to the war they took home. The more immediate consequences of "Acts" are registered in such titles as Robert Bausch's *On the Way Home* (1982), Larry Heinemann's *Paco's Story* (1986), and Larry Brown's *Dirty Work* (1989) — novels of the returned veteran's suffering and alienation. Among both veteran and nonveteran writers, one movement is to a vision of larger perspective: works that integrate the Vietnam War into a reading of the larger American story. Susan Fromberg Schaeffer's novel *Buffalo Afternoon* (1989) is one such effort. Walter McDonald's collection of poems, *After the Noise of Saigon* (1988), is another. Thus, the second wave or generation of works put under the umbrella of Vietnam War literature includes those that represent the plight of the returned veteran in a larger context, some of which look to the earlier and later years of the character's life to understand the experience of this war in a life's context. Hovering between the consideration of the battlefield and the early stages of return are the scars of battle and the memories attached to the percussive world of battle, matters that are explored in chapters 4 and 5.

Even further in time and place from the events of war come imaginative responses to long-term consequences. These are the "shadows"—the works that reveal the ongoing stateside impact, including the presence of Vietnamese in the American cultural landscape, the sense of American destiny and character in the shadow of the war, and the America of the Vietnam veteran as he enters middle age and prepares for the twenty-first century. Such texts are my principal concern in the later chapters, and O'Nan's *The Names of the Dead* and Haldeman's *The Hemingway Hoax* could just as well be discussed there if they didn't also address themes treated earlier in this book. "Shadow" texts can also approach the war obliquely, as does Joan Didion's *Democracy*, or allegorically, like Nicholas Rinaldi's *Bridge Fall Down*, though such writings are not the concern of the present study. Also omitted, but not happily, are works that deal with the protest against the war and of the Vietnamese experience as told by Vietnamese and Vietnamese Americans.

The shadow of Vietnam can also be cast backwards, as I argue in my discussion of Korean War novels. Or is it that the Vietnam struggle is itself the lengthened shadow of Korea? And what of the "literature of return" that has proliferated since the mid-eighties and seems destined to constitute a significant portion of postwar representation? What does it mean that so many veteran writers have taken themselves, and to a lesser extent their characters, back to Vietnam? How do we account for the acceleration of translation projects of writings by American and Vietnamese veterans? Why the growth of bicultural anthologies of war and postwar literature? In imagining the uses to which such questions and their exploration might be put, one is led to imagine—if one is a teacher—the place of such literature in the classroom. Such considerations are engaged at the end of this volume.

IV

There has always been an American literature of war. Whitman's *Drum-Taps*, Melville's *Battle-Pieces*, and Stephen Crane's *The Red Badge of Courage* form the nucleus of a significant literature of the Civil War—yet Whitman was the only major writer who put himself in some proximity to the horrors of battle. Melville was only a casual visitor, and Crane was born years after the war's close. From this beginning (though we could go back further to James Fenimore Cooper's great romance of the French and Indian War), the war literature of American writers has been a mixture of testimony, commentary, and imaginative reconstruction. Though many more creative works about the Civil War were written, only these nineteenth-century visions of that war have come down to us—and Melville's only because of his canonical stature as a novelist. The distant reconstructions of that past include Michael Shaara's Pulitzer Prize novel of 1974, *The Killer Angels*, which treats the battle of Gettysburg, and Stephen Vincent Benét's verse narrative, *John Brown's Body*, winner of a Pulitzer Prize in 1928.

America's best-known literary treatment of World War I is Hemingway's *A Farewell to Arms*, though Hemingway was a veteran of the volunteer ambulance corps, not the army proper. Somewhat less celebrated are John Dos Passos' *Three Soldiers*, William March's *Company K*, and e. e. cummings's *The Enormous Room*. The critical and popular success of Mark Helprin's *A Soldier of the Great War* (1991) reminds us that excellence can reform the canon.

James Jones's *From Here to Eternity* and *The Thin Red Line* are among our classics of World War II, as are John Hersey's *A Bell for Adano*, *Hiroshima*, and *The Wall*. Alongside of Kurt Vonnegut's *Slaughterhouse-Five*, Irwin Shaw's *The Young Lions*, Norman Mailer's *The Naked and the Dead*, and Joseph Heller's *Catch-22* are the retrospective epic treatments of Herman Wouk (*The Winds of War* and *War and Remembrance*) as well as *The Caine Mutiny Court Martial* drama based on his earlier novel. Of more recent vintage is Marge Piercy's highly acclaimed *Gone to Soldiers* (1987).

M*A*S*H is our major literary remembrance of the Korean "conflict," though it is often imagined by the viewers of the television series as a work about Vietnam. More rooted in the specifics of that confrontation are James Michener's propagandistic *The Bridges at Toko-Ri*, James Salter's *The Hunters*, and Pat Frank's best-selling *Hold Back the Night*.

This short checklist of well-known literary responses to our earlier wars reminds us by its very brevity that the winnowing processes of popular and critical acclaim canonize only a small percentage of the imaginative works written on any subject. The rest are left to special interest readers and scholars. How will the writings on the Vietnam War be filtered? Which will survive—and why? The critical enterprise now underway engages these questions.

Why is there such a rich literature about the Vietnam War, a war that for so many years no one wanted to hear about at all? How did that experience stir the nation and discover so many interpreters? There are no conclusive answers to such questions, though some suggestions may be offered.

In the two decades between the end of World War II and our military buildup in Vietnam, the American educational system reached out to embrace greater numbers. The proportion of young men (and women) who achieved a higher literacy (numbers achieved at the expense of a smaller elite no longer attaining the highest literacy) may account for the great number of significant literary responses to the Vietnam War.

Though we read much about the demography of the armed services during the war that describes the disproportionate sacrifice of the disadvantaged and the dropouts, the number of enlistees—and even draftees—who had some college education was not insignificant, and the educational attainments of the young officer corps was high. This is to say that many of those who went to Vietnam had the equipment to turn their experiences into literary documents. And many others would, upon return, gain the skills needed to shape and reshape their memories.

We should note, as well, that among its literary fashions, the sixties ushered in a personal journalism that employed novelistic techniques. Norman Mailer's *The Armies of the Night* (1968) is a classic of this kind. Such a genre was ready-made for the memoirs of the war and for the many autobiographical novels—often memoirs in thin disguise. (Ironically, Mailer's *The Naked and the Dead*, published twenty years earlier, is a model for most of the "old-fashioned" realistic-naturalistic combat narratives of Vietnam. Mailer's own fictional treatment of this war is trendily oblique; *Why Are We in Vietnam?* — 1967 — is a grotesque stateside adventure in macho bloodletting, thus, a study in American character.) The related genre of the nonfiction novel — Truman Capote's *In Cold Blood* (1966) and William Styron's *The Confessions of Nat Turner* (1967) — also influenced the literary climate in which the first writings about the Vietnam War were nourished. And one can hardly imagine the stylistic hijinks of Michael Herr's *Dispatches* without the earlier work of Tom Wolfe.

Aside from anything one might say about the magnitude of cultural upheaval caused by the war, the circumstances of literacy and literature in the United States during the war years help explain the great numbers of writings and the generic outlines of this body of work — a corpus that began to gain momentum in the late 1970s and a decade later became a significant facet of American publishing. The growing commercial viability of Vietnam fiction allowed early works like Ward Just's *Stringer* (1974) to be brought out ten years later in paperback and introduced a new generation of readers to Graham Greene's classic, *The Quiet American* (1955). In late 1995, John Clark Pratt presented a critical edition of this prophetic novel with a fine selection of contexualizing essays.

Many bookstores, new and used, have "Vietnam" shelves. The seemingly endless "Vietnam: Ground Zero" series by Eric Helm (including *The Raid, Incident at Plei Soi, Cambodian Sanctuary,* and *Payback)* is representative of the mass market success of Vietnam material. The "Wings Over Nam" series by Cat Branigan lengthens the bandwagon. Indeed, every paperback house has its Vietnam titles, both fiction and nonfiction, both serious and escapist. There are even a couple of Vietnam bookstores, and several college libraries have undertaken special collections of Vietnam material. Through the 1980s and beyond, Vietnam-related works kept tumbling onto the bookstore shelves. In 1989, Lucian K.Truscott IV's *Army Blue,* John Amos's *The Medallion,* and Franklin Allen Leib's *The Fire Dream* were among the most conspicuous. As the century ends, the flow of new titles continues. The year 1997 brought us Joanna C. Scott's *Charlie and the Children,* Robert Olen Butler's *The Deep Green Sea,* and John Mulligan's *Shopping Cart Soldiers.* In 1998, Wayne Karlin's *Prisoners* appeared; in 1999, Jerome Gold's *Sergeant Dickinson.*

A number of works about the war have earned and gained special recognition, most notably Stone's *Dog Soldiers,* Tim O'Brien's *Going after Cacciato,* Gloria Emerson's *Winners and Losers,* Larry Heinemann's *Paco's Story,* and Neil Sheehan's *A Bright Shining Lie* — all winners of National Book Awards. Pulitzer Prizes have been awarded to Sheehan's book and also to Frances Fitzgerald's *Fire in the Lake,* Lewis B. Puller, Jr.'s *Fortunate Son: The Healing of a Vietnam Vet,* and Robert Olen Butler's *A Good Scent from a Strange Mountain.* Yusef Komunyakaa, who came to attention with his Vietnam War collection *Dien Cai Dau,* received the Pulitzer Prize for a later volume, *Neon Vernacular.* John Balaban's *Words for My Daughter,* a National Poetry Series selection, included many Vietnam-related poems. A production of David Rabe's *Sticks and Bones* was awarded a Tony and his *Streamers* won a New York Drama Critics Award. Earlier, Rabe's *The Basic Training of Pavlo Hummel* won an Obie award for playwriting. Having gained such distinctions, these war-related writings and their authors bid for further attention and for places in an adjusted canon of American literature.

V

The battle among historians and political scientists and politicians who have tried to explain this war is a battle for the perceived *truth* that future generations will share about the reasons for, conduct of, and outcome of this conflict. Our novelists, playwrights, and poets are significant players in this engagement—few, if any, are "above" a political or moral vision, and many works are overtly propagandistic.

Certainly, the fact that the war was witnessed by the American public on television and, however tentatively, in movies does not escape the notice of the literary and dramatic artists who approach it. The constant allusions to John Wayne movies in Gustav Hasford's *The Short-Timers* and elsewhere, the *Ozzie and Harriet* game played by David Rabe in *Sticks and Bones* in which the television doesn't work and David's movie can't be seen, the concern with photographic and cinematic images in Stephen Wright's *Meditations in Green,* Emmett's obsession with *M*A*S*H* reruns in Bobbie Ann Mason's *In Country*, and Sgt. Krummel's comment in James Crumley's *One to Count Cadence* that the maimed VC "flipped out of the tree like a Hollywood stunt man" (282) all remind us of the different planes of perception, intersecting and overlaying, through which the truths of the war are offered us. Indeed, some of the most significant literary art is reportage—Jonathan Schell's *The Real War* and Gloria Emerson's *Winners and Losers* come immediately to mind, and some of that is fundamentally concerned with the act of reporting—of representing—the war to the public. Thus, works like Michael Herr's *Dispatches* are, at one level, about the limits of perception and representation. The works that will last, one must suppose, will be works that transcend the representation of a particular arena of military engagement.

The more provocative stories that unfold in the earlier literature of the Vietnam War are not simply or finally stories of armed conflict in a distant land. They are stories about American society as it evolved through the sixties and seventies. They are understandings, and sometimes underminings, of American myths. As the impact of the Vietnam War extends down through the rest of the twentieth century, imaginative works continue to convey that impact. Among the treasures of this continuing literature are Tim O'Brien's *In the Lake of the Woods* (1994) and Stewart O'Nan's *The Names of the Dead* (1996). A noteworthy effort to represent the continuing legacy of the Vietnam War on the literary imagination is Donald Anderson's *Aftermath: An Anthology of Post-Vietnam Fiction* (1995).

These artistic expressions and the scholarship that responds to them serve the great interest in Vietnam-related studies of all kinds that continues to proliferate on American college and university campuses. That interest comes, in part, from the curiosity of those born after 1975 who are now in colleges and graduate schools. Some are already classroom teachers. These are young adults who are old enough to have fought or be fighting in a war.

Those who lived through the Tet Offensive as young officers (some of whom became authors) were four or five years older than their subordinates. They, and the larger group who came to majority during the 1965–1975 period, are the Vietnam Generation. This generation is now becoming a generation of grandparents—the elders who will lead the United States into the twenty-first century.

As a field of special study, the appraisal of war literature has had sporadic growth. Indeed, fields of literary study centered on the *subject matter* of the literature tend to be considered as marginal, transient, suspect endeavors. While literary criticism becomes more and more concerned with theory and methodology, the questions about what literary works express receive less and less attention and little respect. Scholars who are concerned with myth, paradigm, and genre are making valuable contributions to our understanding of Vietnam War literature. Some critics seem a bit nervous about the "humanities" approach to literature that asks us to find in our study of artistic creations keys to understanding the human condition. As I hope the following chapters make clear, it is what the literature of war tells us—*shows* us—that claims our attention and concern.

Acts

Chapter One

Vision and Tradition

If one goal of literature is to render convincingly a vision of life, to depict it so compellingly that readers are led to share the author's notion of experience, then literary form—as it uses and departs from tradition—is a key means to that end. While the works of fiction that have come out of the Vietnam War tend to share an absurd vision of the war itself, not very many find the innovations in form or technique with which to communicate that vision. The perceived absurdities of the war are manifold: they include confusion over the nature and identity of the enemy, the abandonment of objectives—territory or positions—soon after obtaining them at great cost, conflicting or unreliable information about the goals and status of the war, and constant mismatches of ends and means. If there was, finally, something "unreal" about the fighting man's experience in Vietnam, how best communicate that unreality? The conventions of realism are intertwined with recent, nonromantic traditions of war literature, but they somehow fail to capture the ways in which this war was felt to be different from its predecessors. I review this issue of vision and method by reference to six novels distributed into two categories, then elaborate the discussion by reference to other genres and to two particularly relevant critical works.

The features of the first group of novels include third-person narration with shifting focal characters; a representation that emphasizes the experience of the group, the fighting unit, more than the experience of the individual; the backgrounding of a large cast of characters; and fairly conventional handling of time, place, action, and causality. These are fictions in the realist tradition, filled with the boredom, blood, and pain of men at war. Though each novelist is clearly conscious of absurd conditions, of a unique set of circumstances, the techniques employed are similar to those used by Norman Mailer in *The Naked and the Dead*. And Mailer, I'm sure, found much of what he needed in the novels of John Dos Passos. The works I include here are John Del Vecchio's *The 13th Valley* (1982), James Webb's *Fields of Fire* (1978), and William Turner Huggett's *Body Count* (1973).[1]

15

The novels in the second group share the following characteristics: a severely limited perspective (two are first-person narrations, the other channeled through a single character though cast in the third person); passages of lyrical, surreal description that create distortions of time, place, and action (or illusions of such distortion); and little or no backgrounding of characters. They shred cause and effect assumptions, leaving us to wonder what, if anything, governs human life on this planet. These novels include Gustaf Hasford's *The Short-Timers* (1979), Larry Heinemann's *Close Quarters* (1977), and Tim O'Brien's *Going after Cacciato* (1978).

In the first group, the writers maintain an allegiance to fulfilling several conventional expectations: they tell us where the characters come from, what pre-war circumstances shaped them, and what they might have to return to. The degree to which these pasts, presented through set stretches of exposition or labored flashbacks, inform the present is rarely questioned. They seem offered as a "given" necessity of characterization. The fighting units are rendered along socioeconomic lines, reminding readers about the backgrounds of those people who fought this war for us. Though these novels show us the discontinuities that the war brings to individual lives, they nonetheless work to suggest connections between the characters' experience of war and their larger—or broader—range of experiences.

The novels of the second group seem more claustrophobic, more internal, the characters more detached from any sense of the past's relevance to what kind of people they are now. By defying certain expectations, they may be said to force something closer to the absurd experience upon the reader. These novels blend various components of lyricism, psychological realism, and naturalism.

I

Del Vecchio's work is the most ambitious. *The 13th Valley* slowly but engagingly relates the tale of a major operation, the taking of a North Vietnamese stronghold in the Khe Ta Laou Valley in 1970. The cast of characters includes, most notably, Lt. Brooks, a black intellectual who is torn between his duty to his wife, his duty to his men and his country, and his deep concern for the human condition, and Sgt. Egan, the perfect fighter and point man, a hero to others but a man with nightmares. This callous cynic becomes a mentor to his "Cherry," a radioman without battle experience who slowly turns into a fighting monster. "Cherry" seems to be the author's surrogate.

The characterizations of Brooks and Egan are fairly rich, and the flashback triggers that usher in "the world" are usually plausible and they are certainly well spaced, keeping us in touch with the larger life story of which the current military engagement is only a part.

The novel pays close attention to the details of strategy and tactics, leadership, the effects of battlefield conditions on a wide range of personalities, and the political and moral issues of this and other wars. Del Vecchio provides clear presentations of the various levels of command and their interaction. In fact, Del Vecchio is probably too ambitious, trying to cover too much intellectual ground while maintaining the feel of the various engagements and situations. The political discussions among the men become awkward substitutes for authorial comment.

All in all, this is an impressive achievement, but the broad range of concerns leaves effects diffused, even though there are extraordinary accounts of discomfort, pain, and fortitude. Like many similar constructions, this novel uses the past—the backgrounding of a wide range of characters—to suggest the kind of melting pot or cross section of American society that makes up a fighting unit. Additionally, the more or less conventional past of each character (a fairly predictable sequence of events, purposes, and outcomes) serves to set off the discontinuities of all sorts that characterize the war experience. The inference we may draw is that the characters bring irrelevant pasts to an unparalleled, unpredictable set of experiences.

One of the longest fictional narratives of the war, this book, in fact, is focused on a relatively short period of time. And it is the orderly marking out of events and behavior within a rigid and conventional temporal sequence that overwhelms Del Vecchio's presentation of the flow of experience, a presentation that in certain long passages is handled quite effectively. Nowhere is this irony of how the realistic tradition fails the novelist's essential vision more clear than in *The 13th Valley*, which pays such meticulous attention to time, place, strategy, and tactics. The juxtaposition of maps and official reports of the campaign's progress with invented passages representing the "real" flow and feel of events shows Del Vecchio's constant awareness of this irony. Still, his conventional handling of plot, time, and point of view does not serve to create the "new thing"—the absurd experience—within the reader. His method is a sieve that cannot hold the essential truths of the experience.

Often represented as a vehicle for the celebration of combat, James Webb's *Fields of Fire* is not so easy to pin down. Certainly Webb suggests that, for many of his characters, sharing life-and-death experiences provides a sense of purpose and relationship that nothing outside of combat can provide. However, combat is not a prescription for what ails the world or even the individual psyches of these men.

The special complications of the Vietnam War as they affected the fighting men are seen clearly, especially the nature of the enemy. Other topics include the corruption of those sitting behind desks and the horrors of battle itself. Many sections of this narrative are gruesome.

The inset biographies of the characters, once again, owe much to Mailer's *The Naked and the Dead*. The two main characters, Lt. Hodges and Snake, share our attention and provide our points of reference through the first hundred pages of the novel. Clearly Hodges's perspective is the dominant one for the novel as a whole, and thus his absence from some of the key actions creates a perspective void. In fact, the unsteadiness of point of view is one of the novel's weaknesses.

The backgrounds of the other characters—Goodrich, Phony, Dan (the Vietnamese scout), Gilliland, Bagger, Cat Man, and Cannonball—are layered in at reasonable intervals. And with the introduction of each comes a brief attempt at following the war from this character's point of view. However, each such attempt quickly finds the narrator stepping back into a neutral territory or swinging once again toward Hodges. When we follow Hodges on his Okinawa time-out—the second stage of his romance with Mitsuko—we see, perhaps, Webb's failure to separate the autobiographical "what happened" from the novelist's "what does this story need."

But what are the consequences of the various pasts Webb draws for us? Few of the characters are driven by patriotism or any other ideal. We see them doing what must be done, curiously leveled in spite of all their differences. Is this the message? The war has found them and remade them, and each is equally capable of dying.

Webb is concerned with creating contexts that blur moral issues, often making conventional moral stances irrelevant. Yet his work is at times patently and narrowly argumentative. His patsy is Goodrich, who, though treated with some sympathy, is nonetheless the target of Webb's disdain for intellectuals. Goodrich's attempts at rational perspectives are found wanting, and this part of his character is somehow coupled with his physical cowardice. Such a treatment of Goodrich—a character so obviously drawn to argue a point—compromises Webb's hold on the reader's imagination. Though this case stands out, it does not represent a general tendency of the novel.

Although Webb sometimes seems concerned with characterization as it is found in the best serious literature, more often the characters are there for the sake of the action—the major way in which the popular genres of adventure and war fiction distort esthetic priorities. If the war seems to have discovered and remade these people, then the effort put into giving them pasts becomes an ironically mechanical effort, one which—perhaps unintentionally—underscores the failure of Webb's approach to contain or release his vision. Or is it a failure of vision? These tensions, complicated by the strangely decentralized point of view and the clock-time march of events, underscore the special problems of form and content found in the body of Vietnam War fiction, problems handled even less effectively in *The 13th Valley* and met more sure-handedly in *Body Count*.

One of the most conventionally plotted novels of the war, William Turner Huggett's *Body Count* traces the career of Lt. Hawkins from the time he arrives as a green officer intimidated by his veteran sergeant and eyed skeptically by his men through the various ordeals that prove him worthy of their loyalty and respect. The story of Hawkins's development as a leader helps to give the book a solid shape. Rooted in the realistic tradition, this novel follows a number of vivid supporting characters through major combat operations as well as the lulls in between. The action scenes portray significant stages in the conduct of the war, so that the plot as military history and the plot as officer-coming-of-age run side by side.

Much of the standard lunacy of the war is portrayed, particularly the quick abandonment of positions achieved at tremendous cost and the consequent attitude of men who fought hard, sustained injuries, and saw their buddies die for that temporary objective. Huggett also nails down the tension between the experience of the combat soldier (Marine) and the soft life of those assigned to administrative or supply units. Though Huggett's treatment of the obligatory sex scenes with Asian women seems to break faith with the texture and unity of the novel (see chapter 2), *Body Count* has plenty of saving graces.

Characterization is one of this novel's strengths, but how much of it resides in the backgrounding materials? For me, this relatively unheralded work makes the most effective use of characterization in the realistic mode in handling the absurd elements.

This success is achieved because the range of characters' reactions to the absurdities is detailed and compelling. Huggett allows his narrator to stand behind a half dozen or more key characters, telling parts of the story from the perspective of each (though not in the words of each). By alternating focal characters, Huggett is able to extend the depth of characterization while at the same time fragmenting the "truth" of the Vietnam experience. Del Vecchio lets Lt. Brooks and St. Egan carry almost all of the introspective material (with Cherry representing another pole), and Webb's narrator pushes through the serial presentation of Snake, Hodges, and then the others in a systematic yet self-conscious way. Huggett, on the other hand, cycles and recycles through his main characters, alternating several segments seen through the eyes of Lt. Hawkins, Wilson, and LeBlanc with segments in which various lesser characters are allowed to shape the reader's understanding. There are even segments headed "The Platoon" in which the narrator stands behind the shared outlook of the group. Because Huggett has his plot under control, he is able to find the best character to reveal the nuances of particular events.

Hawkins, Huggett's main character, just barely manages to dominate over the others. Huggett's technique emphasizes the separate identities of the men, even while it is related to the technique of Webb and Del Vecchio that, to various degrees, demonstrates how individual identities are submerged in the group identity of the fighting unit or ground down by the deprivations and exhaustion of the combat situation.

The representations of time, place, and action are realistic, but it is the rich interiority of the novel that makes it so much more than just another fictionalized battle report.

The achievements of Huggett, Webb, and Del Vecchio are genuine, and each novel in its own way is at least a partial success. The scope of *The 13th Valley*, the power and pace of *Fields of Fire*, and the rounded characters and perspectives of *Body Count* show us the war according to the conventions of popular and literary realism. In many ways, these novels are more finished—more complete as fictional structures—than those to be discussed next. Yet the abandonment of clock-time structures for more experiential renditions of "what happened" brings us fictional constructions that seem more capable of recreating the absurd and grotesque awareness that each of the six novelists needs to share.

II

After a powerful treatment of U.S. Marine Corps boot camp, Hasford's *The Short-Timers* loses any kind of standard plot development. The Vietnam material in the sections called "Body Count" and "Grunts" is often beautifully written, sometimes poetic, but rarely directed or shaped beyond what one might expect from autobiographical writing. Events follow one another, but they don't seem to lead anywhere. There is little sense of causality—a feature of the novels more squarely centered in the realist tradition—and, thus, little sense of rationality. Whether these features of the book are intentional or merely the limitations of Hasford's art, they evoke the madness of the war more compellingly than the more programmatically plotted fictions discussed earlier.

The key characters are well displayed, and the brutal and brutalizing aspects of warfare are handled in a convincing and powerful fashion in a style more lyrical than realistic. There is no heroism in this novel—only survival and the ironically dehumanized "being" whose existence is the price of survival. An eerie mixture of the apocalyptic and the realistic, this novel is the basis for the film *Full Metal Jacket,* directed by Stanley Kubrick.

One of the most effective first-person fictions, Hasford's vision is presented as that of Corporal Joker. Joker, however, is not as vivid as many of those he describes: Rafter Man, Cowboy, and Animal Mother. The self-effacing narrator often provides a feeling of merged experience, a sort of a first-person plural "we" perspective that bears some resemblance to "The Platoon" sections of *Body Count.*

The Short-Timers hovers between the Maileresque fictions that envision characters formed by carefully etched histories and works like *Cacciato* and *Close Quarters* that seem to detach their characters from the past. The first section, in boot camp, is conventionally but effectively told, and the variety of characters— of American types—is systematically introduced. While many of these characters are moved into the battle scenes that follow, somehow the two halves of the book are sharply severed. Corporal Joker, the narrator, undergoes changes that turn him into a more powerfully lyrical stylist, and the backgrounding done in the first part loses it relevance as the characters are redefined by the experience of war, an experience that has little association with that of boot camp.

Even the boot camp section is unusual as it presents the characters only in the here and now, as formed identities detached from the freight of history. Hasford's use of the present tense heightens his lyrical thrusting forward. Parris Island is a first rebirth, complete with its own absurdity and brutality. The war itself is a second, its terrors strangely beautiful and other-worldly.

As the novel progresses, Joker's sense of humor becomes more and more grotesque, a dark chuckle at despair. Charged with obtaining atrocity photographs as evidence of the enemy's inhuman cruelty, Joker and Rafter Man approach a mass grave:

> We see corpses of Vietnamese civilians who have been buried alive, faces frozen in mid-scream, hands like claws, the fingernails bloody and caked with damp earth. All of the dead people are grinning that hideous joyless grin of those who have heard the joke, of those who have seen the terrible secrets of the earth. There's even the corpse of a dog which Victor Charlie could not separate from its master.

There are no corpses with their hands tied behind their backs. However, the green ghouls assure us that they have seen such corpses everywhere. So I borrow some demolition wire from the Arvin snuffies and, crushing the stiff bodies with my knee until dry bones crack, I bind up a family, assembled at random from the multitude— a man, his wife, a little boy, a little girl, and, of course, their dog. As a final touch I wire the dog's feet together. (126–127)

In sections like this one, and in the searing, nightmarish account of the skirmish with a sniper who turns out to be a fifteen-year-old girl, Hasford finds the style and the highly charged detail to project his vision. His images are not the images of mere realism, but rather the dream symbols of a fun house for ghouls and madmen.

Though *The Short-Timers* is a novel made out of fragments, at best those fragments become prose poems of unrivaled power. And it is when Hasford is making us experience what is most unreal that he tells us so much: "I try to dream something beautiful. . . . My grandmother sits in a rocking chair on her front porch shooting Viet Cong who have stepped on her roses." There is more in this fleeting dream than in many pages and chapters of "authentic," documentary realism.

Larry Heinemann's *Close Quarters* is a highly stylized first-person narrative that reports Philip Dosier's year of combat. We meet Dosier as he joins a team of soldiers who drive or man armored personnel carriers—tracks—and follow him through a series of ambushes, body counts, and major skirmishes. We witness the spiritual disintegration of Dosier that accompanies his experiences in this war. Dosier's drinking, dope-taking, capacity for mindless violence, and cruelty are seen as the inevitable consequences of what he must learn in order to survive. In this way, Heinemann's work is closest to the conventions of naturalism, with its insistence on seeing man as a creature controlled by instinct and environment and circumstance. Dosier is not to be judged, for without free will there can be no moral judgment.

This is not an original theme, but Heinemann's strategy of keeping a narrow focus through his protagonist's narration gives this treatment heightened power. Many passages attain a poetic elegance unmatched by any other fiction of the war. Heinemann's presentation of fatigue, hallucination, the chaos of combat, and the upwelling of powerful emotions is remarkable. Lyricism, ironically, handles the inner states that tell us so much about what counts in this war. Also of special interest is his handling of Dosier's tenuous reentry into the world, a prefiguring of Heinemann's later critical success, *Paco's Story* (1986).

Like many of the other novels, this one gives us an understanding of the powerful bonds formed among the soldiers, and also the motivations behind their individual and collective hostilities. Unlike the novels in the first group, *Close Quarters* does not depend very much on flashbacks or backgrounding. It's only when we come close to Dosier's future that we get a sense of his past, or in the brief flashback to his relationship with his girlfriend, Jenny, that occurs halfway through the novel—and only then through the trigger mechanism of Dosier's escapade with "Susie," a bar girl he meets while on R & R. What makes him is the strenuous, demanding present. Memory serves that present, joins it, and then dissolves in the rush of events. Only rarely will it become a relevant instrument of identity.

This sense of Dosier as a man recreated in the war, a man who in a special sense has no relevant past, is a significant part of Heinemann's vision. Dosier simply appears, ready to play his part, already molded of the strange stuff that will allow for some kind of appropriate functioning in an absurd predicament.

Repetition of action—the seemingly meaningless cycle of behaviors in which the characters are defined—is caught in the novel's patterns but hardly given editorial comment. The repetition of incident, the endless nerve-numbing or nerve-shattering routines from which there is little relief and for which there is no justifying outcome—this is the full measure of Dosier's experience. Though arbitrarily confined to what the world would call a year, the time of the novel has nothing at all to do with the passage of months but rather with spiraling rounds of madness.

Like many of the novels of this war, *Close Quarters* has a good deal of raw language and raw sex, but it is all convincing and well integrated into Heinemann's determinist vision, a vision in which those best prepared to survive can't make it through while the bunglers somehow hold on.

It is not so much the borrowed authenticity of first-person narration that makes a work like *Close Quarters* so compelling, but the narrowed scale of concerns. While a novel that puts a sharp focus on the individual may not satisfy our demand for explanations of larger political or military issues, it allows us to feel who we might be—or become—as the record of internal events balances or overrides the external record.

Internal event, projected outward as a picaresque romp, is the main concern of Tim O'Brien's *Going after Cacciato*, perhaps the most inventive (along with Stephen Wright's 1983 *Meditations in Green*) of the Vietnam novels until O'Brien's own *The Things They Carried* (1990) and *In the Lake of the Woods* (1994). This surreal fantasy follows a squad's alleged pursuit of a deserter who leads them to Paris on his own naïve separate peace. The men at first believe— or almost believe—in the legitimacy of their mission, but soon come to understand it as a rationalization for their own wishes.

The central intelligence is Paul Berlin, an effective, fully drawn character surrounded by interesting cutouts. Through flashbacks to Paul's periods of duty at the Observation Post, we come to understand what the men have been through that makes their zany chase after Cacciato plausible. The insanity of the war is transformed into their Cacciato obsession, at the same time making that obsessional flight acceptable to the reader. Or are these passages really a hallucination, the presentation of Paul's daydreaming during Observation Post periods or between them? After all, if only one could get up and walk away. If only. Daring to think such thoughts, we allow ourselves to participate in a joyful victory over the war itself.

A consistent explication of Cacciato is difficult in part because the temporal relationships between segments of the novel are hard to pin down. The chapters that record the pursuit after Cacciato form a consistent sequence, always moving forward in a picaresque manner. The Observation Post segments interrupt the chase story, but in themselves don't seem necessarily consecutive. Even if they were, they contain Paul Berlin's memories of battle as well as his contemplation of Cacciato—memories that blur any sure chronology.

More than any other fiction of this war, *Going after Cacciato* develops a complex allegory of the human condition out of its materials. While the specific nature of this war is always in focus, O'Brien's art reaches out to embrace much more. His novel finally leaves the war behind, just as Cacciato does. One thread of this allegory spins off the image of the tunnel.

It is into the Vietcong tunnels that Lt. Sidney Martin urges his men to climb. He gives them directions for the Standard Operating Procedure: first blow the tunnels with grenades; then search for the enemy or any intelligence about the enemy. After two men die following Martin's orders, the others start to organize a rebellion. They plot to frag Martin in order to save their own lives. Paul Berlin is sent to find Cacciato and bring him into solidarity with the group by having him grasp a grenade. Cacciato, found fishing in a rain-filled crater, refuses to participate—more concerned with whether or not there is a nibble at the end of his fishing line. Berlin says, "They say you better touch it. It's hopeless—it'll be done no matter what. And it's for your own good" (286). These are words that ironically argue the call to war itself. Though Berlin presses the grenade into Cacciato's hand, Cacciato never holds it or even feels it. In his excitement over catching a fish, the simple-minded Cacciato escapes complicity in the fragging incident. And in his flight to Paris—or is it Paul Berlin's flight to capture Cacciato's innocence?—he escapes once again, but this time the group follows him. Ironically, Cacciato, the "dumb kid," becomes their unlikely leader.

The journey the men take in pursuit of Cacciato includes episodes called "A Hole in the Road to Paris," "Fire in the Hole," "Falling Through a Hole in the Road to Paris," "Tunneling Toward Paris," and "Light at the End of the Tunnel to Paris." The sequence becomes an allegory of spiritual trial and renewal, of death and rebirth, ironically mirroring the story of blowing up and searching through the mysterious network of enemy tunnels in Vietnam. The men's resistance to Lt. Martin's SOP orders, orders that had already killed their comrades, is linked to their tunneled passage through the sewers to Paris—the Paris of romance and peace conferences—towards which Cacciato lures them.

The ending is difficult to sort out. It suggests a number of rethinkings of the story's meaning. What is unquestionable is the power of O'Brien's work with its mixture of fable and realistic detail that flashes back and forth between literal and imaginative flight. The real and the unreal lose distinction over and over again, becoming part of one another, and this slipperiness is part of the novel's truth about the war.

This lyrical, surreal treatment—with its suspension of time and its provocative Pan myth underpinning—releases understandings of this war's absurd nature far more effectively than traditional or modified realist methods.

* * *

The novels by Del Vecchio, Webb, and Huggett, even while the authors would argue to the contrary, most often create links with previous war literature. Furthermore, by striving after scale and scope, these novels forsake the intensity that can only come through a narrowing of focus. O'Brien's work and, to a lesser extent, the work of Heinemann and Hasford convey the differences by less conventional methods of presentation. These approaches—mixtures of the naturalistic, the lyrical, and the psychological—are handled with sufficient skill to allow for a transformation of reality, or of realism, into something visionary and profound.

III

In his guerilla critique entitled *Fighting and Writing the Vietnam War* (1994), Donald Ringnalda goes several steps further than most critics, myself included, who argue that the traditional realist narratives of the Vietnam War, with their propensity for making sense and seeking order, bungle the task of reflecting the essence of that war. Favoring the fragmentary, the nonlinear, and the experimental, Ringnalda shows how such works as Stephen Wright's *Meditations in Green*, Tim O'Brien's *Going after Cacciato* and *The Things They Carried*, and Michael Herr's *Dispatches* (each author gets a separate chapter) provide experiences for the reader that more closely approximate the experience of the war itself. On the other hand, novels like John Del Vecchio's *The 13th Valley*, in the service of literary realism, disguise the war, domesticating it into something familiar, rational, and safe.

If he had done nothing else but develop and elaborate this key distinction, Ringnalda would have performed a valuable service. But Ringnalda goes much further. He argues that the authors of scores of volumes sharing the techniques and esthetic assumptions of Del Vecchio and James Webb, because they write the war within the mindset of its very fighting, become accomplices—perhaps unknowingly or unintentionally—in the national criminality of our Vietnam misadventure. Such writings cast a convenient but unhealthy closure, promoting cultural blindness and amnesia. This indictment is powerful and shocking, but Ringnalda is up to the task of making it stick. His arguments are compelling, just as his fervor is unmistakable.

Oddly, Ringnalda's approach ushers in no radical alteration of the canon. Most of the works he treats are well-known standards in the Vietnam War literature classroom. In treating the fiction, Ringnalda's main anticanonical gesture is to offer Peter Straub's *Koko* as an example of how stock genre devices can be remade in the service of a radical and cleansing vision. Ringnalda also uses *Koko* as part of his instructive attempt to undermine the privileged status of the Vietnam veteran as official scribe and/or arbiter of the Vietnam experience.

Two sturdy chapters of *Fighting and Writing* examine respectively the poetry and the drama of the war. In each, Ringnalda points out how these genres, in part because of their very marginality, provide tools for bringing the truths of the war home—truths obscured by the very nature of narration, no matter how innovative. Among the poets, Ringnalda gives most attention to John Balaban, D. F. Brown,

W. D. Ehrhart, Walter McDonald, Marilyn McMahon, Yusef Komunyakaa, and Bruce Weigl. The unfamiliar voice Ringnalda introduces is that of Jerry Hansen. For Ringnalda, the power of these poets lies in the fact that they have not covered over or rationalized or romanticized the pain that the Vietnam War produced. They have not sought to control or contain it. In their best work, they make us live with discomfort and disorientation; they force us to counter our national habit of wasting that suffering. While it is easy to agree with these assertions, they seem equally applicable to the work of the best war poets from other eras: Stephen Crane and Wilfred Owen come to mind.

Throughout, Ringnalda elaborates this metaphor: the most significant Vietnam War authors write like the enemy fought. Nowhere does he develop this conceit more effectively than in his chapter on drama, "Doing It Wrong, Getting It Right." Misdirection, collage techniques, and an ostensible poverty of resources underpin a theater of successful guerrilla operations. Along with several plays by David Rabe, Ringnalda explores John DiFusco's *Tracers*, Emily Mann's *Still Life*, Amlin Gray's *How I Got That Story*, Arthur Kopit's *Indians*, and Steve Tesich's *The Speed of Darkness*. Few of the key dramatic works, Ringnalda asserts, are set in Vietnam; thus the plays as a group reveal most clearly that Vietnam begins and ends at home. Along the way, Ringnalda reminds us that these artists have received scant attention from the critics, in spite of (or because of) their effective and affective distance from convention. (Although Ringnalda makes good use of Brechtian theory in his discussion, a reference to Brecht's own war drama, *Mother Courage*, would help prepare readers for Ringnalda's demythologizing of Vietnam War uniqueness.)

Though Ringnalda's commentaries on the special effectiveness of works in the marginal genres of poetry and drama contain valuable insights, I would argue that even within these genres there is a further distinction. Just as with the prose narratives, this distinction hinges on the contrast between traditional uses of genre conventions and visionary works that defy conventions in order to express the war experience with a new kind of verisimilitude. It is important to separate even further the achievement of fine poets like John Balaban and Bruce Weigl, whose approaches attach them to the major traditions of literary history, from writers like D. F. Brown, whose accomplishment is contained in and released by radical, if self-conscious, artistic technique.

Such distinctions, and others, focus the arguments of Vince Gotera's *Radical Visions: Poetry by Vietnam Veterans* (1994), the first comprehensive examination of Vietnam War poetry by participants. In part because he has limited his discussion to the writings of men and women who saw military duty in Vietnam (as distinct from those civilians who, often as accomplished and established poets, chose to write about the war), Gotera's approach leans more toward myth and cultural criticism than literary assessment—and yet there is plenty of the latter. Gotera has carefully worked out an effective critical grid of modes and mythic themes within which to place the concerns and achievement of the various veterans. Taken together, these writers have produced a powerful dissident "poetry of witness and warning." For none of them is poetry an end in itself.

The terms that Gotera employs to describe the poetic modalities are the "antipoetic," the "aesthetic," and the "cathartic"—terms that he understands are largely for the sake of organizational convenience. He considers the antipoetic a chosen literary stance (rather than a sign of stylistic inadequacy) appropriated for its oppositional thrust. The antipoets abandon many of the traditional poetic tools and document their experiences in ordinary language, often employing a "terse, deadpan style" that allows naked horror to reveal itself. Gotera locates such poets as McAvoy Layne, Bill Shields, and Michael Casey within this mode, which he usefully compares to the alienation effect promulgated by Bertolt Brecht, a touchstone thinker for Ringnalda as well.

In the aesthetic camp, Gotera places David Huddle, Walter McDonald, D. F. Brown, and Basil Paquet. These are writers who are comfortable with exploiting western literary traditions, self-conscious as artists, and therefore especially attentive to formal matters. For Gotera, "these writers share a common faith that beauty and vision in poetry are finally salvational."

The cathartic mode is a middle ground. While it shares a documentary impulse with the antipoetic, this mode is energized by self-catharsis. Like the artful lyric, it strives for the epiphanic moment bonding writer and reader. Jan Barry, W. D. Ehrhart, and Marilyn McMahon are among Gotera's representatives of the cathartic mode.

Acknowledging that individual poets write in more than one mode (Gerald McCarthy in particular writes in all three), Gotera observes that "the modes themselves cross over and cross-pollinate." These modal categories do not constitute Gotera's basic organizing strategy. Rather, he divides his material between "The 'Nam" and "The World," distributing through these major sections several chapters focused on mythic motifs: the wild west, the machine in the jungle, Babel, regeneration through violence, and Adamic return. In this regard, Gotera's book resembles studies like John Hellmann's trailblazing *American Myth and the Legacy of Vietnam* (1986) and Tobey C. Herzog's sturdy review of major narratives in *Vietnam War Stories: Innocence Lost* (1992). Essentially, Gotera demonstrates (through examining veterans' poetry) how available, internalized myths, often appropriated by the U.S. government to rationalize the war effort, were discovered to be illusory. In the poetry, these myths are exploited by strategies of ironic allusion, negation, and subversion. On such matters as these, Gotera's findings and those of Ringnalda reinforce one another.

Not all of Gotera's interests fit neatly into his mode/myth grid, and he wisely leaves room for several chapters that look elsewhere. "Warriors Against War" is one such chapter. Here Gotera traces the poetic trail of the Vietnam veteran antiwar activist by paying tribute to the largely unknown work of African American poet Lamont B. Steptoe, honoring the contribution of Jan Barry, and providing a major discussion of W. D. Ehrhart's long and passionate career as an antiwar advocate whose poetic development Gotera examines admirably.

In separate chapters just before his conclusion, Gotera treats the two poets whose writings not only encompass the three modes, but transcend them. Gotera's chapters on Bruce Weigl and Yusef Komunyakaa build upon his earlier work on these two prominent poets, clearly elucidating the themes and manner of each. Weigl and Komunyakaa, as Gotera reads them, have penetrated beyond the dissident stance to reach states of renewal and affirmation, not just for themselves and their personae, but for the nation of potential readers.

In providing the first rigorous overview of this large and varied body of work, Gotera has achieved as well several important if subordinate ends. First of all, he has been industrious in representing the poetic perspectives of women and minorities. In this way, he has not only deepened our vision of the rubric "Vietnam War veteran," but he has opened up the canon of protest literature. Also, by minimizing attention to the conventional literary (read "academic") biases through which we usually assess poetry, Gotera has gone a long way toward the demystification of the hallowed genre. He attends to the personal and societal functions of poetry, bringing us into contact with a body of work that is demonstrably accessible and whose audience can and should be much larger than the withered numbers left in the wake of decades of a diseased cultural elitism. These veteran-poets have reasons to write that go far beyond satisfying M.F.A. requirements. While most readers will never find the enthusiasm for Steve Mason that Gotera manages, they can benefit from Gotera's respectful and generous sensibility.

Gotera's "antipoets" category would seem to best represent the radical perspective that Ringnalda wishes to attribute to the marginalized genre of poetry at large. On the other hand, the idea of a restorative art on the other side of dissidence is attractive and compelling, but it does not serve to fuel the anger and outrage of Ringnalda's guerilla critique in which he reads Vietnam War literature as an indictment of American culture over time. While Gotera doesn't wrestle very much with the question of the war's distinctive features (he in fact provides a concise guide to American war poetry that suggests a continuum), Ringnalda turns the tables on his readers by insisting on how the most telling representations of the Vietnam War shock us with its ordinariness as a manifestation of America's cultural journey.

Once Ringnalda launches the shocking argument that the Vietnam War wasn't so unique after all, his arduous enterprise of honoring defiant structures and styles is called into question: If the war was not unique, then why should its valorized representations be those that defy tradition?

In the last chapters of *Fighting and Writing*, Ringnalda has us turn a corner and confront a ghost. For most critics (and imaginative writers), the problem with writing the Vietnam War is finding the means to render its uniqueness. Indeed, one could read this far in Ringnalda's book and miss a handful of cues pointing away from this standard assumption. But now Ringnalda confronts us with "The Paralysis of Uniqueness." Many, if not all, of the narratives, poems, and plays that he has profiled explode the myth of uniqueness. If read with alertness and imagination, they portray the horrific normality of America's involvement in Vietnam. Atrocities perpetrated by American soldiers, confusion of friend and foe, hostility toward returning veterans, and other supposedly unique features of the Vietnam War are not unique after all. Conscientious historians know this, and so do the imaginative writers toward whose works Ringnalda directs us.

If Vietnam was business as usual, then Ringnalda argues that we can learn no useful lessons from treating it as freakish or aberrant. Indeed, to do so is to participate in a comforting hoax. The Vietnam War was not a time-bound mistake, a lapse of national character, or an exception to the traditions of U.S. military and political conduct. According to Ringnalda, the most significant writers of the war have needed to find extraordinary means to see through the emperor's mythic clothes. The striking and yet radical ordinariness of Maya Lin's Vietnam Veterans Memorial implicates us all, embraces and reflects (in Ringnalda's view) the whole dysfunctional American family across time and space. It reflects the nearby traditional icons of Washington and Lincoln as well as the visitors and its very self. Maya Lin, too, has done it wrong to do it right, has broken with convention to give us a way of seeing what convention blinds us to. To put it another way, the writers whom Ringnalda embraces have not written unconventionally because the war they fought was so very unconventional. Rather, they have done so because only radical statement and technique has a chance of waking us up from our long slumber dominated by comfortable but blinding myths. Visions that break with tradition both in insight and method are inspired by the particulars of time and place, but their meaning cuts a wider swath across the cultural landscape and its history. As chapter 9 illustrates, the perceptions of uniqueness about our involvement in Vietnam fade away when we examine the representations of our preceding Asian war in Korea. In chapter 2, we confront some of the myths, particularly the myth of America's tolerance for difference.

NOTES

1. These works are representative. Other impressive achievements in the traditional mold are Robert Roth's *Sand in the Wind* (1973), Steven Phillip Smith's *American Boys* (1975), and Winston Groom's *Better Times Than These* (1978).

Chapter Two

Sexism and Racism
in Vietnam War Fiction

Attitudes toward women in American society during the 1960s and 1970s underwent significant change as the Civil Rights Movement rallied both men and women to new insight and action. While legislators acknowledged and attempted to correct past injustices, the two-worker household created an economic incentive for a reconsideration of the sexual stereotyping inherited from previous generations. Educated, articulate women joined men in the workplace in greater and greater numbers, often winning positions of responsibility and leadership. Although the liberalization of sexual mores, especially as it affected the psychological and social dimension of marriage, may have been a mixed blessing for women's rights, at least it created a wider range of choices and greater opportunities for women to do some of the choosing on their own terms.

Even in the male-dominated and exploitative media, women were no longer defined solely as wives, mothers, angels, or whores. They were being seen as (and, indeed, living as) athletes, tycoons, thinkers, and opinion makers. They were winning full accreditation as people, not just the weaker sex, in the eyes of men and in their own eyes. Of course, men still held the power of accreditation, and the professional roles that women moved into were roles defined and valued by men. As Otto Rank noted a half-century ago, woman's "professional development in our civilization is only possible along the lines of masculine ideology" (267). Indeed, Catharine A. MacKinnon's argument that "the state is male in the feminist sense" (616) held then as now. However, no one can deny that there was significant progress and the beginning, however tentative, of some new accommodation.

For the men who went to war, though, and for the men who trained them, older and narrower attitudes prevailed. The uncompromisingly male institution of the military thrived on and forced its members to conform to its special blood-and-guts vision of masculinity that polarized male and female attributes, disparaging the latter. The historical and prehistorical dynamic in which "male and female are created through the eroticization of dominance and submission" (MacKinnon

605) was thrown into starkest relief. In wartime military culture, this dynamic becomes an explicit dimension of indoctrination and behavior modification. Killing the woman within is the preparation for killing the enemy without. A soldier's "fear of being considered a woman . . . is the sexual underbelly of combat" (Gerzon 40).

In the nonfiction narratives of the war, the abusive, hostile attitudes and behavior towards women, especially Asian women, are easily documented. Jacqueline E. Lawson has provided a frightening analysis of Vietnam War veterans' memoirs, showing them to reveal the most blatant symptoms of misogyny in contemporary American culture. In the fiction, with its greater obligation to truth than to fact, the revelation of these same attitudes is even more powerful and even more telling. Not only are the old stereotypes played out—in Vietnam, women were once again and forever either mothers, wives, angels, whores, or some painful combination—but the literature of the war sets up hideous and totally convincing equations in which women become both enemy and weaponry. If one is compelled to destroy the woman and to destroy the enemy, it is likely that the categories of "woman" and "enemy" will become identified with one another. Here too, the soldiers' psyche, though strained by particular circumstances, reflects and focuses larger cultural traits. Latent—or repressed—misogyny becomes a psychic platform for effective combat behavior. (For additional perspectives on these issues, see Cooper, Tal, and *Gender and the War,* the 1989 special issue of *Vietnam Generation.*)

The outline of the story about attitudes towards race runs parallel, and may even be thought of as the same story. A society moving toward greater racial tolerance discovered—perhaps invented—a distant enemy that nourished its hunger for racism, ultimately a hunger for destroying difference. Robert Jay Lifton and others have drawn the connections between the "gook syndrome" and the maltreatment of Asian women, and the link between sexism and racism is effectively observed by many writers, including Henry J. Laskowsky in his discussion of Louis Malle's film *Alamo Bay*: "There is . . . a strong sexual component to the harassment of the Vietnamese, as several white youths taunt Vietnamese schoolgirls and threaten them with sexual violence" (138).

In the crude semantic equations of the battlefield, killing gooks is the same as fucking them—and being a man in the military environment means being a killing and fucking machine. The metaphor of fucking the enemy, of course, turns the enemy into women, and vice versa. Thus, in a sense, all enemies are surrogate women. And to the white-bread American grunt, the dusky Vietnamese man—small-boned and sparse in facial and body hair—was a figure simultaneously effeminate and menacing, whether friend or foe.

There are many paths to understanding this equation. According to Arthur Brittan, one way of reading history is that man's subjugation of woman made all other forms of subjugation possible (83). Otto Rank, in his foundational essay "Feminine Psychology and Masculine Ideology," examines the myths expressing man's need for power, his destructive applications of it, and the relation of these to his fear of and consequent need to control sexual power. According to Rank, men fear sex, which they associate with chaos, irrationality, and death. To conquer these fears—essentially the fear of extinction—man exercises his destructive potential. His fear of sex is simultaneously a fear of women and a desire (finally impossible to fulfill) to be independent of them. Man turns his fear of sex into man-power. Thus, as Mark Gerzon puts it, men "have the courage to fight, but not to be naked" (42). (Women, according to Rank, do not fear sex because they accept their basic biology and mortality. What women fear is men.) Combat itself can be seen—and often *is* seen—as a ritual cleansing, a purification of one's essential masculinity from corrupting feminine dross (Gerzon 40).

To reprise the dynamics of sexism, and to a lesser extent racism, in the Vietnam War, I examine four representative novels about the conflict. These are among that war's most highly acclaimed combat novels, novels that have continued to engage readers while scores of similar works have fallen into obscurity. Each is a first novel by a Vietnam War veteran, all but one of whom has gone on to further accomplishment as a writer. These works are among the most successful representatives of their genres, the identity of which has already been examined in chapter 1.

In James Webb's *Fields of Fire,* Marine Lt. Robert E. Lee Hodges has a stopover in Okinawa on his way to Vietnam. At Fort Hansen, he spends time drinking and studying his Combat Leader's Notebook while he awaits processing. Hodges is attracted to Mitsuko, an Okinawan girl working as a waitress in the Officers' Club. She reluctantly agrees to go out with him, and, after he gets her into bed in her apartment, he discovers that she had been a virgin until that night—not at all the experienced hustler that he had imagined all attractive Asian women to be. This warm, romantic interlude—an outgrowth of nothing more than mutual attraction and Hodges's "I'm off to battle" pleading—introduces the rather complex issue of racism and sexism in American culture as it is focused and heightened in the literature of the Vietnam War.

When Hodges first meets Mitsuko, it is in the context of someone hired for her youthful good looks by the O Club manager and who is there to make the customers feel good and to hint, at least, at greater pleasures: "She put his plate down in front of him. He thought he felt her breast against his shoulder. Vague, velvet pressing. Hard to tell. She smiled self-consciously and he squinted, focusing on her name tag. Yup. Same as a minute ago. Mitsuko" (38). Hodges's advances are resisted at first with some talk of an Okinawan boyfriend, but—out of attraction or duty, it is never totally clear—Mitsuko joins him for a night on the town.

She seems humiliated by the events of the evening: the taxi trip that takes them past a beach where Okinawans cannot swim, only American officers; the nightclub where American men are buying the drinks that will lead to buying the favors of Okinawan girls. Hodges senses that Mitsuko is insulted, that she does not put herself in the category assigned to her by this place.

Mitsuko is torn between her likely fate as a sexual and racial conquest to white macho imperialism and her true dignity and pride. And, if she is genuinely attracted to Hodges, she must also cope with the stereotype that brought them together. Webb's treatment of this issue is surprisingly subtle and complex. Hodges is a man of prejudices—the seemingly natural, national ones—but he is also a sensitive man who is alert to Mitsuko's discomfort and the possible reasons for it.

Still, the evening must move on to its inevitable conclusion: she is there to satisfy the needs of this soldier heading off to war. Thus, as she becomes part of the institutionalized structure of available women that always becomes attached to military bases, Mitsuko fulfills the dictum of Marvin Harris: "The training of fierce males requires the training of pliant females" (quoted in Tavris 242). Yet there is something far more personal than formal or institutional about their love-making. Though the circumstances conspire against it, this one-night stand could turn out to be love. Hodges already knows that it is quite special, that he has had his feelings stirred in an unexpected way.

As he reaches the gates to Fort Hansen, he hears "the bar tales of the others coming in from liberty, and all the cruel clichés about oriental women. He thought of the groin-grinding bar girls of two days before, and for the first time understood the sad part of Mitsuko's stare that kept accusing" (45). The affair continues through the next three nights, and, though both know there is no reason to expect that they would ever see each other again, Hodges "hoped deeply that he would. . . . But first there was Vietnam" (46).

This prelude by way of romance is an unusual introduction to the war itself, a war in which such sensitivities and hopes lose relevance. However, through this bridge, Webb presents the issue of racial stereotyping, allowing for the possibility of one unexpressed motive, one strand of the American psyche that contributed to U.S. commitment to and conduct of this war. Fucking one set of gooks, suggests the story line, is a reasonable preamble to killing another set. Yet it does not seem that it was Webb's intention to make this point. There is no hostility in Hodges's treatment of his Asian girlfriend, though there is selfishness. There is, additionally, the suggestion that this relationship, with its respectfulness and tenderness, is the clear exception.

This circumstance raises another issue. Hodges is off to do his duty. His background, his training, his ambition are all pointed toward the battlefield. What place can a woman have in this character's life? What is the basis for their relationship? What will Hodges bring back to her—if, indeed, he survives and is able to come back?

Later in the novel, after being hospitalized for serious wounds, Hodges passes through Okinawa again on his way back to Vietnam. He finds Mitsuko and pushes the relationship to the point of asking her parents to approve their marriage. Webb handles the cultural barriers deftly, and he allows Mitsuko the clearest understanding of why this union can't work. Hodges's enthusiasm wanes, and when he receives an opportunity to be reassigned to a billet on Okinawa, he refuses it. He is anxious to get back to the war, which is in his blood, and to the men for whom he feels kinship and responsibility. There is no way of integrating these two worlds. The potentially gentle, giving, vulnerable side of hereditary soldier Robert E. Lee Hodges is rooted out; the warrior prevails.

In one of the late scenes awkwardly appended to the novel, we find out that Hodges had, unknowingly, left Mitsuko pregnant. Her Okinawan husband has tolerated this Caucasian-tinged boy, often teased by his schoolmates, who learns, at the age of seven, that his real father died a hero. Unfortunately, Webb finds it appropriate for the boy to commit himself to being a warrior. The tradition must continue—a tradition in which the warrior's ethic accepts and fosters the exploitation of women.

While Webb seems to treat his characters and their situation sympathetically, his awareness of sexist and racist motives has only the mildest critical edge. Compared to many other combat novels, *Fields of Fire* treats relatively subdued versions of these tendencies. Not blind to what men put aside to prepare themselves for war, Webb would seem to consider it a necessary sacrifice—a given.

Far less subdued on such matters is Larry Heinemann's *Close Quarters* (1977), a fatalistic narrative that presents a horrifying vision of how attitudes toward Asians and women are heightened by the war experience. The narrator's inflection is so flat that one cannot be sure if the horror is only the reader's. The protagonist's behavior is presented as a series of consequences rather than a series of choices. This naturalistic perspective, then, assumes the animal in human nature and treats the combat zone as a return to the wild. In this novel, we find a most forceful connection between "woman" and "enemy" and between fucking and killing. The soldiers' behavior is described through these equations, but it is hardly judged.

The novel presents three women: Claymore Face, a Vietnamese prostitute who is humiliated and abused by the American soldiers; Susie, a Japanese B-girl with whom Philip Dosier, the protagonist-narrator, has a romantic interlude while on R & R in Tokyo; and Jenny, the girl back home to whom he returns and who aids his adjustment to "The World."

The environment or arena of relationship defines the terms of the relationship and the valuation or status of the woman. In the combat zone, Claymore Face is thoroughly dehumanized; that is, she is turned into an object—or perhaps we should say that the men are, for they become robotic killing-fucking machines. The reader first meets Claymore Face soon after a skirmish in which Dosier sees his first "Charlie"; the connection between the battlefield emotions of kill or be killed and the treatment of "the platoon punchboard" is highlighted by this juxtapositioning: "She snagged a couple takers and took them down the creek to the embankment one at a time while the others stood along the top in a gang, hooting and laughing and lobbing rocks." Comments like, "Goddamn Claymore Face, you sure got the *ugliest* cunt for a hundred clicks around," and "like fucken a washrag soaked in vinegar" are typical (65). The men are privileged to treat Claymore Face as what Mark Gerzon would call a target in a "sexual shooting range" (42).

At one point in the novel, Dosier and the other men, looking for VC, encounter an old woman whose livelihood seems to depend on a water buffalo. Outraged at the woman's denials of knowledge about the VC, and suspecting her of being a VC partisan, they push her around, shoot up and burn the hooches in the village, and pump the water buffalo full of bullets—all on a whim, as Dosier admits: "She was gook. The hooch was gook. The buff was gook buff" (110). The evening following this round of senseless violence—while engaged in a blackjack game with his buddies—Dosier has a vision of a woman.

It is a vision he has often, but it is recorded in the novel at this particular moment, a moment that seems to explain the vision as somehow connected to the cruel behavior toward the Vietnamese mama-san:

> She stands naked in a field of dwarf tundra flowers and red poppies and stiff mustard blossoms. Who are you? I say. I said it every time. She holds tight to her thighs as though squeezing and rubbing a bruise, half from chill and half from the pain of cramps. And the eyes. Black and red they are, with small points of white fire that flash and fade and flash, like the closest stars or two stars together or Mars or Mercury. Her shoulders and chest and breasts are flecked with faded taupe-colored moles. Her skin is scarlet and the dusty black shadows are the shape of taper candles. And the only part of her that shines and glistens is her pubic hair. It is curled and matted and burgundy-colored. And the line of flesh between her torso and hips seems to smile. No, not a smile. A giggle. (112)

Later that night, awakened from a dream to stand watch, he sees her more closely: "I look out over the curved sun shield and the fifty barrel and the claymore wires spread out like fingers, and there she is" (112). The woman never speaks. She teases Dosier, climbs into the hatch of the armored personnel carrier, has sex with him, and then moves off into "the woodline shade with her legs crossed, leaning back against a tree . . . looking me straight in the eye" (113).

In the vision, we find our hero aroused, in part, by the thoughts of bruises triggered by the woman's gestures of suffering. Her "teasing" taps into a sadistic connection that Dosier's experience has made between inflicting pain and sexual prowess, between killing and fucking. Her silent stare is not unlike the accusing look that Mitsuko gives Lt. Hodges in Webb's *Fields of Fire*. The fact that he imagines her juxtaposed against the weapons of war suggests a connection between weaponry and sexuality—a connection made even more emphatically in William Turner Huggett's *Body Count* and with horrifying vividness in Gustav Hasford's *The Short-Timers*, both treated below.

In *Close Quarters*, it is as if the woman is getting back at Dosier in some way. Her control over his imagination, her seductiveness, is a power earned out of her victimhood—a power that taps into Dosier's unacknowledged feelings of guilt, perhaps.

Late in the novel, a mop-up operation following a major engagement shows the men as pure killing machines, ready to destroy anything in their way. They have come to live for the action, the adrenaline high, the nonstop bloodletting. The return to camp reveals their present, savage natures in a sickening episode with Claymore Face. Dosier "started hustling Claymore Face, freakshow fashion, to the fucken new guys" (258). "Quinn and I," Dosier tells us, "set her in back of the Cow Catcher with ammo cans and the blackjack board and blankets and she'd short-time all the dudes there. Quinn and Dewey and a bunch of old-timers would climb on the back and watch through the crew hatch. It got so a regular crowd formed" (259).

Then Dosier and the others start throwing money at her, in the middle of the circle of legs sitting around the crew hatch, and the woman "jumped up and scrambled around, snatching up the money . . . her meaty, sweaty thighs smeared with cum" (260). Finally, Dosier unsnaps the flap of his pistol holster, insisting to Claymore Face that she "got to suck everybody" (260). Which she does, over and over again: "We just sat in that circle while Claymore Face went the rounds again, her eyes darting from gun to gun" (261). They ignore the new guy who keeps telling them they're crazy, but the point isn't lost on the reader. "After that," we learn, "Claymore Face didn't come around much, and nobody much cared" (261).

Is the new guy correct? Are the men crazy? It may be that these men are not crazy at all. In Sylvia Walby's view, "male violence against women should be seen as a systematic phenomenon, which is largely an effect of other patriarchal relations, but which has a degree of influence on them in return" (62). Male violence, far from "being so unusual as to be a sign of mental sickness . . . is endemic" (62–63). Of course, in the combat zone male violence is the unquestioned norm. Thus, by any statistical definition, the men's behavior in Heinemann's scene is, unfortunately, normal.

Claymore Face, as a woman and a "gook" or "dink," has become other than human. She is the enemy—the other—as victim. She is what belongs at the other end of a gun. The men's behavior is only the extreme version of the racism and sexism at large, but most often submerged, in the society from which they come. Heinemann shows us, perhaps unwittingly, a dark cartoon version of the "valorization of male sexuality" (Brittan 55) and with it the transformation of the penis "into a phallus, into a sign of difference and domination" (Brittan 56).

When Dosier has his R & R request approved, he chooses Tokyo, checking into the Perfect Room Hotel because of the images that name conjured up in his imagination: "the cathouse in soldier heaven" (176). In the hotel bar, he meets Susie: "It was an odd, shy moment. The girl sitting next to me was for hire, make no mistake. I would pay her cash, pay it out every morning, but I didn't want any of that 'Say hey, slopehead, fuckie-fuckie? Let's you 'n' me go upstairs, 'cause ol' Deadeye is gonna tear you a new asshole!' . . . 'What's your name?' I asked quietly" (183). It is clear that Dosier's psychological need—his style of manliness, at least—is somewhat different once he is away from the zone of combat where "being a man" always means being brutal.

In the clean luxury of the hotel room, Susie's expertise—her leisureliness, playfulness, and seemingly genuine pleasure—creates a romantic interlude that is explicitly contrasted to the quick half-pleasures with the Vietnamese woman: "I had fucked Claymore Face, when the ache and boredom got to be too much" (191). The R & R environment is different from the combat zone, Susie is a different kind of woman from Claymore Face. Most importantly, Dosier is here a different kind of person.

Susie can show understanding, caring. She can personalize, within limits, her professional relationship with Dosier. He, in turn, can see her in a more human and humane way. They eat lavishly, go to a play, visit an art gallery, and share more than their bodies. Still, when his leave is over, Dosier can erase all thoughts of Susie in an instant: "Then after one more piping-hot bath and a back rub, I dressed . . . packed my suitcase, kissed Susie—or whoever she was—and left" (208). She is only a bathed and perfumed version of Claymore Face after all. The Susies of Tokyo are the paradoxical parasite-victims of the same racist and sexist impulses that threaten Claymore Face with a gun. The only difference seems to be a safe distance from the enemy, good food, new clothes, and clean sheets. The texture of the relationship is different, but its structure is the same. In Heinemann's description of this ritual cleansing, the woman is left behind with the bathwater.

There is at least one other important difference between Susie and Claymore Face. With Susie, Dosier finds himself thinking of Jenny; with Claymore Face, no such comparison is possible. The memory of Jenny that floats to Dosier's consciousness as he counts out three ten-thousand-yen bills to Susie is of "the first made it" (186).

At the end of *Close Quarters*, Heinemann takes Dosier home, and here we meet Jenny: sweet, ready to please, understanding. She is the picture girlfriend and wife for a mid-American depraved soldier. Jenny sets up an idyllic little love nest, takes Dosier there, and points to all the domestic touches that her stereotypical womanly caring has arranged. One part of Dosier notices and appreciates these efforts; another part of him just wants to screw. In fact, there is a sense that Jenny only exists as she relates to Dosier. He is—or has become—so self-concerned that he is only aware of her as a source of pleasure and comfort. Still, his voice has a note of pity: "The first chance we had Jenny and I got married—me because I could not stand sleeping alone anymore; she because she did not know how else to help" (329–30).

Only after their marriage does Dosier start to unburden himself and share his Vietnam experience with Jenny—if "share" is the right term here. He inflicts it on her: "And on those nights we'd make love and make love and *still* I couldn't sleep—even after I started popping Hines V.A. Hospital prescription Librium" (322). Sleep is the goal here. Sex—and Jenny—only the means. Though Jenny is mostly silent, she exhibits the same understanding that Susie did, and is prepared to make allowances for Dosier's condition.

Though we can say that Dosier loves this woman, it is hard to see her as an individual. He never does. She is only defined by Dosier's needs, needs now set in a different environment than Vietnam war zones or Tokyo hotel rooms, but needs that echo the ones filled by Claymore Face and Susie in those other places. Jenny does not carry the stigma of being a gook, only that of being a woman. The end of the novel has less to do with Jenny than with the impact of Quinn's death. Quinn, Dosier's closest friend—the only remaining one when Dosier leaves Nam—is the consummate gook-hater and survivor. When Dosier learns of his death, he visits Quinn's family and begins a long period of coming to terms with his experience. If Quinn had survived, the war might have meant something. Dosier and Jenny keep in touch with the Quinns. A year and a half later, Dosier visits Quinn's grave. After the flood of memories, all Dosier can say, as he clenches and relaxes his fists, is "'Goddamn you, Quinn'" (335). With this resolution, the memory of Quinn displaces the actual presence of Jenny. The strength of male bonding in the combat zone has left little room for other kinds of relationships.

Male bonding is also a principal theme in William Turner Huggett's *Body Count* (1973). This novel, one of the most successful of the conventionally plotted fictions of the war, traces the career of Lt. Chris Hawkins from the time he arrives as a green officer intimidated by his veteran sergeant and eyed skeptically by his men through the various ordeals that prove him worthy of loyalty and respect. Rooted in the realist tradition, *Body Count* succeeds more than most such novels because of Huggett's effective characterizations. Chief, an American Indian, and Wilson, a Black, are among the fully drawn supporting players. However, the obligatory sex scenes with Asian women almost sink the general attractiveness of Huggett's treatment. Shifts in tone suggest that Huggett means to be at least somewhat critical of this rampaging sexism and racism, and yet one cannot deny the titillation factor. Huggett's brand of realism and his very subject demand that he address this material even at the expense of making us unsympathetic toward characters he has otherwise drawn with affection. Finally, Huggett's own position seems ambivalent.

As in *Close Quarters*, the characters in *Body Count* select Tokyo for their contracted five days of R & R. The behavior toward the stewardesses on the flight over is a prelude of what is to come: "Never were three women more rapidly stripped, ogled, and raped than by the lusting minds of one hundred and sixty-five marines on Flight 1400 to Tokyo" (314). Chief's reproduced thoughts are so grossly juvenile, so junior-high-bad-boy, that Huggett's readers will wonder if this is the same novel they had been enjoying up until now.

Once briefed at the R & R Center and checked into his hotel, Chief goes on a manic marijuana high that Huggett handles through stream-of-consciousness. The woman who hustles him (and calls him "Joe," of course) is first perceived through this mind-racing haze, then—the dope wearing off—in sharper focus. Her name is Sayu. They dance, he drinks, and suddenly it is the morning after.

Huggett presents the high-priced ritual of bath-massage-sex-repeat. In the lulls, Sayu instructs Chief on Asian attitudes toward Black soldiers (the Japanese have their own racial prejudices—even the prostitutes). The scene parallels that of Dosier and Susie in *Close Quarters*. The Japanese women are artful, professional, and personal all at the same time. R & R is a sensual Disneyland, but one with its own decorum and respect. Or so it seems.

While Chief has been enjoying Sayu's favors, Wilson has taken up with "Susie-san," one of the Asian women who make Black men their specialty. Upon entering their room and finding the woman asleep under the covers, Chief asks Wilson, "Did you find out yet?" "Find out what?" Wilson replies. "If it's really sideways. What else?" (339). When Wilson claims that it was too dark, Chief takes over, pulling the covers away and spreading Susie-san's legs apart to "solve the ancient mystery of the Orient." And so, roaring with laughter, the men discover a great truth: "*Look. Look. Oh, whole wide world, look. Oriental pussy is not sideways!*" (340).

This scene, perhaps meant to be comic relief, is simply the playing out to its cruel and predictable conclusion the "classic" sexist-and-racist joke. Susan Jeffords argues persuasively that this scene is ultimately an exhibition of sexism, as racial difference vanishes in the likeness of all women and their difference from men (65–66). Susie-san's humiliation is unrecognized. Her feelings, her personhood, do not count. Huggett's relish for such diseased laughter is unexpected, though at least he keeps his main character, Lt. Hawkins, away from this bit of action.

Hawkins's sexual escapades occur earlier in the novel, back in Vietnam, in a chapter called (not ironically) "In the Rear." Here he meets Mel Northcutt, a civilian ("with USAID or somebody") who has accumulated, among other things, an astonishing collection of weapons. Asked by Hawkins about the Swedish K in the gun rack, Northcutt volunteers, "I traded an SKS and two pieces of ass for that" (171). Upon further questioning he adds, cautiously, "Oh, when you work for the Vietnamese, it's always around" (172). Before long, Mel Northcutt brings Hawkins to a shack made of ammunition boxes where two women are provided: "Hawkins got the C minus" (174). The setting is ugly, almost public. The woman is bored at first, then she turns on the smiles: "Hey, GI, you no like *Co* Hue?" (176). Hawkins is amazed that (explode myth number two) "her breasts were really large" (176), but then he discovers "the warm syrupy sweet milk" (177) that tells him she had just given birth, explaining also her wrinkled belly. The lovemaking is quick and mechanical, a sad scene in which Hawkins rationalizes his behavior, turning the woman into an object to excuse himself: "There was only a smile and a girl. . . . You know, that's what I like about whores. . . . You can bang 'em, pop, and roll right off" (178). The woman washes Hawkins, then douches herself in front of him: "He began to feel a little more detached and watched the girl as if she were something in a sideshow":

> How crude that looked. I wonder if that's the difference in Oriental women or just the difference in class. Somehow it would be impossible to picture a cultured girl back home doing something like that. The incongruity of the two images made him laugh. It would be absurd to think of Poo doing a thing like—as if a hammer had hit him, he wished he had never had that thought. He couldn't help it; it had just popped out. Shame, revulsion, and finally a terrible sadness crept in on him at the thought of the only girl he had ever loved. (179)

Hawkins's shame, however, never attaches to his act or his attitude toward Hue, just to his equation of Hue with his girlfriend.

The prostitute hits Hawkins for a couple of dollars more, which he resentfully tosses at her—as if this whole scene was her fault. She is all smiles again, inviting him to return, but Hawkins just wants to flee: "He felt like throwing a grenade . . ." (180).

The relationship of weaponry—exploding or shooting—to the sex act goes through a series of metamorphoses here. First, Mel Northcutt makes weapons and "pieces of ass" equivalent materials for exchange; next, the act itself takes place in a shack made of ammunition boxes; finally, the ugly aftermath of the occasion leaves Hawkins wanting to throw a grenade. Of course, he has already symbolically thrown one.

In these ways and others, the fictions of the Vietnam War continue to reveal what the literature of our previous two wars had begun to discover about attitudes which, though not unique to the military environment, were fostered and heightened by it. The perpetuation of crude stereotypes is the method and madness of basic training. Getting rid of, getting to hate, the woman in one's self is the message of the litany and language of boot camp. Gustav Hasford's *The Short-Timers* shows us how those connections are made in the Parris Island chapter called "The Spirit of the Bayonet."

Over and over again, Gunnery Sergeant Gerheim addresses the new recruits as "ladies" contemptuously: "I can't *hear* you, ladies" (5). To "have balls" is to be capable of any cruelty, to have no soft emotions: "Marines *do not* cry!" (14). At the same time, a contradictory signal is sent by the identification of weapons as women: "I don't want no teen-aged queen; all I want is my M-14" (12). Joker narrates, "Sergeant Gerheim orders us to name our rifles. 'This is the only pussy you people are going to get. Your days of finger-banging ol' Mary Jane Rottencrotch through her pretty pink panties are over. You're married to *this* piece, this weapon of iron and wood, and you *will* be faithful'" (13). The Corps becomes affectionately known as "the Crotch": "'Do we love the Crotch, ladies?'" (17).

One inept recruit, Leonard, tries so hard to follow directions and shape up that he goes crazy: he does make love to his rifle, talks to "her". . . and "she" talks back: "Leonard reaches under his pillow and comes out with a loaded magazine. Gently, he inserts the metal magazine into his weapon, into Charlene" (27). At the end of training, even Joker, the cynical narrator, succumbs: "In my rack, I pull my rifle into my arms. She talks to me. . . . She tells me what to do. My rifle is a solid instrument of death. . . . My weapon obeys me. I'll hold Vanessa, my rifle. I'll hold her. I'll just hold her for a little while. I will hide in this dark dream for as long as I can" (32). Joker, however, clearly sees through his own madness, and Hasford, his creator, is never for a moment other than critical of how the preparation for war inflames and feeds the sexist virus.

The dark dream is a dream of faith in the killing efficacy of Charlene or Vanessa, penises turned into weapons turned into women. It is a dream through which rises an unexpected suspicion: that if fucking is killing, it is also death. So it is death that must be killed. Death is Claymore Face, the battlefront whore, whose name is an ugly reminder of the pockmarked country. She is the enemy without and within. Death is the woman in Dosier's daydream—she whose eyes are black and red, whose "skin is scarlet"—the woman of "strong and beautiful thighs" with whom he "makes it" in the hatch of the personnel carrier: "Are you a witch, I say, or a conjurer? Some soft evil?" (113). Death is what Lt. Chris Hawkins imagines throwing a grenade at: it—or she—waits for him still in the ammo-box hut. And Mitsuko? No, she is not death. Lt. Hodges forsook her for death—his true love. Or perhaps he died twice.

Killing that figures the woman as enemy aims ultimately at the destruction of the species—an ironic suicide. For many, America's involvement in Vietnam was suicidal. For others, the outcome of the war was liberating as it exposed a diseased patriarchal culture. In any case, as Milton J. Bates asserts, "it was America that was castrated on the sexualized battlefield of Vietnam" (143), a symbolic trauma giving rise to post-Vietnam displays of potency in Panama and elsewhere. A masculinist diagnosis might say we had gone soft, inviting the "remasculinization" Susan Jeffords describes in *The Remasculinization of America* (1989).

Jeffords sees in her sampling of literary representations of the war a discourse "linked to the process of remasculinization current in American culture" (185). I would contend, though there is no space here to detail the argument, that a fair sampling of the literature supports no such generalization (even if one granted that such a predictably patterned group of works could be a reasonable index of cultural directions). Moreover, much of the literature *exposes*, in critical and therapeutic ways, the sexist and racist elements in the call to arms. Of those works treated in this chapter, Hasford's novel (as Jeffords recognizes), testifies to patriarchal modes of thought without succumbing to them. The novels by Webb and Huggett come closer to supporting her contention, but Heinemann's work—on one level the most graphically and brutally sexist and racist of the group—can just as well be read as a critique of its narrator's behavior and the conditions that occasion such behavior. Many of the representations of the Vietnam War intentionally respond to issues of gender as they were made manifest *during the war years*, not as readings of the cultural climate in the years of the works' publication. Literature that is inevitably *about* "masculinization" does not necessarily reinforce it. If that were the case, feminist criticism would constantly subvert one of its premier concerns.

In Wayne Karlin's *Lost Armies* (1988), set years after the war, a Vietnamese woman studying English composition writes a theme for her teacher, a Vietnam War veteran named Wheeler, in which she remembers her vision of America's failure: "I am asked to write who I am, but what I am now does not define me. I will tell you what does. Once upon a time and far away I was a whore for Americans. I let them empty their nightmares of the murder of my people into me. Then I made them look into my eyes until they saw me. I knew that one day they would raise a weapon and see me again in the face of their enemy and they would hesitate and die. When they left I knew I had birthed their corpses" (12–13). The narrator concludes, "Wheeler's pen hunted helplessly over the yellow sheet" (13). Reading the American psyche, this whore knew she was death. Wayne Karlin, Vietnam veteran and novelist, artfully exposes that diseased psyche and in no way participates in a "remasculinization" movement. Nor does Richard Currey in *Fatal Light*. Nor did Tim O'Brien in his classic *Going after Cacciato*, a work curiously ignored in Jeffords's survey.

Yet whether or not Jeffords is right about short-term cultural tendencies, there is no escaping the fact that Americans live in a culture in which patriarchal values continue to dominate. Our larger sense of American culture and the dynamics of war might lead us to expect to find women, especially Asian women (twice removed from the "norm" in their otherness), treated as objects. We might expect to find released in this literature—even in our supposedly enlightened times—a deep-seated tear, even hatred, of women as enemy or as a reminder (for male readers) of the feared and hated "womanish" side of one's self. The equating of women with weaponry and killing reveals an even more perverse and dangerous strand of America's patriarchal culture: the ultimate confusion of love and death.

Chapter Three

Vietnam War Writing and Authenticity

If American culture, as projected in the literature of the Vietnam War, maintains an exclusionary or patronizing stance toward women, a stance heightened by the specific culture of the warrior, then what might be said about the status of woman as war-writer? Indeed, what might be said about the status of any nonparticipant author? Responses to Vietnam War literature in the review media often depend upon a high valuation of authenticity that would seem to exclude outsiders, making the domain of war literature a warrior's, or ex-warrior's, domain. Yet the literature of the veteran/warrior can be viewed as only a subgenre of war literature, a narrow if central perspective.

In a 1984 *New York Times Book Review* article, Michiko Kakutani argued that the best literature to come out of the Vietnam War, including books like *Going after Cacciato* and *Meditations in Green*, was "curiously hermetic," reflecting only individual experience. Kakutani did not argue, as I might, that those works which attempted a range of perspectives, like *The 13th Valley*, were of marginal literary value and still had a narrow range: the men in a particular fighting unit. Kakutani awaited the "large novel that embraces the entire scene, that deals with the military and political complexities of the war, its consequences in public and private lives, as well as its reverberations at home" (41).

As Lynne Hanley points out, the soldier's story is "rooted . . . in a particular man's experience of a particular war, a fact that tends "to sentimentalize, but also to dehistoricize our apprehension of war." Hanley goes on to argue that "less myopic versions of our experience of Vietnam . . . occur primarily in literature we overlook in this context because we assume . . . that the soldier's story is the story of Vietnam" (106). Drawing her examples of the "less myopic" from Doris Lessing and Joan Didion, Hanley points to women's writings that answer, in part, Kakutani's challenge. However, Hanley does not imagine the value of a woman author telling the soldier's story and embedding it in the larger scene Kakutani awaits. That is, Hanley does not anticipate a work like Susan Fromberg Schaeffer's *Buffalo Afternoon* (1989).

41

Buffalo Afternoon, indeed, moves in the epic direction anticipated by Kakutani. Largely a combat novel, it still gives us detailed treatments of the particular American milieu from which its protagonist, Pete Bravado, emerges. Schaeffer's handling of three generations of Bravados, a working class Brooklyn Italian family, is a complex rendering of one representative segment of Vietnam era volunteers. Indeed, immigrant visions of America and the future of those visions are part of the ninety-page front porch of the novel.

Moreover, Shaeffer gives us a most ambitious representation of a Vietnamese character, making the young girl Li one of the narrative voices of the novel. Schaeffer goes far beyond the hermetic vision of earlier Vietnam War fiction, in part because the vision she reflects is not her own and in part because she reaches back into the particular tides of American history that shaped Pete Bravado and forward into his life after Vietnam. Part 3 of the novel, "Parades," provides a two hundred-page continuation of Pete's life after his Vietnam experience—the nature of his return and the range of attitudes toward him. Her cast of supporting characters is vast and rich, though in the combat section many of them echo characters found in earlier novels of this war. Perhaps such echoes are inevitable.

Politics and military matters are subdued, handled largely in the ruminations of Douglas Wapniak, a second-tour enlistee with a master's degree who is the replacement sergeant in Pete's unit. Still, there is a political vision inherent in the selection of characters and circumstances.

The reviews of *Buffalo Afternoon* lodge two complaints. The first is that Schaeffer's "outsider" attempt to represent the day-to-day experience of soldiers in Vietnam is outrageously arrogant and inevitably doomed to failure. The second is that Schaeffer is merely manipulating the stereotypes that have become the stock and trade of Vietnam fiction. Both complaints touch upon a central issue in the criticism of Vietnam War literature: the explicit or implicit test of authenticity.

That test, for better or for worse, has become the crucial one in the language of the review media for novels on the Vietnam War. It is explicit in the language selected for the back covers of paperback editions. The paper edition of William Turner Huggett's *Body Count*, for instance, carries the following excerpts from a *Library Journal* review: "First-rate . . . splendid . . . a tense and vivid portrait of combat . . . [crackles] with excitement and authenticity." *Washington Post Book World* finds *Flight of the Intruder* by Stephen Coonts to be "a first novel of impressive power and authenticity." The *Newsweek* review for John Del Vecchio's *The 13th Valley* claims: "Nowhere in the swelling literature about Vietnam does one discover a richer feel for 'what it was really like.'" But who is to make such pronouncements? And what, finally, do they tell us about such literature—or about its audience? Will we have to wait until those who experienced the war are no longer around to give expert testimony before we can begin the business of a literary criticism divorced from testimonials? When we call a literary work "authentic" (or "authoritative"), what qualities are we addressing? Where does authenticity reside?

"Authenticity" has two rather distinct meanings as a term in literary criticism. Popularly, and particularly in review criticism such as that quoted above, it is related to verisimilitude, authority, and the realist tradition in fiction. A work is "authentic" when it accurately renders persons, places, and events against a standard of firsthand experience. This is what "authentic" means in the estimation of Vietnam War literature, even when the term is employed by someone who has no such experience to draw upon. Clearly enough, however, this meaning privileges readers and critics who can speak with the authority of "having been there." As such, it is a meaning that attaches to early responses and can only be offered secondhand by those whose lives have not been involved in the historical events treated in the work. A work's reputation for being authentic feeds an important appeal of fiction—that of providing vicarious experience. As readers, we are allowed to enter imaginatively a world we can't otherwise know with the assurance that the work can be trusted. The authentic work, then, is compellingly mimetic. Its status as a *copy* of something else is inescapable.

The other meaning grows out of more rarified, philosophical concerns. "Authenticity" as applied to literary works (or any artwork) is an extension of Jean-Paul Sartre's concept of authenticity as a measure of human behavior. This esthetic application of existentialist thought is handled succinctly and vividly in Bruce Baugh's essay, "Authenticity Revisited." Baugh relates artistic authenticity to the genuine, the original, and the transformative. His discussion posits that works of art have ends of their own, that the authentic work "allows us to experience the world in a different way. By organizing our experience on the basis of the end of the work's existence, instead of on the basis of our own ends, we give the work a power over us sufficient to alter our experience of the world from its very foundations" (481). Authentic works produce transformations in their readers. Nonetheless, in such transformative authentic works, like those popularly judged authentic but in a different way, "the authenticity . . . depends on their historicity" (482). Further, "authenticity is not retreat into an imaginary world (a *Utopia*), but a transformation of this one." Authentic literary works are not valued as ends in themselves or as copies of experience but because their "power to transform experience reveals new possibilities of existence to us" (485). Thus, such works do not flatly validate the past.

Though there is some common ground between the two concepts of authenticity, there is also clear separation. As soon as a "veteran" critic labels a Vietnam War novel "authentic" according to the first meaning, he would seem to have denied the possibility of this second type of authenticity. If the achievement of the work verifies the reader's memory, then the work's ability to transform the reader's vision is severely circumscribed. Moreover, all of the works perceived as "telling it like it was" may be seen as echoing one another too extensively to make claims for originality. According to Baugh, "Originality lies in returning to the past and reinterpreting it in a way that the present is liberated from the current, dominant interpretation and working-out of its past" (483). The authentic work, in the existentialist sense, recognizes potential and possibility in its world, and it commands our assent to its ends though they are not our own. And it does all this, through its particular conventions, while recognizing the limitations of the shared world that it projects and that readers (independently) inhabit.

With these two concepts of authenticity in mind, let us return to a representative set of assessments in a field where the popular notion of authenticity has had sway. The critics' responses to *Buffalo Afternoon* focus the issue neatly.

Even *Buffalo Afternoon* has been hyped for its authenticity. A *Publishers Weekly* review quoted in an advertisement for Schaeffer's novel called it "A stunning Vietnam chronicle. An authentic testament. A narrative that moves with the implacable power of fate." What kinds of authenticity can a woman who has never set foot in Vietnam give to the story of a young man's experience of that war? Some would say that it just can't be done.

Writing in *Washington Post Book World*, Vietnam veteran and novelist Kent Anderson (*Sympathy for the Devil*) questions Schaeffer's accomplishment; he even questions her purpose. In his review entitled "Pouring on the Gore," Anderson claims that the war section of *Buffalo Afternoon* is not realistic, but "often reads like a kind of gothic science fiction set in a fifth-dimension Asian war. It is filled with ghosts and dream sequences and spiritual visions, passages where the author can 'turn on the prose' for a while." Anderson never wonders whether such a style might be particularly appropriate. He never asks if Schaeffer is striving for another kind of accuracy, one closer to the texture of experience that another Vietnam veteran writer, Tim O'Brien, describes: "For the common soldier, at least, war has the feel—the spiritual nature—of a great ghostly fog, thick and permanent. There is no clarity. Everything swirls. . . . and therefore it's safe to say that in a true war story nothing is ever absolutely true" (*The Things They Carried* 88).

"I had trouble telling," continues Anderson, "which situations were 'real' and which were fantasy because even the parts that I *think* are supposed to be realistic are riddled with absurd technical and tactical mistakes and misconceptions." Although Anderson was prepared "to cut Schaeffer some slack on technical errors," he can't resist making almost half of the review a list of alleged inaccuracies regarding weaponry, communications, and other technical matters. Anderson seems outraged at the amount of mutilation, atrocity, and torture in the novel, and accuses Schaeffer of trying to enhance credibility by "pouring on the gore and tough-guy profanity." He concludes: "It comes down to the hard fact that you can't write convincingly about that war without having been there, and why should a successful poet and novelist like Schaeffer *try* to? I can't imagine what the *purpose* of this novel is, or who the audience is supposed to be."

Anderson's failure of imagination might also leave him wondering why Stephen Crane tried to write about the Civil War or why Shakespeare wrote plays about the Roman Empire. Or perhaps his unspoken concern is that a woman writer has dared to enter a male domain. At any rate, Anderson seems to confuse facts with truth, life experience with the demands of art. Are the lies in the film version of Ron Kovic's *Born on the Fourth of July* as "authentic" as the truths? Is the fact that an author was there any guarantee that a given work will show us how it was with precision, with feeling, and with integrity? As Tim O'Brien reminds us, "A thing may happen and be a total lie; another thing may not happen and be truer than the truth" (89). The telling itself is what counts. Writing "convincingly about that war" does not necessarily mean having the facts straight, though factual errors certainly can jeopardize credibility for readers who fasten upon them.

Although I believe that Anderson's allegations about inaccuracies are not very convincing, I don't want to take the time to rehearse them and argue *on those grounds* the merits of Schaeffer's novel. In fact, whether or not Schaeffer (or anyone else who wasn't there) can write "convincingly about that war" has little to do with technical detail. We need to question the privileged place of participants and witnesses as writers and critics on this war. After all, in reacting to novels and movies authored by Vietnam veterans, readers and viewers who are also veterans of that war do not inevitably agree on which works tell it like it was. Why are we so easily trapped into a naïve hunger for a usually undefined authenticity and authority regarding this material? What leads a reputable scholar like John Newman to write (about John Nichols's *American Blood*): "Nichols did not serve in Vietnam, so his accounts of infantry action in the first part of the book may be suspect to some" (154). Is this cause and effect logic acceptable?

In a *Booklist* review, John Brosnahan comments on Schaeffer's "techniques of magical realism" that "portray her character's descent into madness" (1219). In *Library Journal*, Barbara Hoffert calls *Buffalo Afternoon* a "swift if densely detailed novel" (115). These reviewers, presumably not veterans, have no consequent privilege (or handicap) regarding certain tests of authenticity. (*Library Journal* later named this novel one of its thirty-two best books of 1989.)

Strangely enough, even the most generous response to *Buffalo Afternoon* offers some bows to the authenticity god. Nicholas Proffitt's "Pete Bravado's Peace and War" is the most enthusiastic appraisal of the novel. Proffitt, who was a *Newsweek* correspondent and bureau chief in Vietnam in 1971–72 and is the author of two novels about the Vietnam War (*The Embassy House* and *Gardens of Stone*), does have some useful criticisms to make. He feels that the young Vietnamese girl, Li, begins as a promising character but finally dissolves into being merely a symbol. On the issue of details and authenticity, however, his response is diametrically opposed to Anderson's. He writes: "But it's the details that ultimately convince. All the Vietnam material is authentic: the weapons, the jargon, the leeches, the mud, even the crotch rot. Of course, this isn't the first time that Mrs. Schaeffer has pulled off such a coup. One of her earlier novels, *Anya*, presented such a realistic picture of life in a concentration camp in Poland that it was hard to believe she wasn't a camp survivor herself."

What we might add, of course, is that all these details are there for the taking in scores of earlier Vietnam novels and memoirs. That Schaeffer "spent two years reading oral histories" and that her research included regularly scheduled interview sessions with many Vietnam veterans over this same two-year period tells us something about her seriousness as an artist and her moral sensivity to the act of representation she performed. Her visit to northern Thailand to help develop her "visual grounding" for the novel reflects the same impulse (McGee 26).

Buffalo Afternoon, though a third-person narrative, establishes a male perspective. Schaeffer's most impressive achievement is her ability to render that outlook convincingly: that is her great imaginative act. Schaeffer, a stylist capable of high literary artifice, has drawn in Pete Bravado a character of less literate and literary sensibility than we are used to finding in the serious fiction of the war, a working class head and mouth that is not unduly transformed into a rich linguistic register. Having made that sensibility real, the rest follows. Pete's experience becomes the reader's whether or not a weapon is said to do something that it cannot do. And Pete's experience is capable of changing readers' understandings of the war. Moreover, the combat material is only one section of the novel. What Pete confronts there must be rendered in gut-wrenching detail so that we can understand the two hundred-page treatment of the next twenty years of his life. We know what haunts Pete during his long years of breakdown and rehabilitation, just as we know intimately the young Pete Bravado who went to war. Schaeffer's originality ("authenticity") lies in her rich contextualizing of Bravado's time in Vietnam so that "Vietnam" becomes a felt part of a full life informed by family as well as by regional and national culture.

No *veteran* writer of this war has yet told the "whole story"; that is, none has presented the war—in a single work—as the crucial period (or series of events) in the life of an American male whose larger life is presented in detail. There are novels as big and even bigger than Schaeffer's, but their concerns are more narrowly focused on the war as warfare.[1] Indeed, they may tell us more about it by responding to more of it or by registering the immediate responses of more characters. In most cases, however, the protagonists are curiously detached from their pasts or their futures.

One of the most important Vietnam War novelists, Larry Heinemann, gives us a harrowing combat novel in *Close Quarters* that includes a closing section on the early phases of return. After an interval of ten years, Heinemann published his delicate portrayal of the returned veteran in *Paco's Story*. In neither novel do Heinemann's protagonists fully connect to formative backgrounds. The other major novels of the returned veteran—Robert Bausch's *On the Way Home* and Philip Caputo's *Indian Country*—pretty much leave out the war to get at its consequences. These veteran authors—and others—seem to have fashioned their novels from their personal and artistic mastery over autobiographical materials as those materials became sufficiently distanced to be manageable.[2] Freed from feeding so directly on her own life, Susan Fromberg Schaeffer has been able to give us a more comprehensive vision.[3]

And this is not *because* she is a woman, but because she does not have to contend with the lodestone of memory. Hers is an amazing act of sympathetic projection, more stunning than Norman Mailer's *The Executioner's Song* or William Styron's *The Confessions of Nat Turner* in that its protagonist is a composite. But *Buffalo Afternoon* is not a stunt. It is a fine novel about an American who found it quite natural to be a soldier in Vietnam and then found that nothing was ever again quite natural. It is also about an America that found it quite natural to be in Vietnam. It is a novel about neighborhood and family, dreams and myths, and the first steps of psychic, social, and cultural reconstruction. Is it authentic? Perhaps not in the popular, narrower sense. But that sense cannot comprehend Schaeffer's achievement.

In *Walking Point: American Narratives of Vietnam*, Thomas Myers presents a view akin to Baugh's understanding of existentialist authenticity. Myers states: "The writers who have produced what are likely to be the most lasting documents of the war are those who have assessed and incorporated into their works the battle of words and images that transformed the war into something as much symbolic as real" (142). This act necessitates, according to Myers, an understanding, usurpation, and reformation of the language and rhetorical strategies of "official history"—what he calls "the manager's narrative." Thus, the earlier novelists of the war had no choice but to tell a more limited story, "to retrieve and then recreate the feelings, rhythms, and specific images that remained largely sequestered behind conveniently reconciled history and to place those components in opposition to the dominant text"; that is, in opposition to the manager's narrative of the Vietnam story. Myers recognizes how art depends on other art, and yet how significant art performs a transformation of its material and its readers.

Perhaps only the veteran writers could perform this initial work—or would need to. Without the writings of those veteran authors whose novels preceded hers, Schaeffer's magnificent effort may not have been possible. Like them, however, she has "transformed the war into something as much symbolic as real," and she has also, to borrow Ward Just's formulation, "scaled [it] down to life rather than up to myth" by imagining a life finally larger than the war itself (Myers 143). "And in the end," writes Tim O'Brien in *The Things They Carried*, "of course, a true war story is never about war. It's about sunlight. . . . It's about sorrow" (91).

In a review entitled "Meat in the Tiger's Mouth," Elizabeth Becker complains about the stereotypical patterns in *Buffalo Afternoon*. She remarks that "the teenage GI's bewildering odyssey through Vietnam's battlefields has become the vehicle of choice for expressing anger at the war" rivaled only by "the troubled veteran lost in his own culture, stupefied by his compatriots' disregard for all he has suffered in the line of duty." In Becker's view, Schaeffer has only joined these two genres without demonstrating "why neither the young soldier nor the angry veteran can explain the war or heal its wounds." Asserting that Schaeffer's real subject is madness (as if this were a dirty secret), Becker wonders how novelists can continue to ignore the perspectives presented by *The Pentagon Papers* and by such works as General Westmoreland's *A Soldier Reports*—both possible sources for explanations missing from combat-centered narratives. Becker argues that it is not enough to play on our sympathy for the victims. We must learn specifically who or what caused the war: "Even fiction requires cause and effect, otherwise there is no larger truth to be gleaned. And Americans will continue to dodge the question: Why Vietnam?"

Clearly enough, Becker's complaints question whether Schaeffer's work attains the second kind of authenticity. By calling the work derivative, Becker denies it originality. By calling for a new vision, she seems to accept the transformative requirement of existentialist authenticity. However, by prescribing the nature of the work's end, she shows herself to be finally out of sympathy with the autonomous ends of significant art. Furthermore, Schaeffer's story of disorientation in the American psyche—before, during, and after our military involvement in Vietnam—is much more than just a combining of stereotypes. It is a transcending of them.

While Becker's indictment is provocative, it seems misdirected, a calculated refusal to accept Schaeffer's ends in an attempt to call for the novel about or including national leadership. Schaeffer's novel, in its lower keys, does provide some explanation of "Why Vietnam?" in its sketch of the shifting ethic of three generations of Americans of which Pete's is the last. The inquisitive, knowledgeable Sergeant Wapniak, an important minor character, is the analytical voice in the novel, a more acceptable version of the philosopher-soldiers whose oral exam level discussions shatter verisimilitude in *The 13th Valley*. Becker pays no attention to these dimensions of the novel. She must be waiting for her preferred explanation to be writ large.

Buffalo Afternoon remains a novel of experience, albeit imagined experience. It is a novel of the most cautious optimism about the human spirit's resiliency. It does engage the patterns of other Vietnam novels and memoirs, but perhaps only because these patterns are the inescapable ones. For Becker, a correspondent who covered the war in Cambodia for the *Washington Post* and whose *When the War Was Over* is a major discussion of the Cambodian revolution, the authenticity issue with regard to verisimilitudinous detail is nonexistent. She only worries that Schaeffer "rarely shifts her vision above or beyond the eyes of Bravado" and that "her Vietnamese characters [Li excepted] are stereotypes that deny any serious intent behind that country's war." These characters, of course, are as Pete Bravado sees them, given the circumstances of acquaintance. There are no political scientists or policy makers in this novel.

And perhaps this is a limitation in the fictional treatments of the Vietnam War to date: our writers have only dealt with those who represent the many whose lives were altered by the decisions of the few. On the other side of the issue of authenticity, then, is the issue of persuasive analysis: "This is the way it was" issues are supplanted by "This is why it was." The authority of the veteran is supplanted by the authority of the historian. One offers testimony regarding the "real texture"; the other authenticates "the real answer." Everyone is entitled to have an opinion about *Buffalo Afternoon* as well as any other literary work. Questions of authenticity and such ultimate questions as "Why Vietnam?" are of varying degrees of importance, the latter probably far more important than the former. But I doubt that either question is a fair one to ask of a novel or a novelist. Certainly it is not the criterion on which to base an assessment of what a particular novel has to offer.

Nor should the tests of the veteran or political historian be privileged above other tests. In the future, when no veterans are around to hand down authenticity judgments and when "the real answer" to our involvement in Vietnam is either universally shared or still a matter of controversy, Susan Fromberg Schaeffer's *Buffalo Afternoon* will be seen as a rich portrait of American character. One issue in measuring its achievement will be the issue of gender, an issue complicated by very different notions of authenticity than those of surface detail, much more to do with transforming the reader's vision.

In *The Remasculinization of America: Gender and the Vietnam War*, Susan Jeffords traces connections between "the discourse of warfare" and "the process of remasculinization current in American culture" (185). She finds this body of discourse to be the principal vehicle through which "the constructions of masculine and feminine" are presented "in even firmer and more exclusionary terms" than in other cultural artifacts. It will be interesting to see whether Schaeffer's act of imagination is viewed as evidence for Jeffords's position, as a signal exception to the tendency she describes, or as the leading text among a body of recent works that when taken together refute her argument. What, in these terms, is the cultural significance of Schaeffer's ambition and achievement? Forcefully including herself and her character Li in the discourse, has Susan Fromberg Schaeffer redefined its terms? Is this vision *less* exclusionary? Doesn't the "authenticity" of Schaeffer's work finally depend on the risks she has taken, the desire—through the work—to go beyond and transform herself?

The title phrase "Buffalo Afternoon" has to do with the reassuring constants in life. It tells us that work and hardship necessarily exist, but that they are the preliminaries to peaceful rest. The explanation is given in Li's narrative early in the novel:

> The water buffalo plow, and five hours after noon they are turned loose. This is the time we call buffalo afternoon, when the work is done and the buffalo head straight for their wallows and soak themselves happily in the water or the mud, for they have spent the day beneath the hot, hot sun. When they are finished wallowing, they eat the grass, eating and walking as they gradually make their way along. When evening arrives, they turn homewards, and no matter how far they have gone, they know their way home. . . . (9)

The novel ends with a reference to this vision in the middle age of Pete and his old Army buddy Sal. "'It's *afternoon*,' Pete said. 'It's buffalo afternoon for us, man. We're going to make it. It's the peaceful time. It's time to wander the fields and bring it all back home'" (535). In her splendid novel, Schaeffer invites us to consider a buffalo afternoon for our country.

Given the debate over dramatic license in "life story" works such as the film version of *Born on the Fourth of July*,[4] it is nice to know that Susan Fromberg Schaeffer's novel cannot be criticized for lying. Lying is how it works. Nor do we need to worry about whether Pete Bravado is a thinly disguised version of the author, as Lt. Robert E. Lee Hodges must be in James Webb's *Fields of Fire*. And without that worry, the question of whether the biographical novelist or novelistic biographer is a slave to facts or a violator of them vanishes.

Moreover, Shaeffer's accomplishment takes us beyond Pete Bravado's stereotypical returned vet outrage that says, "After a while, you don't trust anyone who wasn't there." Perhaps Nicholas Proffit has said it best: "Susan Fromberg Schaeffer wasn't there, and she didn't shut up, and for that, Vietnam veterans should be grateful. She can be trusted." What must be added is that it is her achievement as an artist that can be trusted. Whether or not readers can trust the novel's authenticity according to the popular meaning, it has unmistakable authenticity in a more profound sense. It has the capacity to change the reader.

Schaeffer's achievement, with respect to this notion of authenticity, is rivaled by the work of other writers. Among those who were not there is Stewart O'Nan. O'Nan, born in 1961, would have been fourteen years old at the war's end and only seven during the Tet Offensive—the time of his protagonist's wartime service in *The Names of the Dead* (1996). This character, Larry Markham, is thirty-four in the circa 1982 setting of the novel; that is, about the age of his creator during the crafting of this fine testament to the sympathetic imagination. The story O'Nan tells, like many of those to be explored in later chapters, has to do with the presence of a particular past in post-Vietnam America. It is a story evenly divided between acts and shadows.

Larry, whose tour of duty was 1968, finds himself with a failing marriage. His life, beginning with the veterans' group rap sessions that he leads at the local Veteran's Administration Hospital, is invaded by a mysterious Vietnam War veteran named Creeley. Creeley disappears from view, stealing a gun and a deck of cards, but leaves threatening hints (a sequence of playing cards along with notes) and proves by grotesque, ingenious displays that he can maim or murder Larry or those close to him whenever he wishes. Creeley has broken into computer programs and modified records so that his own identity is confused with Larry's.

Larry guesses that they must have crossed paths during the war, but try has he might, he can't remember Creeley.

Suspense builds for the reader as Larry races to discover just who Creeley is, what he wants, and how to stop him before he completes what seems to be his deadly mission. Larry, who drives a delivery truck bringing cake snacks to sales outlets in the Ithaca, New York area, is an unlikely investigator. His life has settled into a routine of quiet ineptitude since his tour as a medic. Larry's stuffy father, a doctor, exudes disapproval; his wife (and mother of his learning disabled child) has had enough of the neglect she feels from Larry's obsessions with Vietnam memories.

Only the oddball assortment of veterans whose stories he encourages seems supportive, along with the police detective who is charged with the Creeley case but, correctly, doesn't think he is getting Larry's full cooperation. In fact, Larry suspects that he won't like the answers he finds, the reasons for Creeley's menace. Avoiding proper channels and enlisting the aid of computer hackers, Larry is able to make faster progress than the agent in uncovering Creeley's background, but he is slow to share what he finds out. He discovers that Creeley is the son of a woman who was Dr. Markham's patient. Larry's imagination plays with the echo of Mrs. Creeley's first name, Ellen, with his own mother's name, Helen. At one point, Larry suspects that his father had an affair with Ellen Creeley, making Creeley his half brother, and that Creeley's motive is based on resentment about his unacknowledged identity, his getting so close to Larry a way of replacing him.

O'Nan alternates chapters of Larry's threatened present with chapters that treat his combat experience, casting them as extended memories. Though his writing is remarkable in many ways, it is most remarkable for the authenticity, in the popular sense, of wartime minutiae. There are few novels of the war that are so intricately detailed with regard to weaponry, clothing, terrain, climate, medical treatment, and the feel of combat. In handling such material, O'Nan rivals the title story in Vietnam veteran Tim O'Brien's classic *The Things They Carried* (1990). The cast of characters in Larry's fighting unit is sharply drawn, as are their speech patterns and superstitions.

Larry's own transition from new guy to hardened grunt is convincing, and his experiences along the way prepare us (as do Pete Bravado's in Schaeffer's novel) for his later stateside difficulties. Larry's ironic progress as a soldier (and medic) includes his passage from pretending to fire his weapon to actually being able to kill the enemy and finally to killing, mercifully, a dying comrade. Later, Larry withholds these truths and others from those closest to him, yet they haunt him, stalk him, even as Creeley does.

Eventually, the insane Creeley forces the confrontation he seeks—and the recognition. Creeley is a soldier whom Larry never truly saw, but during a night-time ambush left for dead. In Creeley's view, Larry should have killed him. Instead, Creeley was taken prisoner and tortured. He was released in 1973. Failing to get Larry to execute him once again, Creeley takes his own life, assured that Larry cannot forget him.

Creeley's haunting exposed secrets that both Larry and his father had wanted to keep hidden. With their exposure, with nothing left to hide, Larry is ready to tell the stories he has kept locked up inside. And the mementos of his lost comrades that Larry has hoarded in his footlocker are also finally released, placed beneath their owners' names at the Vietnam Veterans Memorial.

Like Schaeffer, O'Nan has merged the conventions of the battlefield and returned vet novels, though he has skipped over the immediate problems of return. By focusing on a character in his thirties, O'Nan has lengthened the reach of the war, locating his protagonist in the America of Ronald Reagan's presidency. Like Schaeffer, too, O'Nan has achieved art that reaches that second and higher meaning of authenticity. In an effort of startling imagination, an imagination undoubtedly rooted in meticulous research and sympathetic understanding, this writer answers to the call of transforming his material and opening up to the reader new possibilities. He presents not a copy of something, but, in Baugh's phrase, an original, providing the opportunity to see the world in a different way. In reviewing the book for the *Washington Post*, Marc Leepson claims that *The Names of the Dead* "comes close to being *The Red Badge of Courage* of the American War in Vietnam." The basis for this comparison must include, of course, the distance of O'Nan's life from the war, which he transforms into a universal tale of love, torment, and confrontation.

Schaeffer's story of Pete Bravado is also a story of urban America, while O'Nan's Larry Markham is a son of the small town. The authors know these places and their people well. Schaeffer's Brooklyn and O'Nan's Ithaca are as much the settings for their novels as is Vietnam. What remains a marvel is how they seem to know Vietnam just as well, and how, through their central characters, they have made Vietnam and the home community contiguous places in the American psyche. They have done so in novels that transcend the level of artistry and insight found in most of the works written by those who have "been there."

NOTES

1. One such novel is Franklin Allen Leib's *The Fire Dream*.

2. Ernest Lockridge's *Prince Elmo's Fire* provides a detailed treatment of its protagonist's early life and then takes him through his experience in Vietnam. In his compact *The Second War*, G. C. Hendricks subordinates the protagonist's Vietnam experience to a portrait of the American South that forms him and to which he brings his memories of combat.

3. Evan Hunter's *Sons* records the contrasting experiences and attitudes of three generations of American men at war—Bert, Will, and Wat Tyler.

4. See, for example, Diana West's "Does 'Born on the Fourth of July' Lie?"

Chapter Four

Joe Haldeman and the Wounds of War

In war, combatants are wounded. In representations of war, these wounds often form part of a symbolizing pattern. The wound can be a stigma, a "red badge of courage," a superscription on one's identity. Moreover, the external wound can be a sign of more important spiritual or psychic damage for the individual, the fighting unit, and the society engaged in the military enterprise. The wound, carried (or "worn") long after its direct cause, is always a reminder of mortality and loss. In Stewart O'Nan's *The Names of the Dead*, the wound to Larry Markham's foot is the living symbol not only of his time served in Vietnam but of his failure to keep his platoon alive and of his inability to express his buried anguish. Larry's marriage is failing in part because of his inability to achieve a meaningful intimacy with his wife. Thus, the wound that his prosthetic device hides so well cannot cover his emotional impotence.

When war is viewed as an essentially masculine behavior, and when aggressive masculinity is figured in sexual tropes (as in Hasford's *The Short-Timers*), then the most telling wounds of war will be genital wounds. The symbology of Vietnam War literature includes many examples of emasculating wounds and emasculating trauma. Furthermore, the lost war becomes configured as lost manhood. To once again employ Milton J. Bates's observation, "America . . . was castrated on the sexualized battlefield of Vietnam" (143). Even a wound proximate to the genitals marks a threat to potency on various levels.

Thus, among the more powerful symbols of the Vietnam War are the American M-2 Bounding Mine and the Soviet OZM-3 Antipersonnel Mine, known by the common name of Bouncing Betty. In his *Words of the Vietnam War*, Gregory R. Clark describes this weapon as a "cone shaped mine buried in the ground. When triggered, it bounced about three feet into the air, about groin level, then exploded, causing extensive shrapnel damage to the lower part of the human body" (67). Injuries to lower back, hips, genitals, and legs (including dismemberment) are the usual consequences of Bouncing Betty explosions. While

"Bouncing Betty" sounds like a term of endearment, or a laugh in the face of calamity, it nonetheless is a female personification of male disaster. As such, the term has its place on the allegorical map of Vietnam as gender war described in chapter 2.

In American literature, the prototype of the wounded warrior rendered sexually and spiritually impotent is Hemingway's Jake Barnes, the protagonist of *The Sun Also Rises*, though the precise nature of his wound is not clear, nor do we know of the weapon or device that caused it. John Baird, the wounded Vietnam War veteran in Joe Haldeman's *The Hemingway Hoax*, would seem to be (among other things) a Jake Barnes variant. Jake is an ancestor of the tough guy, literary kin to the hard-boiled detectives of Hammet and Chandler who in turn convey their pedigree to James Lee Burke's Dave Robicheaux, whose Vietnam War wounds are one subject in chapter 8.

A more obvious echo of Jake Barnes, as Katherine Kinney points out, is Tom in Bobbie Ann Mason's *In Country*. While Tom's impotence is war-derived, there is no physical wound—no visible symbol—of his loss. The small lumps on his back from shrapnel have nothing immediate to do with his inability to perform. When Sam asks "Did you get hurt down there too?" Tom replies: "No. It's just in my head. Like a brick wall. The Great Wall of China. I butt up against it" (127).

In Philip Caputo's *Indian Country*, the small round scars on Chris Starkmann's back are the visible signs of his psychic wounding, which is far more profound than the loss of sexual prowess. In fact, Chris is an impressive sexual performer, though he has lost the capacity for true intimacy. Withdrawn, silently and sullenly nurturing the war as his true mistress, his breakdown some years after his war experience is the delayed stress of survivor guilt and the buried self-hatred from having made an error that brought friendly fire down on others. What Chris has lost is his sense of self-worth.

With Larry Heinemann's Paco Sullivan (of *Paco's Story*), wounds and tattoos become a hieroglyph of the war's received messages. As Paco performs his daily tasks at the Texas Lunch, one can almost hear the screws turning in his gimpy leg joints. Seriously wounded and almost left for dead, Paco's postwar life is a kind of living death. He has become positioned outside the normal circle of human contact. He is a gimp, an outsider, and a man living with the spiritual consequences of both his participation in the gang rape and murder of a Vietnamese woman and his status as the lone survivor of a massacre at Fire Base Harriet.

Heinemann's ghost narrator inventories Paco's scars in great detail, and we learn that Paco's penis, too, is "slashed with scars" (172). His sexual fantasies are a yearning for a release from "the stinging ache of those dozens and dozens of swirled-up and curled-around, purple scars, looking like so many sleeping snakes and piles of ruined coins" (173–74). Ironically, Paco's specialty was to rig booby traps like the Bouncing Betty that were "expressly forbidden according to the Geneva Convention Rules of War" (193). Paco is literally a marked man whose inner condition of exile is written on his body.

By turning our attention to the Vietnam War writings of Joe Haldeman, we can explore the territory of one writer for whom the wounds of war are at once realistic detail, characterizing symbol, and a mechanism of cultural critique.

*   *   *

If Vietnam were a science fiction novel, it would be clear who the invading aliens were, complete with inexplicable motivation and futuristic weapons. (*1968*, 239–40)

Although Joe Haldeman is best known as an award-winning science fiction writer, he also claims attention as a Vietnam War author. Haldeman's Vietnam experience runs through a great many of his dozens of works. Not only is it the main concern of three novels—*War Year*, *The Forever War*, and *1968*—but it plays a role in several short stories and a poem, and it touches several other novels in important ways.

Born in 1943, Joseph William Haldeman had earned a B.S. in astronomy before being drafted into the army in 1967. In Vietnam, he served as a combat engineer. Seriously wounded in combat, Haldeman received a Purple Heart and, in 1969, he was honorably discharged. From 1969–1970, he did some graduate work in math and computer science, but dropped out of this program to devote himself to writing. Later, he attended the University of Iowa, earning an M.F.A. in creative writing in 1975. Haldeman began publishing short fiction in 1969.

"Counterpoint," first published in 1972, involves two men born on the same day whose lives run at first along nonparallel lines of opportunity and expectation but whose paths cross in wartime Vietnam. The point of contact does nothing to alter their destinies, as each continues to defy the influences of early environment and develop according to some cosmic plan that Vietnam accelerates by turning the well-born into a vegetable and the orphan into a hero with a pension and a bright academic future. Both, however, die in an instant at the age of forty-two. As their twinned fate is revealed, the narrator makes it clear that they are brothers.

Haldeman's theme of alternative possibilities stirred in the cauldron of the Vietnam War begins here, to be replayed with variations in *The Forever War, The Hemingway Hoax* and *1968*. In these major works and others, Haldeman invests the war wound with rich symbolic suggestiveness on both psychological and cultural levels.

Beyond the direct references and analogies to the war proper, sixties and seventies culture is never far absent from Haldeman's imagination. For example, in *Worlds Apart* (1983), the second volume in a trilogy (which Haldeman considers his best work), he introduces a cast of characters whose names echo icons of the sixties and seventies. The name Berrigan, to choose the most obvious example, ushers in a cultural context that fits oddly with this futuristic saga of postwar horror. Haldeman imagines a world ravaged by war and plague in which Manson cultists invite death as a sacrifice. If humankind can allow itself such immense carnage, Haldeman suggests, perhaps the celebration of death is what we have been pursuing all along. This theme also runs through the works related directly to the Vietnam War. Moreover, the protagonist's choice between personal commitment to her lover and commitment to the renewal of humanity on a distant new world echoes the kind of choice with which many Vietnam era citizens and soldiers found themselves struggling. Choices and their consequences become more and more the thematic ground of Haldeman's writings.

In *War Year* (1970), Haldeman's first novel, the protagonist is the typical "new guy" through whose questions the reader learns about the material and cultural realities of the war. The more experienced men are always explaining slang, abbreviations, and so forth — and John Farmer passes his new knowledge on to us. We learn about weapons, explosives, fire bases, C rations, and almost everything that touches the daily life of a combat engineer as he prepares for and performs his duties.

John Farmer is nobody special. He is an innocent whose exposure to war has little intellectual or philosophical dimension. Experience is learning to deal with death and to deal it out. Haldeman's most revealing scenes depict the horrors of burial detail. Farmer's manhood is challenged by his early sickness over the maimed, bloated, decomposing bodies. Soon enough they are only slabs of meat. *War Year* presents vivid battle scenes, but little close contact with the enemy. Mines explode, artillery rips, but face-to-face conflict is minimal. Attached to Bravo Company engineering corps, Farmer blasts down trees to clear landing zones, sets up barbed wire perimeters, and generally learns the ways of explosives. Eventually, he is seriously wounded by a Bouncing Betty mine that kills his friend and mentor Prof. These wounds to thigh and knee, no doubt autobiographical records, reappear charged with literary significances in Haldeman's later novels, *The Forever War*, *The Hemingway Hoax*, and *1968*.

Returning to his company, Farmer soon finds himself in an ambush during which limbs and other body parts are flying around. Assigned to clear a landing zone, he nearly finishes the job when his narration is cut off in mid-sentence. Another voice tells us that a captain is about to deliver the KIA message to Farmer's mother.

This early effort is a rather slim representation of the title year, but it nonetheless gives much of the flavor of men at war. It is a novel with little political slant (though Farmer does notice that every other soldier seems to be an African American) and with almost none of the absurdist flavor characteristic of premier Vietnam War fiction. Farmer is a deadpan narrator without any particular way of looking at this war or war in general. It is hard to find in this novella Haldeman's vision of things. Well-flavored dialogue, keen description, and a concern with war as a natural atrocity are the main hallmarks of this work, a work that seems naïve by the standards of the larger body of Vietnam War literature and by Haldeman's own later writings. In fact, it is little more than a slightly fictionalized memoir.

War Year is dedicated to "Farmer and Doc and Sergeant Crowder," suggesting that the novel carries a strong dose of Haldeman's own life. These same names appear toward the end of Haldeman's narrative poem "DX," a work in which the narrating character is "Professor," another moniker from *War Year*. Since Haldeman was himself a college graduate when he was drafted, it is likely that "Prof" in both works is close to him in some ways, while Farmer, who survives in the first (hardcover) edition, is close to him in other ways.[1]

"DX" covers some of the same experiential ground as *War Year*, but it is more markedly polemical. In the poem, for example, Haldeman notes the absurdity of digging a hole, filling sandbags, and using logs and the sandbags to fortify the hole for one night's rest, then emptying the sandbags the next morning before moving on to do this all over again. "Rural urban renewal," he calls it. The men in the poem are combat engineers who need to pack their various explosives and accessory devices with care each time they move on. They come upon an enemy camp at which explosives have been left behind. The "X-Rays," jargon for combat engineers, have to DX this pile of untrustworthy explosives. They had detonated such leftovers on many previous occasions. This time, the DX was a trap, radio-detonated by the enemy. Doc is killed, as is Farmer. Sgt. Crowder loses a foot and dies in the hospital where Professor is treated. Professor survives, his injuries including those to knee, thigh, groin, and genitals that echo in part Farmer's injuries in the novel and anticipate the wound symbolism in *The Hemingway Hoax*. The poem's tone is heavily ironic and knowing, unlike that of *War Year*. Also, its technique is experimental, while that of the early novel is straightforward prose narration. In fact, the technique of the poem, a pastiche of columns that can be read horizontally or vertically, linearly or spatially, allows for alternative versions or readings. This technique parallels the collage methods of some of Haldeman's later novels.

In *The Forever War* (1975), Haldeman's first science fiction success, his futuristic premise has to do with expansions of time that allow a person to age according to one time dimension while "living" through much longer stretches. Through this concept, and through the title, Haldeman images America's long involvement in Vietnam as well as the load of experience packed into the single year of service that was customary. Compared to *War Year*, this novel is politically savvy. Haldeman takes hits at inappropriate training: in the case of the future encounter, the earthlings, called Terrans, are trained for combat in extreme cold but have encounters in extreme heat. The objectives of the war are unclear, as are the goals of specific missions. Little about the enemy is understood. In fact, in the imaginary version the enemy Taurans are seen for the first time. Nonetheless, part of Private William Mandella's training has involved a kind of brainwashing during which the enemy is demonized and thus made easy to kill. In the first encounter, unarmed Taurans are massacred by heavily armed Terrans in a manner that echoes My Lai.

In a later encounter, Sgt. Mandella and the strike force to which he is assigned meet a far more sophisticated Tauran force. Before that encounter, however, the group has become demoralized because of the long period of waiting. Boredom is as threatening as the enemy (as we learn from many Vietnam War memoirs). In the course of the battle, and in its aftermath, it becomes clear that intelligence about Tauran tactics and resources has been poor. Moreover, the Taurans seem to be improving rapidly (in terms of the premise, this is because much more time is passing for the Taurans than for the time-travelling Terrans). The slow acknowledgment of the enemy's capabilities parallels the slow realization that the North Vietnamese forces and the Vietcong would not be so easily defeated as first thought. To keep readers thinking about Vietnam, Haldeman reminds them that his main characters, William and his lady friend Marygay Potter, were trained by people who were from the last generation of Vietnam War veterans. Also, they embark for the war at collapsar Yod-4 from Tet-38, a Hebrew letter used in the collapsar numbering system that eerily parallels the name of the Vietnamese New Year celebration and thus the January 1968 military offensive associated with it. After suffering heavy losses, the Terran commander decides to risk court-martial by returning to home base for an assessment of damage that can lead to a clearer picture of enemy technology. This decision coincides with the end of Mandella and Potter's enlistment terms. They are warned about changes on Earth before they return, to decide whether to remain civilians or to reenlist as training officers.

The great changes that have taken place during their twenty-six years of absence serve to dramatize the returned veterans' sense of alienation and exile. (Mandella and Potter have in fact served two-year terms.) This interest was developed more fully in an early draft of the novel. The material that was removed before the publication of *The Forever War* has been separately published as the short story "You Can Never Go Back."

In this episode, Mandella and Potter discover that the world government has been seriously misrepresenting the nature and conduct of the war to keep support high. Both characters are interviewed, but their words as presented to the public are fabricated. They are told that they will not be able to find jobs, and that the likelihood of updating their skills is small. The war effort's drain on the economy demands that they return to soldiering, even though that return is not administratively forced. They seem to have no other option. While this last issue has no clear parallel with conditions met by the returning Vietnam War veteran, the others sound all too familiar. And maybe it does have a parallel in the feeling expressed by many that Vietnam, as a psychic landscape, had become the only home in which they could flourish.

The second half of *The Forever War* has much less Vietnam-related material than the first half, though the excised material that makes up "You Can Never Go Back" is in itself an important part of the "returned veteran" literature of the Vietnam War. Haldeman preferred the version of the novel that included this extended stay back on Earth, but he admitted that it stopped the adventure's action. In the excised material, he imagines more fully the reaction of the general public to a war that has gone on for so long that its purposes and presence have long faded from consciousness. In Haldeman's imagination, few veterans ever return, so their experiences have little impact on earth politics. The people "were angry in the abstract that it took so much tax money to support [the war], they were convinced that the Taurans would never be any danger to Earth; but they all knew that nearly half the jobs in the world were associated with the war, and if it stopped, everything would fall apart" (250). To the extent that the arts reflect the times, we are told that "Painting and sculpture were full of torture and dark brooding" (237).

In H. Bruce Franklin's words, "*The Forever War* fantasizes and extrapolates America's longest war into an 1143-year intergalactic combat instigated by generals and politicians, waged for profits, and conducted as a devastating fiasco from beginning to end" (350). William Mandella always carries guilt and pacifist leanings, but he never has the strength to resist the momentum of the war. Through him, Haldeman urges us to reject the thrill of a technology of destruction and leaves us horrified at the cultural path that has led and still leads us to ennobling our blood lust.

We should not leave this novel without reference to the wound that Mandella suffers in a later encounter—one in which the enemy now has clear superiority. This wound takes away a portion of his leg. Super-prosthetic techniques allow for the full restoration of function as well as near-indestructibility of the restored limb. In this futuristic setting, the physical wound becomes an occasion for technological regeneration: a wish-fulfillment device for any seriously injured combat soldier. On a deeper level, Mandella's wounds are psychic or spiritual. The combination of dislocation, the deeds he has performed and observed, and the sense of betrayal—"The 1143-year-long war had been begun on false pretenses" (226)—have left him an exile, as has the time-skipping premise of the novel.

Beyond this, *The Forever War* has an undercurrent of anxiety regarding homosexuality. Mandella is for some time labeled "Old Queer," and the future civilization Haldeman posits has a growing—perhaps species-threatening—homosexual dimension. Clearly, the wounding (on whatever level) has some connection with this concern about lost or altered sexual identity:

> I'd gotten used to open female homosex in the months since we'd left Earth. Even stopped resenting the loss of potential partners. The men together still gave me a chill, though. (139)

The many novels and stories that follow *The Forever War* offer occasional references to Vietnam, for Haldeman's work is generally set in the near future in which Vietnam looms as past experience or memory. A character in one of his novels is called the world's oldest living Vietnam War veteran.

In several of Haldeman's more recent novels, he has experimented with other genres and only given his sci-fi followers a glimpse of the premises that they are used to. His Cold War thriller, *Tool of the Trade* (1987), has a mind control premise that springs the plot but is hardly the center of interest. The conventions of the spy novel dominate here, and there is one character whose background as a Vietnam veteran has some significance.

The Hemingway Hoax (1990), one of Haldeman's most engaging titles, is a kind of literary thriller with a minor key premise of intersecting and alternative time-worlds. The protagonist is a Vietnam War veteran, now a college professor, whose war wounds become curiously interwoven with those of Hemingway and Hemingway's characters. John Baird, about to finish running through an inheritance and be forced to live exclusively on his salary, encounters a con man who tempts him into forging a manuscript of one of those lost Hemingway stories. In the course of the novel, the hero regularly measures himself against Hemingway. In particular, his wounds suffered in the Vietnam War are compared and contrasted to the wounds suffered by Hemingway in World War I. Baird doubts Hemingway's claim of having carried another wounded man "back to the trench, in spite of being hit in the knee by a machine-gun bullet" because Baird himself "was hit in the knee by a machine-gun bullet . . . and didn't get up for five weeks" (11). Nevertheless, Baird chooses to draw upon this link, the common experience of war, in order to choose his story material: a war story.

The question of potency resonates on many levels, including creativity and sexual performance, as the war wounds undergo metamorphoses each time Baird is killed by a superhuman entity who is trying to stop him from stirring up an interest in Hemingway that may lead to planetary doom. The wounds, of course, are some combination of knee, thigh, and genitals—the usual injuries found in Haldeman's fictions. Each "kill" sends Baird into a new iteration of his possible lives, and each life brings him closer to Hemingway, until finally he and Hemingway phase in and out of identity. The war, here and elsewhere, is an opportunity or a necessity for man's killing nature. Moreover, the business of completing the hoax becomes a life and death struggle between Baird and the con man, one that also involves Baird's wife and a bookish ex-prostitute who is hired to put Baird in such a compromising position that he can't back out of his commitment to the hoax. Haldeman carefully interweaves sexual lust and bloodlust.

For the historical and mythical Hemingway, for John Baird, and for Haldeman himself, this novel raises the issue of the war creating the writer who re-creates the war—of the wound opening up a flow of words that reconstitutes the wound. In many ways the most self-reflexive of Haldeman's fictions (he, like, Baird, is a wounded Vietnam veteran, a writer, and a college teacher), *The Hemingway Hoax* presents a series of "what ifs" through its intersecting planes of time and event. However, all of these alternative paths seem to blend into a common, unified destiny, so that for all of its complication and nuance, *The Hemingway Hoax* presents a vision that contains a strong thematic echo of "Counterpoint" and the gritty determinism of *War Year.*

Finally, Haldeman returns to the literal war novel in *1968* (1995), a work in which he presents his most sophisticated treatment of the Vietnam War both on the battlefield and on the home front. The protagonist of *1968*, John Speidel ("Spider"), is (like his creator) a draftee from the Maryland suburbs of Washington, D.C. Like John Farmer of *War Year*, he is assigned to a combat engineer squad after early duty on burial detail and graves registration. Also like Farmer, he works with a character nicknamed "Prof" and is witness to various maimings of legs and genitals. Moreover, Haldeman's need to find strategies through which to explain the specialized terms and practices of the war is just as powerful. However, though Spider is something of an innocent, the narrator of *1968* is not, and Haldeman's narrative strategies as well as his vision become rewardingly complex.

One important difference between the two novels is the enriched historical context of the more recent one. The narrator is savvy about political and military events and about sixties culture in ways that allow Spider's experiences, and those of other characters, to collect meaningful overtones. We visit not only the battlefield and Walter Reed Army Hospital in Washington, D.C., but also the assassination of Robert F. Kennedy in California and the police riots in Chicago during the Democratic National Convention. Additionally, the narrator of *1968* is a grand ironist, and even Spider's dimensions of perception are far beyond those granted to Farmer.

Structurally, the novel works on three levels: chapters that are units of time in which we first encounter weeks, then months, then seasons. There is less that needs to be filled in as the character and the reader accumulate knowledge, as we move from the battlefield to hospitalization and stateside adventures. Also, Haldeman is more careful this time about fully representing a year than he was in his first novel. Within the time-focused chapters are subdivisions with various, sometimes whimsical, headings focused on topics. Some of these headings recur with enumeration, suggesting the nature of the war, and of history, as both progressive and cyclical, linear and spatial. Most of the headings, like "Three Contributions to the Theory of Sex," promote the whimsical strain in the novel's complex tone. The third structural device is alternation of central consciousness between Spider and his girlfriend Beverly. Her life as a marginal player in the civil rights and peace movements parallels Spider's as a minor player in the year of the Tet offensive. These latter strategies, with the effect of fragmentation and alienation, are refinements of devices Haldeman uses in his science fiction efforts and also remind one of his technique in the "DX" poem.

The traumatic center of Spider's experience is the shock of the ambush in which his squad is annihilated and he is unaccountably spared. Like his predecessors in Haldeman's Vietnam War stories, Spider suffers a thigh injury, but his physical rehabilitation is a minor issue compared to the psychological impact of this wounding. Spider's trauma, though treated somewhat comically through the portrait of his inept and self-seeking psychologist at Walter Reed, is a composite result of experiences of which the ambush is only the most intense. Spider has already been having hallucinations ("seeing ghosts"), and his memory of events is compromised or complicated by the interweaving of different layers of perception and reality. In fact, Haldeman narrates several "versions" of the ambush story, leaving the reader to piece together a full and satisfying ur-story—or to despair of ever doing so. Thus, the treatment of Spider's wounding in an otherwise "realistic" narrative has parallels with the versions of John Baird's wounding, and versions of the missing Hemingway manuscripts episode in *The Hemingway Hoax*. (Indeed, there are uncanny parallels between the alternative story-truths offered in both of these novels and the "versions" of Kathy Wade's disappearance in Tim O'Brien's 1994 *In the Lake of the Woods*, a novel set in the aftermath of Vietnam atrocities.) The knowability of truth on a literal level is denied, yet as the patterns take on symbolic suggestiveness, a concern with truths that transcend facts emerges.

One means to that end is that the latter versions of the trauma tale emerge as fantasy and sci-fi renderings in which Spider's experience is transformed by his imagination and his reading. From the beginning of his wartime experience, Spider has been reading science fiction, beginning with Robert Heinlein's *Glory Road* (1963), itself considered a prophetic pre-Vietnam War vision of American destiny. Moreover, one of the "versions" of Spider's story is, the narrator tells us, "loosely modeled on *Starship Troopers,*" another Heinlein novel. The habit of mind that demonizes enemies and obsesses over technical gadgetry receives a satiric glance here. In fact, by making Spider a sci-fi fan who can refashion his war experience in that genre, Haldeman, quite knowingly and engagingly, directs our attention to his own career, a career in which various protagonists try to hold on to individuality and principle while in the service of corrupt systems that foster empire building and dehumanization. Whether Spider's trauma drives him insane or simply amplifies a preexisting tendency toward schizophrenia, the war enterprise itself is viewed as a collective madness whose rationalizations are shattered by Haldeman's insistence on mankind's perverse hunger for death and death-dealing.

In *1968* and elsewhere, Haldeman's inquiry into human sexuality complicates his analysis into particular and universal warfare. In some works, homosexuality is viewed as a desirable or at least necessary state that will help stabilize populations. Alternatively, Haldeman connects macho mentality and behavior with both sexual insecurity and the propensity toward killing and war. This connection is a major motif in *The Hemingway Hoax*, a work in which Haldeman underscores the critical vogue of discovering homosexual leanings and fears beneath the great hunter-warrior image that Hemingway so carefully calculated. He has us imagine that John Baird's hoax will stir up a destructive interest in Hemingway and Hemingway's celebration of macho style that will be harmful and thus needs to be terminated by the supernatural beings who intrude upon Baird's intentions.

In *1968*, Spider is haunted by memories of his graves registration stint and by a vision of his sergeant's masturbation with the severed and decomposing head of an enemy soldier. The image of the faceless skull follows him, though it loses its overt sexual connection through much of the novel. For several reasons, including some physical symptoms, Spider is diagnosed as being a homosexual. The "Li" he mutters about, a Vietnamese prostitute, is confused by Captain Folsom, the analyst, with "Lee," Beverly's new boyfriend. Through Folsom and Spider's father, middle class America's homophobia is examined as part of the psychosocial problem that leads to war. Thus both *The Hemingway Hoax* and *1968* provide complex images of homophobia and exaggerated macho stances born of sexual insecurity as causal factors in the dynamics of war.

The general direction of Joe Haldeman's Vietnam War representation has been from naïve description to sophisticated analysis, and from battlefield experience to the larger historical and cultural setting of wartime America. There is a linkage in his work between imagining what humans are capable of doing and remembering what Vietnam showed him about death's simultaneous horror and lure. Throughout, the presentation of literal and symbolic wounding has challenged readers with a range of meanings, including the suggestion that macho cocksureness is a causal factor that finds an appropriate revenge or threat. The exploding of male genitalia (or the threat of such) is figured as both the cause and consequence of the warrior condition. In addition, Haldeman characteristically keeps the reader occupied with pondering alternatives, questioning the inevitability of who we are and what we can make of our lives. Always, Haldeman is a great entertainer, his later works growing in comic and satiric shading without ever softening or undermining the importance of the serious issues he pursues.

NOTES

1. According to Haldeman, the paperback ending is the true original; the version in which the protagonist lives was written to placate the publisher of the first edition, which appeared in hardcover. Nonetheless, Haldeman is already contending with alternative possibilities.

Chapter Five

Vietnam as Noise

Anyway, Paco always said you could pretty much tell if you got a kill or just a hit by how solid the *whomp* was.

—Larry Heinemann, *Paco's Story*

And thunder is the pounding mortar.

—Bruce Weigl, "Song of Napalm"

Our gravel-crunching boots tear great / holes in the darkness, make us wince / with every step.

—W. D. Ehrhart, "Night Patrol"

While the scar or other physical marker is a constant reminder of its cause and context, the psychological wounds of war, large and small, are often attached to sensory experience and thus can be aggravated by sensory triggers. Indeed, simply as memory, the war exists as a complex weave of emotion, sensation, and pieces of story.

Among the literary reflections of the Vietnam War are many works with passages that put a premium on auditory experience. In most of these works, the particular uses of auditory imagery suggest a unique situation in which the usual dominance of visual perception is challenged or overthrown. Many passages help us understand the special ways in which one thinks, feels, and operates in this night world of sound. In certain works, auditory images accompany key moments of thematic underpinning or structure. Still others reveal the lingering effects of auditory experience on traumatized veterans. Though such imagery has become a literary convention in writings about the Vietnam War, it is rooted in the experience of those writers who served there. In their various ways, these writers suggest that you cannot see the truth of Vietnam; maybe you can only hear it.

Of course, such experiences and representations are not unique to the Vietnam War. Many literary treatments of the battlefields of modern warfare convey the sounds of cannon, bomb, machine gun, ricochet, and the chugging and clanking of combat vehicles. Hardy's "Channel Firing" comes to mind here, and the opening lines of Owen's "Anthem for Doomed Youth":

> What passing-bells for these who die as cattle?
> —Only the monstrous anger of the guns.
> Only the stuttering rifles' rapid rattle
> Can patter out their hasty orisons.

Narratives of ancient warfare rehearse the clash of blade and armor. For Vietnam, however, the auditory experience has become a special signature, accompanying such icons as the helicopter (with which it intersects) and the pungi stick, which is later replaced, in history and representation, with the Vietcong mine (see Hall 156–58).

In Perry Oldham's poem, "War Stories," a character named Howard brings home a tape recording so that he can share his experience of the war with family and friends. Not movie footage, not photographs, but a tape of sounds. Howard, like many of those who served in the war, has fastened onto its sounds as the most revealing, the most truthful images.

> Have you heard Howard's tape?
> You won't believe it:
> He recorded the last mortar attack.
> The folks at home have never heard a real
> Mortar attack
> And he wants to let them know
> Exactly
> What it's like.
>
> Every night he pops popcorn
> And drinks Dr. Pepper
> And narrates the tape:
>> Ka-blooie!
>> Thirty-seven rounds of eighty millimeter—
>> You can count them if you slow down the tape.
>> There's an AK.
>> Those are hand grenades.
>> Here's where the Cobras come in
>> And whomp their ass. (Ehrhart, *Carrying* 209)

Though all wars strain all human senses, and though many wars have involved significant night-time actions, the memory of the Vietnam War and the literary expressions of that experience have stressed the intensity of such light-starved encounters to the point where this aspect of the war has become mythologized. This is the war in which our usually dominant sense of sight went underground. Combatants had to learn to see in the dark, and special optical instruments that improved night vision—starlight scopes—were standard equipment for watch-standers. But one also depended, sometimes almost exclusively, on feeling and listening.

Basil T. Paquet's "Night Dust-off" is one reminder of this world of sound in which light is artificial, intermittent, unreal:

A sound like hundreds of barbers
stropping furiously, increases;
suddenly the night lights,
flashing blades thin bodies
into red strips hunched against the wind
of a settling slickship.

Litters clatter open,
hands reaching into the dark belly of the ship
touch toward moans,
they are thrust into a privy
feeling into wounds,
the dark belly of all wound,
all wet screams riven limbs
moving in the beaten night. (Ehrhart, *Carrying* 217)

A typical narration of night combat is the following one from John Del Vecchio's *The 13th Valley*, told almost entirely in images of noise. There are pages of such noise-saturated description:

Amid the explosions and the continuous small arms cacophony came the popping sounds of the NVA mortar tube below Company A. The enemy mortar team was firing furiously. Brooks grabbed Cahalan's handset, threw it back and scrambled for Brown's. He keyed the handset bar furiously, interrupting Bravo's artillery adjustments. "Armageddon Two, Armageddon Two, this is Quiet Rover Four, over." He unkeyed. "Come on you bastard, I got a fix on the tube." Brooks keyed again. "Armageddon . . ." He paused. Everyone else had frozen. The twelve howitzers on Barnett were all firing. The booming from Barnett and the explosions across the valley increased. Brooks violently shoved the handset into FO's hand. "Get Arty. Tell em you hear the tube. Tell em you'll adjust by sound." (295)

Such noise-dominated experiences forge connections between battlefield noises and the whole spectrum of combat emotions, connections that are not likely to be obliterated. The impact of such sounds is given eloquent testimony in this passage from Charles Durden's *No Bugles, No Drums*:

But the sound was what got me. Rockets whinin' 'n' screamin', then an earth-rattlin' boom. Shrapnel whippin' past, buzzin' like a flock of hornets. The machine guns chatterchatter-chatterchatter, two or three different pitches accordin' to what kind they were. The '16s poppin'. The M-79 grenade launchers . . . when they go off it sounds like somebody's pulled the cork on a twenty-gallon wine bottle, sort of a deep *pong*! Grenade explosions, mines blowin', gasoline goin' off, screams from the dyin', screams from the livin', pure fear personified in falsetto vibrations so unreal in other moments that a man would deny he's ever made noises even remotely similar, and prove it by tryin' and failin' to imitate himself. (193)

It is not only the description that is important here, but the narrator's testimony that "the sound was what got me," the suggestion that sound is the lasting, characterizing imprint of the war. The cacophony of death symbols made a chilling concert, at once recognizable and unfamiliar, unpredictable and unavoidable.

In *In Country*, by the time Bobbie Ann Mason's 1980s teenager, Samantha Hughes, tries to trick herself into an awareness of the circumstances the father she never knew met in Vietnam, the whole sonic rigmarole of the war had become well known to her generation of high school graduates. Their popular culture had enshrined it. She had learned, as had all reading, television-watching, and movie-going Americans, that the Vietcong "conducted their business at night" (214). At Cawood's Pond, as Sam forces an imagined combat night upon herself, she conjures up the flashes of night-fire from her Uncle Emmett's descriptions and from her reading. She recalls that the "soundtrack" of the war is made up of "the *whoosh-beat* of choppers, the scream of jets, the thunder-boom of artillery rounds, the mortar rounds, random bullets and bombs and explosions. The rock-and-roll sounds of war" (214). Sam's awareness of a sonic environment, her way of thinking about it, consolidates the stories that we have all heard and read, and that many veterans have told. In so doing, it underscores the mythic dimension of the represented auditory barrage—the soundtrack.

One of the tellers is W. D. Ehrhart, whose memoir *Vietnam-Perkasie* contains a passage that might have fed Samantha Hughes's imagination:

> It was never really silent in Vietnam. Night after night; all the way to the four horizons, there was color and sound all night long: the flash and boom of artillery . . . the fast orange zip of tracer bullets . . . the tat-tat of small arms fire; and always the thump and whine of choppers and jets prowling the skies with their rotating beacons and winking wing lights. (69)

In such an environment, one's sensitivity to sound is heightened. Anxiety and noise are inseparable, as in these lines from Ehrhart's poem "Night Patrol": "Our gravel-crunching boots tear great / holes in the darkness, make us wince / with every step" (Ehrhart, *Carrying* 93). Tim O'Brien's description of night guard duty in *The Things They Carried* makes the point:

> After a while, as the night deepens, you feel a funny buzzing in your ears. Tiny sounds get heightened and distorted. The crickets talk in code; the night takes on a weird electronic tingle. You coil up and tighten your muscles and listen, knuckles hard, the pulse ticking in your head. You hear the spooks laughing. No shit, *laughing*. (231)

How many more tricks would the imagination play on someone who had LP (Listening Post) duty, "where a fire team went outside the perimeter in order to give advance warning of any probe or attack" (Webb 343)?

In O'Brien's *Going after Cacciato*, Paul Berlin's night duty in the Observation Post tower gives rise to his fantasy of Cacciato's extended flight in a reverie framed by harsh sounds. On a nighttime watch, Berlin would depend on hearing as much as on visual observation to detect enemy action.

Noises of explosions link the outer and inner stories. Near the beginning of the action—the pursuit of Cacciato—Stink Harris takes the point and walks right into the trip wire that Cacciato had set. "There were two sounds. First the sound of a zipper suddenly yanked up. Next a popping noise, the spoon suddenly releasing and primer detonating" (34). The mixture of fear and the inhalation of the red smoke lead Paul Berlin to pass out. There was no lethal explosion, only the anticipation of one. At this moment, Paul's fantasies begin. At the end of his long reverie, as he and the others are about to corner Cacciato in a Paris hotel, Paul becomes aware of his fear: "The sound spun him around. His ears exploded" (388).

Red tracers turn back into brilliant red threads and then into the dissipating red smoke from the grenade. The noise that won't stop is the noise of Paul's own automatic rifle firing, which he has gripped in panic and can't let go of. "How did it start? A kind of trembling, maybe. . . . Then the shaking feeling. The enormous noise, shaken by his own weapon, the way he'd squeezed to keep it from jerking away from him" (392).

Here and elsewhere, the auditory image marks the threshold between orientation and disorientation. Imaginative flight and reentry are marked by the framing punctuation of sound, the latter bringing Paul Berlin back to the mundane just as Keats's speaker returns from his reverie upon the tolling of a bell-like word in "Ode to a Nightingale." In Keats's poem, however, the flight of imagination is not a mechanism of coping with traumatic fear.

Interpreting sounds is the business of the night soldier. Just as Del Vecchio's Lt. Brooks will have his forward observer make such an interpretation before telling artillery where to fire ("'Tell em you'll adjust by sound'"), so in Larry Heinemann's *Paco's Story* the narrator remembers that "Paco always said you could pretty much tell if you got a kill or just a hit by how solid the *whomp* was" (192). And Ehrhart's *Vietnam-Perkasie* records how a soldier would "learn to distinguish which sounds were okay and which were not. It was only a new sound, or a different sound, that sent a distress signal from the ear to the brain. The sounds you heard night after night rapidly became something to ignore. . . . Something subconscious heard the sounds and discarded them" (69–70).

Of course, the enemy could adjust by sound too, as clients of popular culture were reminded in Billy Joel's retrospective anthem of the war:

They heard the hum of our motors
They counted the rotors
And waited for us to arrive . . . ("Goodnight Saigon")

Perhaps the most clinical observer and recorder of the Vietnam War's auditory environment is Larry Heinemann. In his brilliant novel *Close Quarters*, the constant noise of the war becomes lodged in his main character's sensibilities—a nagging irritant, almost a disease, that affects his responses. Noise and its absence become poles of disease and health, victimhood and release.

Before looking closely at how this works in Heinemann's fiction, let us observe analogous uses by other writers. I suggest that "noise" has, for some Vietnam veteran writers, become a kind of code word. Walter McDonald's poem "After the Noise of Saigon" gives us no rendering of noise or of Saigon. Instead, we find a man hunting cougar in a spruce forest, working something out of himself in isolation:

> These blue trees have nothing
> and all to do with what I'm here for
> after the noise of Saigon,
>
> the simple bitter sap that rises in me
> like bad blood I need to spill
> out here alone in the silence
>
> of deep woods, far from people I know
> who see me as a friend, not some damned
> madman stumbling for his life. (65)

Carrying that noise is a form of damnation. It is an invisible scar: the scar under the other scars. It is the war as it has followed the veterans home. It is "The Sound of Guns"—the title phrase in Gerald McCarthy's poem that ends:

> Seven winters have slipped away,
> The war still follows me.
> Never in anything have I found
> a way to throw off the dead. (Ehrhart, *Carrying* 181)

But then it is not anything quite so particular as a *sound*. *Noise* is something else.

In *Close Quarters*, Heinemann's protagonist, Philip Dosier, drives an amtrack or "track." His world, in this case even his daytime world, becomes one of vibrations and noise: "The vibrations jolted my hands and arms and chest. The CVC muffled the grinding and shrieking and thumping of the treads, the throttled roar of the engine, but after that day I always had a buzzing, crackling, rushing hum in my head" (31). This noise becomes something Dosier carries with him through and beyond the war. It is compounded, modified, and sometimes relieved (as when he is on R & R in Tokyo), but it is the war internalized. Even when the war's ongoing din is squelched, Dosier's inner noise remains.

There is an extended description of a night battle that summons that noise: "All that noise like cackling and throaty rattling, a junk box poured out on the ground, all clatter and jangle and screaming" (230). After pages of continuous sensory description, we come to the point at which "Suddenly the sun rose over the trees" (234). Then all the fighting, and the noise, stops. But the inner noise does not.

Dosier's vision of health, of normalcy, is a vision at the other end of that buzzing in his head:

> But most of all it will be quiet. One morning I will be reaching sleepily for the burner to make the coffee or slipping a fresh blade into my razor or bending over to pick up a snippet of thread from the floor, and that buzzing in my head will cease—simply pass away. (298)

This silence is what he waits for. But it may be a long time in coming.

Though the psyches of veterans are scarred by all kinds of images, a hypersensitivity to noise is a recurrent theme. Early in *A Rumor of War*, Philip Caputo writes: "I had . . . an intolerance of loud noises—especially doors slamming and cars backfiring—and alternating moods of depression and rage that came over me for no apparent reason" (4). Such noises frequently trigger flashbacks. In Bruce Weigl's "Song of Napalm," an otherwise idyllic scene is turned into a memory of dread for a Vietnam veteran many years home when a storm comes up "and thunder is the pounding mortar" (34). Perhaps the strength of the auditory image, and the power of sound as a flashback trigger, comes from its association with explosive, percussive phenomena that are not only heard, but felt in the shuddering response of the whole body, as in the Heinemann passage presented earlier.

Post-traumatic stress disorder, an illness of Vietnam War veterans characterized by increased autonomic system response to perceived symbols of war trauma, is, after all, a refined understanding of those symptoms previously associated with the term "shell shock"—a term whose metonymic roots are obvious. The relationship of assaulting noises to pain and the witnessing and fear of death are so strong that individuals who are continuously exposed to such noises do not become habituated to them, as they might to visual or olfactory stimuli. And uncontrollable conditions always produce a higher degree of stress than controllable ones—so that firing at a pistol range will not have the same effect as battlefield explosion or a tire blowout.

Such phenomena are clearly keys to the prevalence and power of auditory images in the imaginative literature of the war. Explored in the rich clinical literature on auditory stress and post-traumatic stress disorders, they cannot be detailed here.[1]

In one of the finest unheralded novels of the war, Rob Riggan's *Free Fire Zone* (1984), the protagonist's post-Vietnam perception mixes the sound of the chopper with the accompanying fear. To the other person in the scene, this "noise" not only doesn't mean anything, it isn't even heard.

> Away, up river, the sky began to vibrate. Gradually the noise filled the valley, became louder and louder, hammered at me. I turned and saw a woman hanging out her clothes behind the farm house. I wanted to reach for her. My hand slid through the grass. She didn't seem to hear anything.
>
> God help me! My eyes welled up. I looked across the canal, toward the trees above the towpath, and waited as the noise crashed around me, up against the hill. For a year I'd heard that sound, been thrilled by it. Now the land was quiet and it brought terror.

It passed. The propeller sound of its wake, the steadier drumming faded into a soft chop as the Huey vanished over the trees where the river road wound up into the escarpment. The woman was watching me, puzzled. How long had she been watching me? She smiled tentatively. She had never looked up, never heard it! (original in italics, 176)

Certainly the propeller sound of the Huey is the trademark auditory image of Vietnam. Billy Joel's "Goodnight Saigon" lays down a track of prop noise at the opening and close. ("We held the day / In the palm / Of our hand / They ruled the night / And the night / Seemed to last as long as six weeks / On Parris Island . . .") In Philip Caputo's *Indian Country* (1987), this very song—with its reproduction of "the rhythmic whisper of helicopter rotors" (205), becomes a flashback trigger for Chris Starkmann's harrowing memories, memories that flood the present and return him to the time of his Vietnam trauma.

The wish for an inner silence is implicit here, as it is in Heinemann's *Close Quarters*. Chris Starkmann's dream is revealed to us as a refashioning of the scene in which he is rescued. In the dream, everything is idealized and other-worldly. The helicopter is not green, but white. As the chopper ascends, Chris's blistered face is cooled. He feels safe and serene as the "fabulous bird" moves heavenward: "He no longer hears the roar of the engine, only a wondrous silence" (347). Chris has escaped what Alasdair Spark calls "the unmistakable slap-thud of the ubiquitous Huey" and its authority of noise (91–92). This silence is an attribute of the desired state of forgiveness—a state that Starkmann will attain later in the work.

Parenthetically, we should note that Chris Starkmann's return to the United States was an entry into additional turmoil, turmoil characterized by noise: "the pop of tear-gas guns, the chants of angry crowds rising above the choirs of police sirens, the sounds of an America gone berserk" (106). His move to the desolate upper peninsula of Michigan was a journey into solitude and silence, but only an exterior journey.

To conclude this brief survey, let us attend to another passage from Riggan's *Free Fire Zone*. Unlike the one mentioned earlier in which the narrator is aware of noises unheard by others, this passage presents him coming to an awareness of certain other noises—non-threatening noises—for the first time. In the passage, Riggan gives us a clue to the daytime and night-time operations of one veteran's senses:

I can hear diesels whining through the woods, northward, black like the night. For almost six months, I've lived across the river from these same tracks, but until tonight, I never knew the trains were so frequent. I didn't hear them. In the daytime, one doesn't hear sounds so much. It's easier to hide in the day. (15)

For people who have lived and almost died in shadows, the clarity of daylight is obliterating and the buzzing of psychic wounds is masked by absorbing fields of vision. The sounds are there, but pushed back and down, just as the enemy guns were often silent during the day. But at night, in darkness, one is exposed and sound becomes spectral.

Bruce Weigl's poem "Noise," found in *The Monkey Wars* but curiously not included in his 1989 gathering of Vietnam materials, *Song of Napalm*, also addresses the persistence of that noise in the veteran's psyche and the longing for silence. Weigl's narrator, now many years beyond his war experience, reports the 3:00 a.m. argument of newlyweds, the loud noises of passing trains, and the anger he carries within himself. The external noises are magnified by his anger and become part of "a triangle of nervous noise / Because the noise is in my head too, / The noise is always in my head." In such ways, the literature reminds us of lingering disease in the aftermath of our nation's longest war. The noise in the speaker's head is also a shadow on his soul.

NOTES

1. Interested scholars may turn to R. Pary et al., "Post-traumatic Stress Disorder in Vietnam Veterans"; R. K. Pitman et al., "Psychophysiologic Responses to Combat Imagery of Vietnam Veterans with Posttraumatic Stress Disorder versus Other Anxiety Disorders"; N. L. Carter, "Heart-Rate and Blood-Pressure Response in Medium-Artillery Gun Crews"; and A. Brier et al., "Controllable and Uncontrollable Stress in Humans: Alterations in Mood and Neuroendocrine and Psychophysiological Function." See also the splendid annotated bibliography by Norman M. Camp et al., *Stress, Strain, and Vietnam.*

Shadows

Chapter Six

Vietnamese in America

When, in 1987, John Clark Pratt proposed a structure to the canon of Vietnam War literature in his excellent "Bibliographic Commentary," he divided the material—fictional treatments—into five "acts" (corresponding to stages in the battlefield progress of the war itself) that the literature, regardless of publication date, represented. The acts in Pratt's "Shakespearean tragedy" are surrounded by a prologue and an epilogue ("everything after 1975"). A mere thirteen years ago, then, Vietnam War literature was primarily defined as combat literature. However, a year after Pratt's essay appeared, William J. Searle, in his *Search and Clear*, provided a selection of commentary that recognized an important second stage of Vietnam War literature. In a section on "Return and Partial Recovery," essays by James A. Robinson, Vince Gotera, and Searle himself provide an early map of the war's consequences in terms of representations of the veteran's return. Such representations (like Larry Heinemann's prize-winning *Paco's Story* and Philip Caputo's *Indian Country*) explore not only the veteran's condition but also the represented America the veteran reentered. Many of these titles have a temporal sweep that overlaps the chronology of the war itself.

In his study of veterans' poetry (*Radical Visions*, 1994), Gotera collapses the literature into two neat categories, "The Nam" and "The World." Works in the former group reflect primarily battlefield experience, while those in the latter group—a group having grown in size and importance—portray the returned veterans' ongoing trauma, problems of reintegration into U.S. society, and (less often) the more general theme of Vietnam as a continuing cultural pathology or syndrome.[1] If extended into fiction (including books by nonveteran writers), the latter category would include such works as Bobbie Ann Mason's *In Country* and an expanding library of detective fictions featuring protagonists whose Vietnam War backgrounds influence the conduct of their cases and their lives.[2]

Another group of writings, perhaps distinctive enough to constitute a separate category, is beginning to claim attention: representations of the Vietnamese in

America. One consequence of the war is the growing number of stateside Vietnamese communities. These communities are directly investigated in several monographs and in a special issue of *Vietnam Generation* entitled *Southeast Asian-American Communities* (1990) that contains a comprehensive bibliography. The imaginative literature, particularly prose fiction, reflecting this new ingredient in our cultural landscape explores or at least hints at the meaning of this presence both to its members and to the majority culture.

While there is a growing body of literature by Vietnamese Americans, representations of the Vietnamese in America by writers from the majority culture reveal something about that culture's ability to perceive and to absorb this new element. Significant among literary treatments of these Vietnamese residents are Robert Olen Butler's novel *The Deuce* (1989) and his short story collection *A Good Scent from a Strange Mountain* (1992). Other noteworthy representations include Wayne Karlin's *Lost Armies* (1989), which conjures up a Vietnamese community in southern Maryland proximate to the nation's capital, and Charlie McDade's *The Gulf* (1986), in which Vietnamese refugees try to take up their traditional occupation of shrimp fishing in coastal Texas. T. Jefferson Parker's mystery thriller, *Little Saigon* (1988), examines the turbulent Southeast Asian community in Orange County, California. Four of these five works have as background or foreground a love relationship between an American man who served in Vietnam and a Vietnamese woman he met there, a circumstance that suggests a tentative embrace of cultures and a healing potential even as it harkens back to a longer tradition of wartime romances about American GIs who had affairs with and sometimes married Asian women.[3]

Renny Christopher's *The Viet Nam War / The American War* (1995) elaborates the larger context for these concerns. Christopher's subtitle—*Images and Representations in Euro-American and Vietnamese Exile Narratives*—suggests the comprehensiveness of her study. In her chapter on "Euro-American Representation of the Vietnamese," Christopher offers provocative insights into the titles by Butler and Karlin, as well as dozens of other related titles. Though she, too, is concerned with racism and xenophobia, Christopher does not attend to the issue of community nor to the repeated pattern of relationships between American war veterans and Vietnamese women that is at the heart of the present examination.

The body of literature addressed here involves Vietnamese characters whose ongoing lives (of partial acculturation and accommodation) are informed—haunted, almost—by memories of their homeland and of the war that scarred it and led to their exile. For many, the unresolved tensions of Vietnam's history live on in the United States. If Vietnam as a set of cultural conditions has always had its home in the United States, now, in a more literal and permanent way, Vietnam is here for good.

In *Lost Armies*, Wayne Karlin imagines a Vietnamese refugee community in southern Maryland. Many of its members had fled the urban confusion of the "Little Saigon" already established in Arlington, Virginia. Karlin has them employed at "high-tech service companies near the Naval Air Station base" (3). One family, the Trans, owns a 7-Eleven and has a granddaughter who won the high school science fair. These people seem to have adopted the American dream long abandoned by many Americans. This and other fictional representations of Vietnamese in America bear out the statistical evidence summarized by Darrel Montero: "Since arriving in the United States, most of the Vietnamese have found jobs" (42), though many suffered "downward mobility" in occupational status after coming to the United States (39). Still, as early as 1977, Vietnamese refugees had moved "steadily toward economic self-sufficiency" (55).

In Karlin's novel, a new wave of immigrants is pressuring the Maryland community, especially as community leader Lily Minh's plan of having them work in crabbing and lobstering threatens the watermen's thin economy (18). They do some farming while they wait for Lily to supply boats. In setting up this complication, Karlin explicitly refers to the well known troubles of the Vietnamese immigrants who attempted to engage in shrimping in the Gulf waters of Texas, the premise of McDade's novel of three years earlier. Among these immigrants is Xuan, a mysterious and attractive woman who is one of protagonist Wheeler's students in a special English class.

Lily Minh, daughter of an ARVN general, has connections with Congressman Mundy (who makes another appearance in Karlin's 1993 novel *US*) and is using Mundy's influence to help support the Vietnamese trailer camp community she has founded. Madame Aleyn, a Vietnamese woman married to a Frenchman, runs a Vietnamese restaurant, Chez Aleyn, where Xuan and her brother work. She and everyone else do favors for Lily. Lily's mysterious power, the reader suspects, has sexual origins, just as Xuan's eerie sexuality taps into the interplay of power and powerlessness, victim and exploiter, that forms the psychological dynamic of Karlin's novel.

The unfinished business of the war presents itself as the mystery of a series of slain deer discovered with their tongues cut out, an echo of wartime mutilations that forces Wheeler, a burnt out reporter and Vietnam War veteran, to investigate. These grotesque deeds may be a mad signal from Wheeler's boyhood friend and wartime buddy, Dennis. The emotions of betrayal and revenge, and the destructive madness of a Vietnamese refugee tortured by his own earlier betrayals of others, energize the plot. Often, Karlin employs the metaphor of dealing with the dead, with ghosts, with souls who are not at rest, and with the living dead who left some part of themselves in limbo. He capitalizes on the Vietnamese belief in spirits to explain their stateside terror of the slain deer, but he also makes that belief palpable for the reader.

Christopher provides a detailed plot analysis that won't be attempted here. Karlin's use of setting, however, deserves special attention. Karlin uses the dense marsh ecology of Southern Maryland as an environmental echo of places in Vietnam, solidifying his themes of the presentness of the past and the American origin and final destination of our Vietnam tragedy. In this novel, as in Parker's *Little Saigon*, frail hope emerges from the ashes of spent antagonisms. A vicious destiny plays itself out, leaving the survivors, Wheeler and Xuan, with the slim but serviceable tools of understanding, compassion, and the strength born of dealing with loss. As individuals, they find their private ways of putting the war to rest and, however tentatively, moving on.

More importantly, Karlin's representation of a living Vietnamese community in the United States focuses the ongoing consequences of our involvement in Southeast Asia. That community is both an unwanted looking glass and a redefining factor in the larger culture. Vietnam is now *in America,* permanently.

In Parker's *Little Saigon,* the setting reflects the actual Indo-Chinese (largely Vietnamese) community in Orange County, California. The capital of this community is Westminster, a community so large it is considered to be "the neocapital of the Vietnamese" (Steltzer 9). The town's name has ironic echoes that Parker exploits ably. This Anglophile town with Anglophile architecture grafted upon the Southern California landscape bears the name of the church where Britain's illustrious dead are entombed. Now it houses a "Little Saigon," with all the attendant oddness of cultural juxtaposition magnified. To magnify the ironic grafting of one culture upon another even further, Parker places his precipitating event, a kidnapping, during the town's annual "Saigon Days" festival.

Though only about ten years old at the time of the novel's action, this community is sizable, mature, and relatively independent. Every kind of tradesman, shopkeeper, and professional seems to exist, as do warring gangs of street toughs. Parker's portrait reflects the observation made by a Westminster businesswoman in Ulli Steltzer's photographic study of Southern California immigrants: "Here in Westminster we are lucky to live among Vietnamese people. We can almost forget that we are not at home" (136).

Indeed, the Vietnamese community in Westminster has developed its cultural, religious, and economic institutions to the point that, to a large extent, stability has been achieved. However, as Paul James Rutledge remarks about Vietnamese communities in general:

> The one destabilizing influence that remains is politics: politics relating primarily to Vietnam and to the process of establishing relations with the Socialist Republic of Vietnam. The deep division among refugees on this issue may be seen in the violence which has erupted as a result of opposing views. (142–43)

Noting that violence from the right or the left is equally possible, Rutledge continues, "Staunchly anti-communist in composition, many Vietnamese communities have contributed to a fund which is directed at supporting insurgents in Vietnam" (143).

In Parker's novel, the local police force puts its Vietnamese-American detective, Minh, on the case when Li Frye, a well-known Vietnamese singer and wife of Bennett Frye, war hero and heir to an immense real estate fortune, is abducted during a performance for the "Saigon Days" celebration.

The novel's protagonist is Chuck Frye, Bennett's ne'er-do-well younger brother, a former surfing celebrity and (like Karlin's Wheeler) small-time reporter who is going through a divorce and has just been fired from his job. Eerily, the chase after suspects leads through Little Saigon shops with hidden trapdoors down into tunnels reminiscent of those subterranean networks devised by the Vietcong during the war.[4] As in Karlin's novel, aspects of setting shrink the distance between past and present.

Various communities of interest intersect in the Little Saigon neighborhood. These include: former ARVN General Dien's waning forces, now focused on helping Vietnamese in America; Vietnamese refugees active in supporting resistance movements in Vietnam through funds and arms and moral support (the war continues); self-interested entrepreneurs taking money in the name of the resistance; MIA fund-raisers; and gangs. Local police and FBI agents jockey for position in the investigation, while various other interested parties conduct their own investigations. Some suspect an aging Hanoi official charged with quelling resistance forces at home and abroad. The theme is that anything can happen in Little Saigon: it is a dangerous, mysterious place in which political and personal intrigues intersect, bringing fear and death. So too, the Vietnam-like swamps of Karlin's setting.

This story, again like Karlin's, is rooted in betrayals that took place during the war, betrayals in which trusted Vietnamese turned out to be working for the communists—if only temporarily during some crucial juncture. In both stories, the war casts its long shadow into the present to extract vengeance, penance, or a mix of both.

In *Little Saigon*, Lucia Parson's activities on behalf of the MIAs bears fruit, at least with regard to fund-raising, promises, and partial results, but her sincerity is compromised: she sees her success as a staging platform for a congressional seat. She has a place in Parker's political vision akin to that of Congressman Mundy in Karlin's *Lost Armies*. Or perhaps she is a Ross Perot stand-in. Her brother is Burke Parsons, an utterly corrupt power-seeker and manipulator (and former CIA operative) whose own quest for power amidst these political concerns knows no loyalties.

Parker's story is backgrounded by events in wartime. Lt. Bennett Frye's suspicions of Lam, his Vietnamese intelligence accomplice (and rival for Li) led him to suspect a bomb when only three bottles of champagne were sent to him via Li for a marriage celebration. Bennett ordered Lam killed, but Lam survived: the surviving, vengeful disfigured Lam is reborn as a Hanoi tyrant whose official role becomes squelching resistance. Lam comes to California to settle the score (he was the kidnapper); Bennett and Lam (now known as Colonel Thach) are both killed. After the litter of corpses, a note of hope infuses those who remain: Li, Chuck Frye, Chuck's love interest Christobel, and a chastened and humbled Frye family.

Though in both Karlin's and Parker's novels the elements of suspense and intrigue are the primary ingredients for reader engagement, each writer has also made the Vietnamese in America real, not only as individuals, but also as a people. They have broadened their readers' understanding of America's changing cultural landscape, its causes, and its consequences. Both novels, also, take us back to events in wartime Vietnam whose unfolding continues into Reagan-era America. The convenient demarcation of the war's end and the fall of Saigon (the 1975 close of Pratt's fifth act) is erased by the reader's consciousness of a vivid continuum in the outer and inner lives of those whom the war involved. In each novel, a spiral of personal betrayals hints at a larger theme of betrayal, a dark antimyth of national character clouding the inherited myths of frontier heroism, manifest destiny, and altruistic purpose.[5]

Charlie McDade's *The Gulf*, the earliest of the novels treated here, also involves a former serviceman whose time in Vietnam, once thought buried, is reactivated by the presence of those with whom he once crossed paths. In this case, a Vietnamese woman (Nancy) he loved while in-country is part of the community that comes to the small Texas fishing town. McDade's focus is on the hostile attitude of the townspeople toward the intruders, an attitude based on economic rivalry and racial difference. His veteran character, David, works through a version of survivor guilt, as (to a lesser extent) do Karlin's Wheeler and Parker's Bennett Frye.

The Vietnamese community in Witman, Texas does not get the same sort of scrutiny in *The Gulf* as do the communities in the two thrillers. In fact, the Texas town is detailed in all of its friendly narrow-mindedness long before the Vietnamese appear in its midst. Thus, there is little Vietnamese community structure to examine. The locals' attitude toward the growing Spanish community and toward one newcomer, a Jewish doctor, predicts the harsher treatment that the racially different and economically threatening Vietnamese are likely to receive. Other story lines are developed before the Vietnamese arrive: (1) the attempt Vietnam veteran David Hodges makes to renew the relationship with his former girlfriend Kate even as her brother (Pat), a big-shot bigot and deputy sheriff, makes his life difficult; and (2) the relationship between David and his brother Peter, a young man who fled to Canada rather than serve. This latter process of reconciliation interacts with the theme of reconciliation with the Vietnamese and with our continuing obligation toward them. As the novel progresses, an additional complication is added when David discovers his wartime Vietnamese bedmate, Nancy Diem, among the leaders of the refugee community.

McDade details the efforts of those who choose to help the Vietnamese. These include Peter, Al Rodriguez (a priest), and Luke, a lawyer. These men persuade the Vietnamese to study English, and they set up a class in the church basement. Members of the small community of thirty-five nervously begin to appear. While some, like Mr. Dong, know English fairly well and can assist, others, especially the children, have no formal schooling of any kind. As the townspeople become divided over what to do about the Vietnamese, David strains to remain neutral: he doesn't want to help them, and he doesn't want to join efforts to get them to move on. Ironically, his draft-dodger brother becomes their English teacher.

A confrontation between "enemy" shrimping trawlers leads to violence and to a town meeting at which compromises cannot be reached. Inevitably, a bunch of locals attack a Vietnamese boat and kill David's brother Pete, Nancy, and one of Nancy's brothers. The new war at home finishes what the war in Vietnam left undone. In the novel's ultimate violence, Kate's brother Pat and David kill each other. The ending is one of total despair: no bridges of aid or welcome or peacemaking are strong enough to withstand the festering hostility of ideological partisans and of racism. In contrast to Karlin's and Parker's novels, no one is left standing in McDade's *The Gulf* to prefigure a hopeful future. Loss begat loss, and hatred engendered only more hatred.

The same impulse that finally leads David to confess to Kate about his affair with Nancy also forces (or allows) him to admit that he had unknowingly killed

Kate's brother Donald to stop him from massacring Vietnamese children. Shut out by Kate, David finds himself accepting Nancy's embraces for solace just as he had as a lonely American soldier years before. More than that, he finds with her a mutual acceptance. Nancy's death cuts off the false hope of reconciliation figured in the couple's last embrace. But that embrace, for each, was a moment of belonging.

Those familiar with Louis Malle's film *Alamo Bay* will note many similarities with McDade's novel. Both represent the tensions in a small Texas shrimping town between the locals and the new Vietnamese interlopers. Both works prefigure the reception of the Vietnamese by presenting the Anglo attitudes toward Mexican Americans, both involve violence against the Vietnamese, and both present at least one Vietnamese who is willing to take a stand and fight for his rights. Though their casts of characters and plot details are quite different, McDade and Malle both suggest that America's foray in Southeast Asia was essentially a racist impulse, and both remind their audiences that the "gook syndrome" is alive and well. (For more on this theme, see Laskowsky's "*Alamo Bay* and the Gook Syndrome.")

In each of the three novels so far examined, the plot depends in part on a Vietnamese woman's relationship with an American serviceman. Xuan had been Dennis's mistress and becomes Wheeler's lover, Li had forsaken Ham for Bennett Frye, and in *The Gulf* David finds a former in-country girlfriend, Nancy, among the leaders of the refugee community.

In all three novels, the sexual giving or exploitation of the Vietnamese woman partakes of a range of symbolic significances that reverberate back to Graham Greene's uses of his character Phuong in *The Quiet American* (1956). The Vietnam veterans, like Greene's Alden Pyle, have fallen in love with Vietnam itself without quite knowing what lies beneath the beauty and strangeness that has drawn them to her. Though Greene, through his narrator Thomas Fowler, belittles Pyle's naïve, do-gooder dream of marrying Phuong and turning her into a happy American wife, more than three decades later that dream seems somewhat less naïve and its fulfillment perhaps necessary, perhaps even inevitable. Through a confused metamorphosis, rape and less violent masculine aggressions have given way to balanced, normative relationships which, though troubled, are the harbingers of reconciliation. This gender story may be an enactment of the cultural and political story in progress. In the mythos of Vietnam War representation, Vietnam is always a woman, and the theme of regeneration through violence (in combat) has had a peculiar issue in violence toward Vietnamese women. These stateside novels, while reminding us of the warrior regeneration myth, suggest different paths of regeneration for the veteran cleansed of his warrior code who is now preparing to mate—to partner—rather than dominate.

Had there been children of these affairs, as there were of the many they resemble, one child may have grown into the title character of Robert Olen Butler's *The Deuce*. This finely crafted novel focuses on the identity issue of a "child of dust" raised in the United States by his Vietnam veteran father from the age of six. As a consequence of war and his father's sense of responsibility, Saigon-born Vo

Dinh Thanh has become Anthony James Hatcher. And Tony Hatcher, partly as the result of his uncertain identity, has become "The Deuce"—a Manhattan street person whose chosen name reflects his adopted community around Forty-second Street. Having almost lost one culture and not quite fit into another, the teenaged hero-narrator runs away from his second home and struggles through a terrifying ordeal of self-making.

Ironically, Deuce's guide to this underworld is an experienced street denizen named Joey, a Vietnam veteran who, as Deuce puts it, "could've passed through my mother's bed" (138). Joey is a con who plays on people's sympathy to collect money, but he carries a burden of guilt that is somewhat lightened in his fatherly relationship to Deuce. As with the other novels, the past is woven into the present; the man and the boy each carry Vietnam around inside of them. Joey's death eventually returns Deuce—Tony—to Kenneth, his real father, and to the rebuilding of that relationship. Deuce's life in the urban jungle of Manhattan has unexpectedly brought some stability to his sense of self, and with it some measure of self-acceptance.

Butler's portrait of this half-Vietnamese youngster of certain parentage but uncertain belonging is distinctive in that he is biologically a Vietnamese American. However, his tensions and confusions are much like those of other people called Vietnamese Americans, that is, Vietnamese immigrants who have made the United States their home.[6]

Butler's Pulitzer Prize short story sequence, *A Good Scent from a Strange Mountain*, develops this same identity theme while looking more closely at the texture of Vietnamese life in America (around New Orleans). Unlike the first three novels, the point of view of these stories is that of the Vietnamese. Each has a Vietnamese narrator whose perspective on self, past, and community is quite different from that presented in the novels by Karlin, Park, and McDade. To Butler's credit, what could have turned out to be merely an intriguing literary stunt becomes a journey into the kind of sympathetic understanding that can truly heal. Butler builds his sense of a Vietnamese-American community not through the convenient polarity of leaders and followers, but rather through a spectrum of individual voices registering differing mixes of Vietnamese memory and heritage and American culture, language, and style. Though these individuals, indeed, reside in immigrant communities, they do not represent types defined within community roles.

Butler's imagination has pulled him far into the personal, social, geographical, cultural, and historical worlds of these Vietnamese refugees. He has found the range of voices needed to let these men and women narrate their tales of dislocation, difference, accommodation, and acculturation. One remembers a young Ho Chi Minh in his dreams; another is the owner of a shoe once belonging to John Lennon; yet another has won a vacation trip on *Let's Make a Deal*. Citizens of Lake Charles, Louisiana, or the Versailles neighborhood near New Orleans, they speak the haunted English of layered selves. To give them life, Butler had to become the other. Moreover, these people are not instruments in a political or ideological plot. They are not decor. The plots of these stories are their very lives and perceptions, perceptions in which we, the comfortable majority of Euro-Americans, are perceived in all our strangeness. Even more than in the works by Karlin and Parker, these Vietnamese are at the center of the imagined world. It is *their* world that mainstream readers enter, not a world of people like themselves that includes an unexpected pocket of Vietnamese.

Three years before Butler gave us the imagined voices of *A Good Scent*, James M. Freeman published *Hearts of Sorrow: Vietnamese-American Lives*. Freeman has collected narratives derived from forty interviews with Vietnamese immigrants. The latter chapters have to do with their lives in America and stress cultural contrasts and accommodations. Reading these narratives, one is left marveling at Butler's accomplishment. Though Freeman's transcriptions, often translations, are in the service of presenting "Vietnamese-Americans as *persons*" (4), in many ways Butler's fictions do a better job. Freeman's transcriptions get the facts straight, but not the voices. Telling one's story to an interviewer or a tape recorder is not quite the same as telling a story that interests you or has a special meaning for you. Butler's spokespeople are not interviewees or merely representative types. Their narratives include place names, neighborhoods, sights, and smells. They include humor. They are expressions of personality rather than expressions of pondered experience. While the narrators in Freeman's collection, for example, expound about contrasting notions of family, Butler's characters give such an issue feeling tones and immediacy. They are being themselves, not posing for the camera.

In various ways, then, mainstream American authors have begun to explore, in imaginative fictions, the unmelted Vietnamese strand in American's cultural stew. Although they are subordinated to the machinery of detective thriller plots, the Vietnamese portrayed by Wayne Karlin and T. Jefferson Parker have artful shading as individuals and attachment to believable communities, goals, and pasts. Both writers tap into the mythic and psychic dimensions of America's Vietnam War, Karlin more provocative here than Parker. Both also imagine social and economic contexts of Vietnamese in America, Parker's handling of place more detailed in this regard.

The genre of detective fiction (the seekers here journalists rather than public or private investigators) has a particular utility, the search for the truth of guilt on the level of plot generating larger issues of national and cultural complicity in the many crimes that constitute the war itself. It is important that such investigations take place in the United States because the cultural indictments and the sought-after justice attach themselves to American actions and attitudes.

Charlie McDade, a far less accomplished writer than Karlin, Parker, or Butler, does little to distinguish his Vietnamese characters, perhaps staying closest to newspaper accounts of Texas Gulf troubles for his plot details. Nonetheless, he brings home to readers the strife between communities and the ways in which the dominant culture resists its responsibilities. His book, unfortunately, underscores an undercurrent of need to be at war with the Vietnamese, even the Vietnamese newly making their way in American society, rather than the need to make peace.

For Butler, in his more recent books relating to Vietnam, the Vietnamese-American lives *are* the story.[7] Theirs are the perspectives he brings to the forefront in his daring first-person narrations. His Vietnamese are caught in their various ways of being Americans. Indeed, the ambiguously directed title of his longest story, "The American Couple," points simultaneously to Frank and Eileen Davies and to the newer Americans, Gabrielle Tran and her husband Vinh—the men both veterans of the war—as the couples meet while enjoying their prize vacations as quiz show winners. While sharing this commercial fantasy version of the American dream, the men indulge in dangerous war games, only stopping when this other American dream of prowess in battle becomes too real, both men Americans now. The couples themselves are tentatively mated, foreshadowing a strand of the new, post-Vietnam American community.

The shared contribution of all of these works is, on the one hand, a broadening of the range of what constitutes Vietnam War literature—and on the other hand a broadened, complicated sense of nationhood and culture. "Vietnamese in America," the title of this exploration, transforms into a metaphor of "Vietnam in America," with all the power of "Vietnam" as a generative image.

Already, American bookstores and libraries are offering new representations of their American lives by the Vietnamese Americans themselves, works that follow from Tran Van Dinh's *Blue Dragon. White Tiger: A Tet Story*, praised by Renny Christopher (in her contribution to *Reading the Literatures of Asian America*) for its evocation of bicultural experience, and Tran Dieu Hang's stories of the Vietnamese "refugee consciousness and unconscious" in southern California (Qui-Phiet Tran 274). Readers can anticipate more novels, like Vo Phien's *Intact* (1990), that imaginatively extend the understandings available in such nonfiction accounts of relocation and acculturation as Le Ly Haslip's *When Heaven and Earth Changed Places* (1989). However, the writings about the Vietnamese by members of the majority culture will continue to act as registers of that culture's capacity for acceptance, for respecting difference, and for extending the margins of its peripheral visions.

NOTES

1. One could argue that another category, stateside protest literature, coexists in counterpoint to the battlefield literature.

2. For example, James Lee Burke's ten "Dave Robicheaux" novels, James Crumley's three novels featuring C. W. Sughrue, and John Maddox Roberts's *The Ghosts of Saigon* (1996). Such works, examined in the following chapters, share quite different ends than the "returned veteran" genre and may be thought of as a distinct category. They tend to be stories of middle-age masculinity in the post-Vietnam era defined so well in James William Gibson's *Warrior Dreams*.

3. The earlier "battlefield" literature contains many such romances, several of which portray American servicemen falling in love with Vietnamese women, often women working as prostitutes in order to support themselves in a country ravaged by war. In several of these tales, the relationship is severed and the woman is exploited. The romance is not transportable back to the United States; it is rather a relationship confined to the particular needs of men at war, a feature shared with the backgrounding material in *The Deuce*.

4. The tunnel theme is developed on a much broader scale in another thriller, Joseph Flynn's *Digger* (1997). Vietnam War veterans have created a Cong-style network of tunnels under a Midwestern American city. This network helps them counter the villainy of a corrupt businessman, who in turn hires a former Vietcong member, now a citizen of the Vietnamese immigrant community in Westminster, California, to destroy the tunnel rats. See also the discussion of Michael Connelly's *Black Echo* in chapter 7.

5. These and other mythic reflections of American culture as found in the earlier literature of the Vietnam War have been explored by many, beginning with John Hellmann in *American Myth and the Legacy of Vietnam*. A more recent treatment is Milton J. Bates's *The Wars We Took to Vietnam: Cultural Conflict and Storytelling*.

6. Young Tony's passage to America is romantic but far from typical. The fortunes and misfortunes of other "children of the dust" are related in Thomas A. Bass's *Vietnamerica: The War Comes Home*.

7. In his Introduction to the *Vietnam War Literature* catalogue published by Ken Lopez, Bookseller (Hadley, Mass.: 1990), Butler writes: "it is fine to examine Vietnam with our minds, but more importantly we must not forget the way life happened in Vietnam moment-to-moment, in the sense-based, unabstracted experience of individual sensibilities. And when works of art ask us to enter these sensibilities, don't forget that this war involved Americans only secondarily. We had our one-year tours into Vietnam and our own souls, but we came back to a place that was our own. Even those Americans who continue to struggle with their experiences have a country and a culture and representative government to rail against. The Vietnamese had no home away from the war, and now 800,000 of them live among us with a sense of loss that we can only vaguely imagine. Read about Vietnam and all that we Americans suffered and learned, but also remember the Vietnamese."

Chapter Seven

Hard-Boiled Nam I

The Vietnam War in Detective Fiction

As we have seen, the American literature of the Vietnam War has undergone several phases. The first phase is centered on battlefield accounts, while the second explores the immediate situation of the returned veteran. A third phase explores, in part, the nature of the Vietnamese immigrant experience in the United States while still following the lives of Americans who served in that war. More recently, we have begun to see works that use the Vietnam experience as transforming background in the lives of fictional characters some fifteen or more years after service in Vietnam.

A prominent genre of "transforming background" narrative is hard-boiled detective fiction in which the protagonists' Vietnam experiences are portrayed through flashbacks, dreams, and dialogue. The protagonists, thus, are nearing or well into middle age, but still depending on skills, attitudes, and sometimes a network of specialist acquaintances developed during the Vietnam War. Some, like James Crumley's C. W. Sughrue, are private detectives. While solving problems outside of the constraints placed upon government law agents is the traditional domain of the private eye (as well as the soldier of fortune), "outsider" psychology comes naturally to one brand of Vietnam Vet, as we shall see. Others, like Michael Connelly's Harry Bosch, are law enforcement officers who find themselves in conflict with the institution they serve, as was likely the case, sooner or later, in Vietnam. Most notable here is James Lee Burke's Dave Robicheaux, who is treated in chapter 8. Still other hard-boiled protagonists have no career connections to professional law enforcement but are drawn into the same investigative concerns and must function like detectives. These include Robert Olen Butler's Wilson Hand, Gustav Hasford's Dowdy Lewis, Jr., and Charles Durden's Jamie Hawkins. These post-Vietnam hard-boiled detectives, like their forebears, are descendants of the Wild West frontiersman.

In *Gunfighter Nation*, an examination of the frontier myth and the qualities of the frontier hero, Richard Slotkin juxtaposes "the husbandman's life of laborious cultivation" with that of "the hunter-hero"—a prototype of the warrior-hero. Though the latter acts on his own initiative and often without conventional moral constraints, his function "is to make the wilderness safe for a civilization in which he is unsuited (and disinclined) to participate." By definition an outsider, he is paradoxically a defender of those commercial values he escapes through "his purifying regression to the primitive" (34).

In his earliest incarnation as an Indian fighter, the frontier hero absorbs some of the skills and allegedly primitive ways of his enemy—the Indian. In one of his later incarnations as a private detective (or public peace officer with a private agenda) in the mythic frontier of urban-centered crime, the warrior must also be "one who knows Indians"—or criminal classes. The earliest dime novel detectives were at once outlaws and heroes. Slotkin argues that "By turning outlaws into functional approximations of detectives, these dime novels augment the moral authority of the outlaw as symbol of a critical stance toward the ideology and practice of industrial and finance capitalism" (150). This outlaw-hero's functional twin, the designated detective, serves and "defends the progressive social order, but does so *in the style* of an outlaw, always criticizing the costs of progress and often attacking the excesses of the privileged classes" (154).

Paraphrasing Raymond Chandler, Slotkin writes that "The hard-boiled detective's answer to the constriction and corruption of the post-Frontier landscape is to labor with wit and violence to create a small space or occasion in which something like traditional justice can prevail and in which the 'little man' or the 'good woman' can be protected against the malignity of the powers that be" (218). In the novels of our own time, those powers are not only foreign and domestic crime syndicates, but big business and big government. The detective-hero's perception of justice, and his motive for pursuing it, remains personal, even as it overlaps with traditional understandings. His successes are limited and symbolic: "The justice which the detective achieves affects persons, not classes; it changes situations but does not transform orders" (Slotkin 228).

As every student of Vietnam War representation knows, America's frontier myth was alive and well in Vietnam as a late stage both of manifest destiny and of domino theory rationalizations of the drive to restore national (perhaps racial) virility through combat and conquest. As a cleansing cauldron of rediscovery and rebirth, however, Vietnam held many surprises that challenged the mythic underpinning of the frontier-taming enterprise. Foremost among these surprises was the consciousness of participating in a corrupt and/or bungled mission. In Vietnam, the warrior not only came to "know the Indian"—the other who threatened to destroy or contaminate one's kind—but to become the Indian: an abomination. The plain of potential conquest known to the grunts as "Indian Country" became a scene of shame on many levels: a scene of failure, a scene of personal horror, a scene of betrayal of values. The first generation of Vietnam War literature and the critical endeavors tracking that literature explore the scene and its crimes.

Within the present generation of detective fictions is a subset that links the old hard-boiled detective recrudescence of the frontier hero with the more recent representations of the frontier warrior in Vietnam. The post-Vietnam mythic landscape is filled with vivid descendants of the heroic type created by Chandler and Hammett. These heroes are cynical men who cling to a traditional concept of personal honor even as they break the law in pursuit of justice. Hard-boiled detective characters like those created by James Crumley, John Maddox Roberts, Michael Connelly, and James Lee Burke are among our newest frontier heroes, agents of regenerative violence who incorporate many values of the mythic frontier. These men are carefully imagined and sharply drawn individuals, but they have much in common. Not the least of these commonalities is their shared participation in the Vietnam War. To varying degrees, these detective heroes remain in contact with the self reshaped by Vietnam, and to varying degrees forces let loose in the Vietnam War roll through their present lives and create either their cases or their methods of operation or both.

These serialized detective heroes have peers among the later efforts of key Vietnam War writers who came to prominence with battlefield fictions. As follow-up efforts, both Gustav Hasford and Charles Durden have attempted to exploit the detective genre. However, the way had been shown by Robert Olen Butler, whose *Sun Dogs* (1982), the second novel in his intriguing Vietnam trilogy (surrounded by *The Alleys of Eden*, 1981, and *On Distant Ground*, 1985) initiates many important motifs.

Butler's protagonist, Wilson Hand, is hired to investigate the disappearance of records and the feared misuse of secret information stolen from the remote Alaskan station of a major oil company. However, Hand's investigation seems less an exercise in methods of detection than a journey into the mysteries of his tormented psyche. His broken marriage and his tendency toward self-destruction are hinged to his memories of incarceration by the Vietcong. Butler employs the primitive majesty of his Alaskan setting as a symbolic frontier for Hand's combined expiation, exile, ritual cleansing, and final sacrifice. As Philip D. Beidler has noted, Butler's symbolic use of the Alaskan setting is much like that of Norman Mailer in *Why Are We in Vietnam?* (54). The novel's suspense has little to do with the immediate case, and almost everything to do with the mysteries of character connected to Hand's haunted past.

Hand acts as if he is still a prisoner. Certainly, he is a prisoner of his dreams. Beyond this, his search for a special place to work out his fate is clearly a search for resolution of the war's myriad loose ends. Hand is contaminated, as is the energy industry and the hungry nation it feeds. The defilement of this last great natural realm is, for Butler, another version of America's venture into Vietnam. In a sense, then, Hand's journey to Alaska is a figurative "return," similar in meaning (indeed, as a quest *for* meaning and peace of mind) to the literal returns to Vietnam of other Butler protagonists. Like the frontiersman-turned-detective of Slotkin's formulations, Hand's justice is personal. His loyalty is not to institutions, not even to those that hire him. In this case, the institution itself is corrupt. Only individuals can be helped, or brought down.

A very personal sense of doing the right thing motivates Wilson Hand. It also motivates Gustav Hasford's Dowdy Lewis, Jr. in *A Gypsy Good Time* (1992). Dowdy, who served as a Marine in Force Recon operations near the close of the war, is an ex-policeman now running an antiquarian book business in Los Angeles. Investigating the disappearance of Yvonna Lablaine, a young woman with whom he has just begun a torrid affair and who is caught up in her own plot with drug dealers, Lewis assumes the frontier warrior mindset he had developed in Vietnam, a mindset never far below the surface of his postwar existence. His tough-guy, antihero stance is coded by a single utterance that is also the authorial stance of his creator: "I am the man who killed Audie Murphy" (110).

Fast-talking, darkly humorous Dowdy is the middle-aged (almost forty) reincarnation of Hasford's James "Joker" Davis, protagonist of *The Short-Timers* and *The Phantom Blooper*, two classics of Vietnam War fiction. In both, but particularly the first, Hasford participated in the symbolic killing of Audie Murphy, the archetypal World War II hero, by exposing the deadly irrelevance of World War II notions of romantic heroism to the realities of the Vietnam War.

Dowdy's moment of what Slotkin calls the "purifying regression to the primitive" is carefully marked out and tightly bound to the self developed in wartime. "War is the only home I ever had," exclaims Dowdy, "I was born in Vietnam, Republic of. The Vietnam War is stuck in my mind like a bullet in a post" (103).

His case having reached a momentary dead end, Dowdy is energized by the addictive force of deadly power and by the hungry vengeance that comes when a friend is threatened or killed: "The old feeling comes back, the power feeling, the awful magic of the angry gun" (102). And one more quotable Dowdyism: "revenge is the best revenge" (103).

The passages that most strongly link Dowdy's present actions with his Vietnam experience occur about two-thirds of the way through the novel. They are cast in an evocative, poetic prose mixing landscape, philosophy, and narrative, much in the manner of Henry Miller. At one point, Dowdy questions the authenticity of his surface motive—his desire to protect Yvonna:

> Maybe I didn't love Yvonna after all. Maybe I'm just using Yvonna's disappearance as an excuse to arc-light the city. It's not easy finding a way to die a heroic death in a public relations world, a world full of paper heroes. There were no heroes in Vietnam, only dead friends and survivors. I should be grateful for this opportunity, good Alamos are hard to find.
>
> War is a Cinderella story in which men turn into soldiers. (103)

But Gustav Hasford knows that war is not a male version of the Cinderella story; rather, it is too often *told* as one. The traditional war story, like the traditional detective story, is usually rooted in the cultural assumption that the hero must be an outsider-warrior. The alternative frontier tale, what Slotkin calls the husbandman's story, the "life of laborious cultivation," rarely presents itself as a vehicle for heroism.

The Hollywood beat that Dowdy Lewis patrols for his own purposes is at once phony and savage, at once an effete mecca of superficial values and a place in which greed and erotic longing provoke deadly warfare. Dowdy's only license is his heart, and his primary map is a map of Vietnam War memories. From

Dowdy's post-Vietnam and Hollywood-dazed perspective, the Gulf War was "the mother of all publicity stunts" (103). Tough, cynical, witty, and fearless, the protagonist of *A Gypsy Good Time* is a unique contribution to the hard-boiled detective genre. As it concludes, Dowdy decides to set himself up as a bounty hunter, a more conventional (capitalist) version of the lone wolf warrior-hero. Clearly, Hasford was hoping to create a character that could continue through several more novels.

The curious but eventually familiar mix of drug money and right-wing fanaticism provides the villainous motive in Charles Durden's *The Fifth Law of Hawkins* (1990). Hawkins is Jamie Hawkins, a Vietnam veteran whose war story is told in Durden's fine absurdist novel, *No Bugles, No Drums* (1976). Hawkins's war experiences, alluded to frequently in *Fifth Law*, have deepened his natural cynicism. However, he is a sucker for a righteous cause—as he sees it. For some time an itinerant small town reporter (with, like his creator, a Vietnam War novel to his credit), he finds his way onto a major Philadelphia newspaper when one of its owners hires him to be a puppet in her power play for control.

What Hawkins's investigation turns up is a conspiracy among officials and ultra-conservative business leaders, most important among them the police commissioner, to build a secret counterterrorist force. Durden's portrait of Commissioner Reichmann begins with his fascistic name.[1] Reichmann sees contamination of American purity everywhere, and he fabricates terrorist activities in order to provoke a public demand for the kind of operation he has secretly and illegally assembled.

Though legally an office holder and part of the establishment, Reichmann is driven by the same urges that fuel the grassroots independent paramilitary organizations of diehard patriots whose rallying cries are cries of hate. In Brother James Academy, what passes for a religious school covers the antiterrorist training of individuals not on the official police payroll. The basement of a major public art gallery houses the command center and arsenal of Reichmann's operations.

Jamie Hawkins is no career detective, public or private, but as an investigative reporter he is the next best thing.[2] A constant rule-breaker, a torment to his employers and supervisors, this heavy-drinking, dope-smoking rebel cannot let his cynicism deflect his core moral compass. He has to bring the bad guys down, and with the help of some accomplices, he at least puts a check on their activities. Angelo Finori, a Philadelphia policeman who aids Hawkins's plot, also helps him pass as the real thing by giving him the credentials of an Atlantic City narcotics detective. He also gives him a gun. With this touch, and through a series of female bed partners whose feelings Hawkins treats with woeful indifference, Durden signals to readers that Hawkins belongs to the hard-boiled detective tradition.

In a review article that addresses both of these novels and several others, Kali Tal notes that the protagonists are characterized by a "death-in-life" state that not only reflects the spiritual outcome of much Vietnam War fiction but is a hallmark of hard-boiled detective fiction as well. This similarity, she suggests, helps explain the lure of the Vietnam veteran writer to the detective fiction genre. Both genres, she asserts, are ultimately tales of the man alone, though detective fiction

often "depends upon the body of the feminine 'other' to carry the story to its conclusion." Tal continues:

> Female characters appear to be as integral to detective fiction as they are incidental
> to war stories. As far as I can tell, most detective stories are inscribed on the female
> body, the "body in the bed," which is either sexualized or slaughtered, or both. (141)

While one cannot deny the utility of this generalization, an interesting feature in
the writings of Roberts, Connelly, Crumley, and Burke is a reshaping of the ways
in which female characters are employed.

Charles Durden's *The Fifth Law of Hawkins* is clearly a sequel to his Vietnam
War novel, but only the repeated central character links the two works. Several
writers have launched series within the detective genre with characters whose
Vietnam War pasts have shaped their later lives. Among these writers are John
Maddox Roberts, Michael Connelly, and James Crumley.

Roberts, who has had a successful career in many genres including fantasy, science fiction, and mystery, began the Gabe Treloar series in 1994 with *A Typical
American Town*. Though Treloar is established as a Vietnam War veteran who had
seen duty during 1968 as a military policeman in Saigon, little about this part of
his background is exploited as a key to his decision, after a forced exit from the
Los Angeles Police Department, to work as a private investigator. Nor, in this
novel, do his attitudes about law or life reflect lessons learned during wartime.

The transformative power of the Vietnam War experience is somewhat more
significant in *The Ghosts of Saigon* (1996), Roberts's second "Gabe Treloar Mystery." What is even more important, as the title suggests, is how Roberts connects
the war to the present situation in which Gabe finds himself. Now working for the
Knoxville branch of a large detective agency, Gabe is hired by Mitch Queen, with
whom he had served as an MP, to investigate threats to Queen and to the lead
actress in a movie about Vietnam and the war that Queen is preparing to produce.
Someone wants this movie, *Tu Do Street*, cancelled.

The someone would seem to be Martin Starr, a man whom Gabe and Mitch had
arrested back in Vietnam and were transporting to prison, but who escaped and
became legendary in the deserter community. He is the premier ghost of Saigon.
Gabe's failure to deliver Starr, or to kill him during his escape attempt, is having
consequences twenty-five years later.

Soon after the investigation begins, Gabe learns that the brother of his deceased
wife, a Vietnamese woman named Rose, has been murdered by Vietnamese
agents of an international Asian mob. The cases are vaguely connected, and the
solution to each requires that Gabe revisit Saigon.

Gabe is teamed with Connie Armijo, who has been hired to protect the actress.
Connie works for an all-female detective agency. By coincidence, she had been a
Navy nurse in Vietnam in 1975.

As the plot develops, we learn that Mitch, in alliance with Martin Starr, has
involved Gabe in a hoax. Starr is really the author of the screenplay, the details of
which reveal criminal acts of United States officials during the war. In 1968, before

going underground as a freelance wheeler-dealer in Southeast Asia, Starr had been a CIA agent, and his captor, Major Gresham, another rogue operative, had been trying to find a way of getting rid of him because Starr had information on Gresham's activities. In the present time, it is Gresham, now living under an alias just as Starr had for many years, who is trying to make sure the movie isn't made.

The story is a variation on a common theme in this generation of Vietnam War literature: The past not only haunts but directly affects the present. The corruption that was American involvement in Vietnam bred even more corruption by way of covert operations (CIA operations that aided drug trafficking), and corrupt operatives became freelancers whose only loyalties were to money, thrills, and power. Vietnam released and/or created addictions that drive behavior, individual and collective, decades later.

In this novel, the unusual twist is that the mysterious, effete Martin Starr seeks some kind of redemption. His play script is meant to bring his old enemies out of hiding, making them vulnerable. In a crescendo of violence, Gresham and his partners are killed or arrested. Starr, perhaps not fatally wounded, falls upon a Japanese sword to end his own life. Among Gresham's accomplices are the murderers of Gabe's brother-in-law.

Among the conventions of this generation of post-Vietnam fictions that Roberts's novel includes are (1) the protagonist's fate in the present being linked to wartime events in Vietnam, (2) the recognition of Vietnam-in-America through the representation of Vietnamese-American communities, and (3) the modulation of attitudes toward women from the rampant sexism of traditional wartime adventures to something more appropriate to the antiwarrior stance of the new hero proposed by James William Gibson in his cultural study, *Warrior Dreams*.[3] The professionalism and physical hardiness of Connie Armijo make her at least Treloar's equal. Though they have an affair, clearly Connie is in charge of her life and not dependent on Gabe in any way.

Another convention is Gabe Treloar's cynicism about the corruption of values reflected in or set into motion by U.S. conduct in Vietnam. Roberts expounds on the "follow the money" cliché of detective work as follows:

> At big-business and government level, crimes of passion are rare, but crimes of greed occur in overwhelming profusion. I've been told that, above a certain level, big business, big crime, and big government become almost indistinguishable. This could be an exercise in cynicism, but you never know. (103)

This equation links Roberts's work with that of all the other detective novelists treated in this and the next chapter, though Gabe Treloar in other ways is not a full-blooded hard-boiled type.

Michael Connelly's Harry Bosch debuted in *The Black Echo* (1992—Edgar Award Winner) and has been continued through five more novels.[4] In the premier work, Bosch is established as a Vietnam War veteran who served around 1970 as a "tunnel rat," searching for, entering, and destroying the tunnels used by the Vietcong as an important infrastructure. Twenty years later, a fortyish Bosch emerges as a cynical fifteen-year veteran of the LAPD, a homicide detective whose hotshot career had been derailed by not being a "family man" on the force, but rather a lone wolf who couldn't keep from doing things his own way. Also, Bosch had been accused of making a "bad shoot" on a criminal who was later found to have no weapon. Though cleared, he was reassigned from the central homicide bureau to a less prestigious job at the Hollywood branch. Having made enemies, Bosch always seems to have the IAD (Internal Affairs Division) looking over his shoulder.

The present case has to do with a man named Meadows with whom Bosch had served. Accidentally, Bosch is assigned to investigate what seems to be an addict's OD death. A witness had called 911 about a man discovered dead in a concrete water pipe frequently used as shelter by bums. Entering this closed place to check the body is one of many burrowings into tunnel-like enclosures that bring back the emotion of Bosch's tunnel rat assignments.

As it happens, Bosch's discovery of Meadows brings special attention to a case that would otherwise be written off as a routine OD. Bosch quickly perceives it as a homicide and pursues the case, the accident of his past association with Meadows ruining a well made plan to steal diamonds that has its origins in the evacuation of Saigon in 1975.

As the mystery is uncovered, we learn that corrupt Vietnamese captains on the Saigon police force had turned their protection and drug wealth into diamonds and had been given special consideration by Americans running the evacuation program. Among those assigned to the American Embassy at this time was Meadows, who had reenlisted several times since Bosch had served with him and was involved with drugs and other illegal operations. Meadows, while in prison and upon release to a halfway house called Charlie Company, met others ready to join in the plot of a former army lieutenant for whom Meadows had worked, a man who was now in full control as the FBI's senior investigator on this very case. Somewhere along the way, Agent Rourke developed the plot to steal the diamonds kept in supposedly secure vaults by the former policemen who were now influential businessmen in their Vietnamese-American communities. Rourke has built his team of Meadows and a few others, a team with tunnel rat experience, because the plan required moving through the LA storm sewer system and then drilling under and into a bank vault and a vault in a private security company.

As in other post-Vietnam detective fictions, corrupt practices of Americans in Vietnam inscribe the war as a moral turning point in American culture. Meadows and Rourke are only a few American operatives, civilian and military, who turned the war situation to their own gain and who later—back in the States—found ways to feed their addiction to wealth and power.

Meadows had been killed because he broke faith with the gang. In the first robbery, of the bank vault, the team had taken valuables from hundreds of deposit boxes to obscure the fact that they were after the diamonds in one particular box. They knew that the owner of that box, the former Saigon police captain, would not be able to make a claim for his illegal gains. But Meadows pawned a valuable piece of jewelry, thus compromising the operation. He had to be eliminated, and he was. However, a teenaged delinquent named Sharkey had seen the body dumped in the pipe and called 911.

Sharkey is soon eliminated, and Bosch feels guilty about not having taken precautions to protect this witness. But with Sharkey's elimination, Bosch knows that there is an inside leak because only those connected with the investigation can have discovered that Sharkey was a witness.

The novel is powerful in developing Bosch's character (especially his independent streak), his mastery of investigative procedure, and his relationship with Eleanor Wish, an FBI agent who is teamed with him on the case. It is Agent Wish who articulates Bosch's relationship to the institution he serves: "you are an outsider in an insider's job. You made it to RHD and worked the headline cases, but you were an outsider all along. You did things your way and eventually they busted you out for it" (95). In this and in Connelly's later novels, Bosch is often outside the law in his private pursuit of justice.

Through the successive Harry Bosch novels, Bosch's Vietnam War background remains a part of his memory package and a convenient source of occasional metaphors, but he is not obsessed or haunted by it, nor do incidents from his Vietnam past or the pasts of other characters become part of a case. In the fifth novel, *Truck Music* (1997, in which he is reunited with Eleanor), Bosch remembers an episode of being separated from his unit with another man and "waiting under the jungle canopy for Charlie to stumble onto them." We learn that he frequently remembers that night, a close escape, "when he was alone on a stakeout, or in a tight spot" (297) as he is now. Camouflaged and waiting to trap a suspect in darkness, he also remembers the tunnels: "Coming upon an enemy in the darkness. The fear and thrill of it. It was only after he had left the place safely that he acknowledged to himself there had been a thrill to it. And in looking to replace the thrill, he had joined the cops" (299).

Another notable ingredient of *Trunk Music* is the delineation of Bosch's relationships with Kizmin Rider, a young black woman with whom he is partnered on this case, and Lieutenant Grace Billets, Bosch's immediate superior. Connelly does not allow Bosch to be patronizing or in any way awkward with these effective professionals who gain his respect by their skills and dedication. Even after learning that these women are involved with one another, Bosch assesses them as professionals and finds them reliable, even admirable. He treats them accordingly. Like Roberts's Connie Armijo, they are part of a pattern in which contemporary hard-boiled detective fiction partly redeems its sexist heritage in the adjusted attitudes and behavior of men who had served in Vietnam.

In *Black Echo*, Eleanor Wish has a James Crumley novel on her shelf (201), and it is no accident that Connelly pays homage to Crumley. The prototype of the Vietnam vet detective may be James Crumley's C. W. ("Sonny") Sughrue, who first appeared in Crumley's well-received *The Last Good Kiss* (1978), in which the Montana private eye drops occasional remarks about his three Army hitches and his service in Vietnam.[5] We learn that he once "grenaded a hooch and killed three generations of a Vietnamese family" (212) and that he left "Vietnam in irons." To avoid a term in Leavenworth, he agreed to spend two years "as a domestic spy for the Army; sneaking around the radical meetings in Boulder, Colorado" (22). The latter details establish Sughrue as someone with an authority problem and a distrust of government, traits without which a hard-boiled detective isn't worthy of the name. However, there is little in *The Last Good Kiss* or the recent *Bordersnakes* (1996) that makes Sughrue's Vietnam background more than an authentic-sounding decoration for someone of his generation.

The early novel does establish Sughrue as a drug-taking, authority-bashing loner whose personal code of conduct transcends rules and regulations. The frontier he rides through takes in Montana, California, and Texas—especially the back roads and backwaters where the promise of the frontier has decayed into a jaded cynicism punctuated by irrational moments of hope and courage.

It is only in *The Mexican Tree Duck* (1993) that Crumley infuses the present with the past and explains Sughrue's behavior as well as his country's condition through a web of references to Vietnam. Sughrue's case brings him into conflict with thugs whose large-scale operations make the novel's conflict analogous to war. Vehicles and weaponry (all Vietnam-era), as in battlefield novels, engage across a forsaken landscape—now a desolate American west, a morally decayed frontier. As in the representations of war in Vietnam, enemy and ally are frequently confused. Betrayal is constantly in the air. Moreover, the fighting unit that Sughrue puts together in order to fight the war that his case becomes is made up of a band of buddies from Vietnam. As they pursue what is essentially a rescue operation, their talk rings with Vietnam veteran lingo. They seem to be trying to finish something that had been left unfinished, to redeem themselves. A member of the team says of himself and a close friend, "neither one of us has had a nightmare since we hooked up with you, Sughrue" (204). Barnestone, a riverboat commander and a SEAL in two Vietnam tours, has been a drug kingpin for twenty years (202). Now he is part of the "good guy" action. The "bad guys" also have Vietnam War pasts. Joe Don Pines, a former intelligence officer, attempts to run Mexican crude across the border to fill his dry oil wells. Another character has a list of offshore bank accounts of CIA drug money. The elicit enterprises have pointed parallels with the Golden Triangle drug trade during Vietnam.

Crumley's blurring of good guy/bad guy, good vet/bad vet, and government/ underworld lines is a convention of hard-boiled detective fiction that originates in the outlaw heroes of western fiction and accelerates in post-Vietnam writings. The catalyst for this acceleration is the perceived corruption of American leadership during the war. Often, Crumley employs flashbacks to happenings in Vietnam as if they "explain" the present. As Sughrue puts it, "the American military and political establishment used the war for their own benefit, then manifestly displayed all the meretricious mendacity of a Mafia don or a Hollywood whore . . ." (223). In the post-Vietnam present, a connection between CIA drug money and Mexican politics blackens the convoluted workings of power like a curse from the dying lips of butchered Vietnamese civilians.

Cases involving corrupt officials link many of the hard-boiled detective stories. The police commissioner in Durden's *The Fifth Law of Hawkins* has conspired with other high officials. Corrupt FBI agents are the enemy in Connelly's *Black*

Ice, while buried secrets of corrupt officials and power brokers spring the plots of his other novels. In *Trunk Music* (1997), corrupt police officers in both Los Angeles and Las Vegas have to be put down. The criminal antagonist in Roberts's *The Ghosts of Saigon* had been a CIA agent. Corrupt policies of government agencies show up in Crumley's work and elsewhere. The dilemma of distinguishing enemy from ally learned in Vietnam, along with the worry over government purposes and policy, turns into an uncertainty about placing trust in law enforcement officers and government officials in the middle-aged world of these wised-up tough guys. For the hard-boiled detective who plays a closed hand under the best of circumstances, this malaise leads him into an even deeper sense of exile. As in war, friends are few, and among them loyalty runs deep. Cases are personal. Power, especially the power that releases deadly force, is intoxicating for the evolving frontier hero. For many, this power is related to the risk and thrill addictions caught in wartime.

While their lives bring them into contact with women who fill the stereotypes of the old macho traditions: bimbos, whores, leeches, and even a few impossible goddesses (the female interest in Hasford's novel combines these types),[6] some of these new warriors (Gabe Treloar and Harry Bosch) have moved into new territory in their private and professional relationships. Partnered with women, they are finding their way towards a productive equality in love or lust and in the war that is their work. And it's still the same work: making the wilderness safe for a civilization in which they don't quite belong.

NOTES

1. Reichmann's key associate is named Gentry!

2. Other Vietnam vet journalists involved in mysteries include Wayne Karlin's Wheeler and T. Jefferson Parker's Chuck Frye discussed in chapter 6. Winston Groom's Beau Gunn in *Gone the Sun* is yet another such character. A Vietnam War veteran, Groom is best known for his sprawling, traditionally fashioned war novel, *Better Times Than These,* and for *Forrest Gump*.

3. Parts of Gibson's critique will be summarized in chapter 8.

4. These are *Black Ice, The Concrete Blond, The Last Coyote, Trunk Music,* and *Angels Flight.*

5. Of the four series creators discussed in this chapter and chapter 8, only Crumley is a Vietnam War veteran. His first novel, *One to Count Cadence,* closes with several chapters set during the clandestine early stage of our military involvement in Vietnam.

6. Butler's Marta Gregory (in *Sun Dogs*) is somewhat unusual in this regard, a woman defined by her own transcendent erotic longing.

Chapter Eight

Hard-Boiled Nam II

James Lee Burke's Dave Robicheaux

While James Crumley served in the Army at the outset of the Vietnam War, James Lee Burke's Vietnam is a place Burke has only imagined.

James Lee Burke, whose first six novels gained critical acclaim but not a mass audience, hit the jackpot with his detective series featuring Dave Robicheaux, a Cajun homicide lieutenant whose service in Vietnam has helped form his outlook and sense of self. In the first novel of the series, *The Neon Rain* (1987), we meet Robicheaux as a mid-fortyish veteran on the New Orleans Police Department. He is a man who has troubles with liquor, with his memories of Vietnam, and with authority and regulations. During much of *The Neon Rain*, Robicheaux is on probation from NOPD; at the end, though reinstated, he retires and opens up a boat rental and bait business at which we will find him in each of the nine novels that follow.

The case itself has to do with paramilitary forces, some having government connections, involved in gunrunning to Nicaragua and Guatemala. One of the leaders is a retired army general whose son was tortured in Vietnam and forced to set mines around My Lai, causing the losses of American personnel that "justified" the massacre. Robicheaux suspects that the general's association with this right-wing crowd grows out of his emotional reaction to what happened to his son. Just as the general has come to justify and accept his lawbreaking, so, on a less obvious level, has Robicheaux, who is always abandoning regulations and personalizing his conflicts. Robicheaux forces situations that allow him technically legal kills of people he wants out of the way. He has a vigilante streak.

Burke establishes Dave Robicheaux as a sophisticated and sympathetic version of the New War warrior described by James William Gibson in his provocative study *Warrior Dreams: Violence and Manhood in Post-Vietnam America*, though in important ways he transcends this type. Moreover, the Robicheaux environment is very much like the America of Gibson's analysis. It is an America that can no longer define itself as the land of the winners. Following Vietnam, America (and particularly American men) faced a "disruption of cultural

101

identity" amplified by the victories of the civil rights and feminist movements. Gibson argues that:

> American men—lacking confidence in the government and the economy, troubled by the changing relations between the sexes, uncertain of their identity or their future— began to *dream*, to fantasize about the powers and features of another kind of man who could retake and reorder the world. And the hero of all these dreams was the paramilitary warrior. In the New War he fights the battles of Vietnam a thousand times, each time winning decisively. Terrorists and drug dealers are blasted into oblivion. Illegal aliens inside the United States and the hordes of non-whites in the Third World are returned by force to their proper place. Women are revealed as dangerous temptresses who have to be mastered, avoided, or terminated. (11–12)

Burke's Dave Robicheaux does not reflect all of these tendencies (he treats women and minorities fairly), but he moves through a world that is permeated with characters who bring these dreams to life as mercenaries for or principals in crime clans and hate groups. A domesticated, thinking man's Rambo, Robicheaux carries the Rambo-like bitterness of betrayal and suspicion of authority into a plainclothes pursuit of New War justice. When he pursues a drug dealer, the case does not end with a trial, but with a showdown in which Robicheaux's violence— and the vigilante nature of his motivation—prevails.

Robicheaux's personality profile overlaps, in part, with those Gibson describes as becoming contract killers, mercenaries, or right-wing warriors:

> First, they were deeply affected by the Vietnam War: their participation or their failure to make a personal appearance on the battlefield was a crucial event in their lives. Second, . . . these men drew the same conclusion from the defeat of the United States in Vietnam . . . [that] dark forces of chaos had been unleashed and dangerous times make it not only permissible but morally imperative for them to take their personal battles far beyond law. (196)

In Robicheaux's case, what's legal is a moving line, often distinct from what's *right*. Always in trouble with his superiors, sometimes on suspension or a leave of absence, Robicheaux's effectiveness comes through turning his cases into personal battles that require personal solutions. The "dark forces" are often criminal cadres involved in drugs, gunrunning, gambling, prostitution, and other rackets. Some live on the edge of respectability, as eager politicians and entrepreneurs mix with them in the course of feeding their own appetites for power.

Robicheaux's Vietnam experience is laid out as follows:

He served early, his ten months straddling part of 1964 and 1965. He carries two wounds, and they are repeated in each of the novels like a refrain. One is a scar "from the dung-tipped *pungi* stick" that has the appearance of "a broken gray snake embossed on my stomach." The other is a welter of scars on one thigh resulting from the explosion of a Claymore mine.

The story regarding the second wounding is told many times in many ways, often in flashbacks or feverish dreams. In *The Neon Rain*, Robicheaux tells the story to his girlfriend, Annie, a woman he later marries. Calling himself "a hotshot lieutenant with a degree in English who thought he could handle the action," Robicheaux recounts walking into an ambush of North Vietnamese regulars, who had suckered the Americans into a mined area. "We lost ten guys in fifteen minutes, then the captain surrendered." Afterwards a gunship spotted them and "a bunch of rangers and pathfinders came through that same mined area to bail us out. We were the bait in the rat trap." The point of the story, here and in later novels, is for Robicheaux to admit that "I was glad someone else was getting shredded into dog-food instead of me" (60-61). His hatred of the enemy was topped by this other emotion, and he knows that his sense of honor does not include ending up dead.

These wounds form part of the iconography of the Dave Robicheaux landscape. The vulnerability of gut and thigh are near the surface of consciousness at all times, both for Robicheaux and for Burke's readers. Another icon in Robicheaux's world is the .45 automatic that he carries along with or instead of his police issue weapons. It is his souvenir of "Saigon's Bring-cash Alley, out by the airport" (72), notable for the damage it can inflict.[1] The wounds and the weapon are the overt signs of how Vietnam is carried or worn by Robicheaux each day of his life. In later novels, Robicheaux digs for evidence with his army entrenching tool (*Black Cherry Blues* 294), another icon from his past.

But the impact of Vietnam has extended roots deep into Robicheaux's psyche. His present experiences always make connections with his Vietnam combat past. As a villain shoves Robicheaux's head into a filled bathtub in *The Neon Rain*, Robicheaux feels himself slip "down through the depths of the Mekong River, where floated bodies of other fatigue-clad men and whole families of civilians, their faces still filled with disbelief and the shock of an artillery burst . . ." (56). In such ways, Burke, through his protagonist, rehearses the enormous carnage that was Vietnam, as well as the damage it has done to the souls of the survivors. The shadow of Vietnam is always present.

That damage includes the taste for the kill, and in that first Robicheaux novel readers discover the "adrenaline-fed sense of omnipotence and arrogance" in killing, some "secret pleasure" that Robicheaux first experienced in Vietnam and that is shared by many thousands of others, good citizen or criminal, whether they know it or not (100).

Three quotations from *The Neon Rain*, quotations that have echoes in the succeeding novels, sum up Robicheaux's version of lessons learned:

- In a hallucinatory state, Robicheaux hears a character called the pencil man say, "The government will mess you up." (133)
- "Like many others I learned a great lesson in Vietnam: Never trust authority." (146)
- "Who wants to be a good loser?" (155)

Vietnam lies in the background of the other good guys who populate the Robicheaux novels, and the bad guys as well. Indeed, the blurring of the line between good and evil is one legacy of Vietnam that Burke underscores through this distribution of characters and backgrounds as well as through other means. I have already mentioned General Abshire, who has allied himself with right-wing paramilitary operations in Central America that involve the transport and exchange of drugs and guns.

Another adversary, Bobby Joe Starkweather, a crazed gunman in the outlaw crew, wears "a tattoo of a grinning skull in a green beret with crossed bayonets under the jaw and the inscription KILL THEM ALL . . . LET GOD SORT THEM OUT" (51). Treasury Agent Fitzgerald, a Robicheaux ally, says that Starkweather is reputed to have fragged an NCO in Vietnam and, of course, that he has worked for the CIA. Fitzgerald also tells Robicheaux of paramilitary training camps in Florida and Mississippi somehow involved in illegal right-wing enterprises. The problem is that Starkweather is the underside of Robicheaux himself.

Heaven's Prisoners (1988), the second in the series, contains less Vietnam-related material, but perhaps assumes readers' familiarity with *The Neon Rain*. Each Robicheaux novel gives enough background to raise the specter of Vietnam, and each can be read independently, but taken together they make a major statement about post-Vietnam America as well as about the "New South." In this novel, trouble finds a retired Robicheaux (now married to Annie) when he rescues a young girl from a small plane crash and later finds out that someone he saw in the plane is not officially listed. That person had "a green and red snake tattooed above his right nipple and something in my mind, like the flick of a camera shutter, went back to Vietnam" (7). Robicheaux has stumbled upon a countermove in an operation meant to help illegal immigrants get into the United States. The pilot, a priest, had been rescuing people from El Salvador for some time. Before long, Robicheaux makes an enemy of Monroe, an agent of the Immigration and Naturalization Service, by hiding the young girl and denying her existence. Monroe's job is to thwart such activities, not to act on any sympathy for anyone's oppressed condition. He is one in a series of well-meaning, tunnel vision bureaucrats who populate Burke's novels.

Robicheaux tries to find the missing tattooed man by tracing a swizzle stick he had found in the dead man's pocket. He's Johnny Dartez, a lowlife who worked for Bubba Rocque, Robicheaux's childhood friend who is now a crime kingpin in the New Orleans area. Robicheaux connects with a DEA agent named Minos P. Dautrieve who is on the case from another angle. They both aid and annoy each other. Dautrieve, who served in Vietnam in an intelligence unit, says that Dartez was a narcotics transporter for Bubba Rocque.

The DEA had been after Dartez and Victor Romero, another Rocque henchman, as a means of putting Rocque out of business. In keeping with Burke's vision of government effectiveness, DEA and Immigration won't cooperate.

The young girl, whom Robicheaux renames Alafair and later adopts, gives a description of her squalid home life that reminds Robicheaux of his time in Vietnam (46–47). Through her, but in other ways as well, Burke develops the subtheme of exploited, tortured innocence that runs through the entire series. A flashback to a Saigon burn ward (49) forms part of the pattern. Reminders of Vietnam trigger, once again, Robicheaux's memory of the dust-off operation that saved him after he was seriously wounded (53–54). This time, he also remembers being among prisoners urinated on by North Vietnamese regulars (60).

Annie, whom Dave has married, is murdered in his place by the Rocque forces, actually now controlled by Rocque's wife, Claudette. Rocque has been involved in people-smuggling from another angle. He brings in Colombian drug lords to do business. Upon Annie's death, Dave joins the local (Iberia Parish) sheriff's office to pursue the murderer of his wife, but as is his passionate way he breaks all the rules and tries the patience of his sympathetic boss.

Through the remainder of the series, Robicheaux is more or less connected with this department, though sometimes suspended and sometimes on leave.

We learn, with Robicheaux, that Dartez worked for Immigration in some way (perhaps as an informant), as well as for Rocque. The plane was blown up to kill Dartez, not the others.

Perhaps the government has made his body disappear. Such an intermingling of gang and government agency hirelings runs through the series, complicating the moral ground. Often, this odd coupling is linked back to the CIA operations during Vietnam in which Air America transport operations benefited the drug lords of the golden triangle.

Robicheaux's stint as a lieutenant in Vietnam and his long experience as a police officer have led him to an understanding of violence that he articulates in this way:

> Most people think of violence as an abstraction. It never is. It's always ugly, it always demeans and dehumanizes, it always shocks and repels and leaves the witnesses to it sick and shaken. It's meant to do all these things. (108)

But Robicheaux is a man who uses violence as much as he hates it. He knows that it lessens him, but he can't remove himself from the cycles of violence that permeate not only his narrow world but the America that Burke portrays. Post-Vietnam America is a place where individual and corporate appetites are larger than national interests or loyalties, and where violence is the only effective exercise of power.

Robicheaux's dreams elaborate this infection of violence. In one, he remembers seeing a chopper gunner firing on people and villages and understands the disease of this addiction to violence and power (123–24). There are always innocent sacrifices to this addiction, which, like the addiction to drugs, seems to have America's Vietnam adventure as its catalyst. The gunner in the flashback shoots long after there is no enemy:

> There were no people to shoot anymore, but no matter—his charter was clear. He was forever wedded and addicted to this piece of earth that he'd helped make desolate, this land that was his drug and nemesis. The silence in the dream was like a scream. (124)

The violence, the thrill of it, can become its own end.

In the present action of this novel and the others, violence and weapon firing always turn Robicheaux's imagination to action in Vietnam. And the hard-boiled cynicism that he brings to his job and his expectations has its roots there, too: "You declare a difficult geographical and political area a free-fire zone, then you stand up later in the drifting ash and the smell of napalm and define with much more clarity the past nature of the problem" (135).

For Burke's Robicheaux, the free-fire zone has leapt across time and space to the American continents where lords of violence and addiction destroy whatever gets in their way. They have inherited the Vietnam War method of problem solving. If Robicheaux can describe himself as a "new colonial" in Vietnam (173), then the drug kingpins, weapons dealers, and gambling czars are the new colonials back home. And their enterprises have no boundaries; nothing is off-limits. What saves Robicheaux, what separates him, is his obsessive sympathy with the victims.

In *Heaven's Prisoners*, characters besides Robicheaux have their Vietnam pasts and stories. Victor Romero, the man who mistakenly killed Annie while trying to assassinate Robicheaux, was a sniper in Vietnam (189). He is a hardened survivor who "ate bugs and lizards for thirty-eight days and came back with eleven gook ears on a stick" (214). Vietnam made him fearless and indifferent to the misery of others. He continued to be a sniper.

Minos Dautrieve, on the other hand, refused to murder an incompetent, stupid, malicious major whose foolishness got agents tortured and killed. He didn't cross the line, and, even though that major is still out there "fucking people up," Dautrieve's hands are clean: "I don't have to live with a shitpile of guilt. I don't have to worry about the wrong people showing up at my house one day" (251). Though Dautrieve respects Robicheaux, he worries that Robicheaux killed Romero unnecessarily. Could Robicheaux have made an arrest? Did he want to? The reader can't be sure.

At the end of *Heaven's Prisoners*, Robicheaux quits the sheriff's department just as he had quit the NOPD at the end of *The Neon Rain*. We expect that it won't be long before he picks up his badge again.

With *Black Cherry Blues* (1989), Burke became an award-winning author, garnering the Edgar Award for mystery writing. The story line has to do with an old college friend and former rockabilly star, Dixie Lee Pugh, who comes to Robicheaux for help. Dixie Lee had fallen into trouble through his work as a leasing agent for Star Drilling, a Louisiana company looking for opportunities in Montana. Dixie Lee had been manipulating the company's purchases and leases so that they could be later obtained by Sal Dio, a mobster out of Las Vegas. Two Star coworkers, Vidrine and Mapes, found out about Dixie Lee and wanted in on his action, then wanted more. Also, Dixie Lee discovered that the pair killed two Montana Indians who were working to block private takeovers of land to which the Indians laid claim. When a drunk Dixie Lee threatened to turn them in, Vidrine and Mapes set out after him.

Robicheaux tries to help Dixie Lee, but gets falsely accused of killing one of the pursuers after he beats the two up with chains. Actually, Mapes had killed Vidrine. Threats against Alafair and the need to clear himself lead Robicheaux to Montana, where most of the action occurs. He works as a detective for no one but himself, but does have the usual ambivalent alliance with a government agent (DEA man Dan Nygurski) who works the case from his own limited angle. Robicheaux's age is forty-nine in this novel. His state of mind is revealed in terms of moving through his fiftieth year.

This novel has no extended Vietnam flashbacks, but includes the usual references to the pungi-stick scar and other incidental details that establish Robicheaux's background. The text is sprinkled with quick references like this overheard conversation among prisoners planning criminal action: "'It's like war. You make up the rules when it's over'" (16). In his own way, Robicheaux has developed a similar philosophy toward dealing with the violence that enters his life. There are also the familiar references to Robicheaux's dreams, here summarized: "In my dreams is a watery place where my wife and some of my friends live. I think it's below the Mekong River or perhaps deep under the Gulf" (37). On a rainy night, Robicheaux dreams that he hears Annie's voice reminding him that his platoon buddies didn't like the rain because it gave them jungle sores (63). Repeated from *The Neon Rain* is the theme of guilt in Vietnam "when the man next to you was hit . . . you were glad it was him and not you" (51–52).

Once again, a key Robicheaux adversary shares the Vietnam War background. This time it's Mapes, the killer who worked for Star Drilling and is now after Robicheaux for helping Dixie Lee. Early in the novel, Robicheaux is threatened by a package that includes a photograph: "A pajama-clad Vietcong woman lay in a clearing by the tread of a tank, her severed head resting on her stomach. Someone had stuffed a C-ration box in her mouth" (55). The photo is accompanied by a hypodermic needle and a note outlining Alafair's daily routine. We later learn that it was planted by Mapes, who had been a helicopter pilot (173) and who reportedly spoke of blowing up a VC nurse in a spider hole (99). Mapes's weapon turns out to be "a 7.62-millimeter Russian Tokarev, a side arm often carried by NVA officers" (282).

Black Cherry Blues reunites Robicheaux with Clete Purcel, his former partner (in *The Neon Rain*) on the NOPD. Clete, also a Vietnam War veteran, talks a version of the talk and walks a version of the walk that Robicheaux does. However, Clete is even more of a line-crosser. He has mixed with criminals to the point where some of their mind-set has rubbed off on him. In this novel, Robicheaux finds Clete working security for a drug dealer, Sal Dio, who is building his Montana territory. In *The Neon Rain*, Clete had just about betrayed Robicheaux, but they now reach an understanding that allows the old friendship to surface and grow. They begin working together, as they have one bond that is stronger than anything that separates them. This bond is Vietnam and the special mutual insight and implicit trust it can afford. Burke allows Clete to make the kinds of observations that explain the blurred moral lines of post-Vietnam America: "The CIA deals dope, guys in the White House run guns. You [Dave] used to say it yourself—we keep the lowlifes around so we can have a dart-board we can hit" (88).

On several occasions in *Black Cherry Blues*, Burke uses Robicheaux to reinforce the distance between those who have seen combat in Vietnam and those (like the priest whom Robicheaux visits) who have not: "his day [is] obviously ordered and serene and predictable in a way that I could not remember mine being since I walked off the plane into a diesel-laced layer of heat at Tan Son Nhut air base in 1964" (188). As much as Robicheaux will resist letting people blame their present situation or behavior on the war, telling them to get over it, at bottom the war has worked to form him and separate him from others who have never faced ordeals that required them to question who they are: "They have never heard a shot fired in anger, done time, walked through a mortared ville, seen a nineteen-year-old gunner go apeshit in a free-fire zone" (243). Unlike the smug innocents, Dave Robicheaux needs someone to tell him he's all right.

A Morning for Flamingos (1990) finds Robicheaux involved in an undercover operation for the DEA while still in the employ of the New Iberia Sheriff's Department. He teams up with his old buddy Minos Dautrieve (from *Heaven's Prisoners*). Clete, who now owns a bar in New Orleans, serves as both official and unofficial backup. Robicheaux needs to bring down Tony Cardo's drug operation, and to that end he infiltrates Cardo's system as a buyer and then a buddy. The relationship is complicated by Tony's genuine care for his disabled son (Robicheaux is a soft touch for fatherhood), as well as by Robicheaux's understanding and sympathy for Tony's addiction and Tony's Vietnam War demons. Another plot element is Robicheaux's wish to pay back Jimmie Lee Boggs, a lowlife who shot and seriously wounded Robicheaux when Robicheaux was transporting him from the local jail to state prison. Questions of Boggs's whereabouts and near encounters with him lurk through the novel.

The two plots eventually come together when Boggs is at the other end of a drug buy that is a setup not only by the DEA but also by Houston and Florida gangsters who want to take over Tony's Louisiana action. Boggs is killed trying to escape when Tony sets a meeting-place hangar on fire and Robicheaux lets Tony escape. Other complications include Robicheaux's new girlfriend, his old college flame Bootsie (running a mob-connected business), whom he marries at the end, quitting police work and going back to his boat rental and bait business.

The emotional center of the novel concerns Robicheaux's feelings for his counterpart, Tony Cardo, possibly a good man doing bad things. The power of his attachment and confusion is felt in Robicheaux's confession to a priest regarding his sense of guilt over betraying people (as an undercover agent), a confession that ironically falls on ears totally unequipped to help him (228).

Early in *A Morning for Flamingos*, Robicheaux is shot by his prisoner, Boggs, and the sucking chest wound he receives triggers the first of many Vietnam flashbacks. (The wound from this encounter is added to Robicheaux's physical iconography for the rest of the series.) Exhausted and traumatized, Robicheaux relives a Bouncing Betty episode that left him "disbelieving and voiceless in the scorched grass" (15). As he recovers, Robicheaux's dreams are haunted by a metaphoric figure who could be any old adversary as well as "old Victor Charlie" (20). Fear has once again entered Robicheaux's life, and this novel is largely about Robicheaux forcing himself to take risks, to push the fear away.

In order to talk out his problem, Robicheaux visits Minos Dautrieve. Minos reminds Robicheaux that he has two Purple Hearts and assures him that he'll be okay. With the help of Minos, Robicheaux begins to right himself. Only another Vietnam veteran, one assumes, could do this. For Robicheaux, the difference is that this time he saw it coming, while in Vietnam his wounds were surprises. However, Robicheaux's Vietnam nightmares continue, now reworked with Boggs in them. In one dream, Robicheaux rescues a soldier named Martinez who has a chest wound, confronts the enemy who has used Martinez as bait, and the enemy VC transforms into Boggs (49–52). With such devices, Burke keeps the present and the past interactive and interdependent. Clearly, the serious wounding by Boggs is worse psychologically than the wound that took Robicheaux out of Vietnam: Robicheaux doesn't know if he still has his physical courage. He's not sure if he can go through with the undercover task (54). But of course, he does.

As is usually the case, Robicheaux needs his own reasons for action. It doesn't satisfy him to know that he is working for a presidential task force. He tells Dautrieve, "The head of the DEA says the contras deal cocaine. Reagan and Congress give them guns and money. It's hard to put all that in the same basket and be serious about it" (53). Robicheaux's cynicism about the government and its bureaucracy knows no bounds. Minos urges Robicheaux to play by the rules, reminding Robicheaux of his shaky track record.

As he enters his assignment, Robicheaux gets his body into shape and takes inventory. Burke provides the familiar reference to "the scar tissue where a bouncing Betty had gotten me in Vietnam [that] looked like a spray of small arrow points under the skin of my right thigh and side" (60). (Over time, Burke's initial reference to a Claymore mine has changed to a Bouncing Betty.)

From the first reference to Tony Cardo being a Vietnam veteran (71), the series reader is eager to see the ways in which Robicheaux's false friendship develops. After all, this is the fourth novel in which Dave Robicheaux's present challenge involves an adversary (or adversaries) to whom he is linked by the shared Vietnam past. Bobby Joe Starkweather, General Abshire, Victor Romero, and Harry Mapes lie in the foreground of this encounter. There was always some hint of identification in these conflicts, the other side of the reason Robicheaux turns off a movie on television featuring a "famous actor who had been deferred from service during the Vietnam War because he had been the sole support of his mother" (110). The difference this time is that Robicheaux has to get close to Tony Cardo; he has to enter his life—and then betray him. Thus the moral grounding is more complex, as is the psychological threat of even stronger identification with the adversary.

In many ways, Tony Cardo is likeable. He considers himself some sort of patriot, according to a lowlife named Fontenot who also adds that Tony "likes to talk about 'nape'" (napalm) (97). Soon after Robicheaux works his way into the Cardo "family," the men begin to exchange Vietnam stories. Tony was wounded, too—an additional ingredient of bonding from a shared past. But when the conversation reveals that Tony saw action near Chu Lai, Tony gets tense; he seems to have a secret regarding his activity there (129–30). He is haunted in ways with which Robicheaux is familiar. Robicheaux asks "Why watch the replay the rest of your life?" and Tony responds, "Some guys say the war's never over." Lines like this are James Lee Burke's code for the sorry condition of post-Vietnam

America. Even Dave Robicheaux's life can be considered a series of replays. And yet he is less static than most of his fictional peers. One always senses that he is pushing for a way out of his Vietnam-enclosed cycles of behavior.

Robicheaux requests Cardo's military record (140), but receives only a partial version (193). Something about the record is not right. Robicheaux discovers, over time, that Cardo's present condition of drug addiction began in Vietnam, but that he had been locked up in a psychiatric unit rather than treated for addiction (261).[2] The incarceration had been a terrible ordeal in itself. In an attempt at recovery years later, Tony had a bad experience with a patronizing analyst who made fun of his Vietnam trauma (232). Finally, Tony tells Robicheaux his story. After he was wounded, he was not sent back to join his platoon but reassigned "to a bunch of losers." Men in his new company raped teenagers and blew up a Vietnamese hut. Fearing to tell anyone what happened, Tony volunteered to work in the mortuary at Chu Lai (266–69). He thinks he showed cowardice, but Robicheaux says maybe not—maybe he chose the gruesome mortuary work as his penance. Robicheaux wonders why Tony can't forgive himself. But Robicheaux has the same kind of problems with self-esteem (and fights his own addiction to alcohol): "I got four of my men killed on a trail because I did something reckless and stupid" (272).

Finally, though, Robicheaux doesn't want to let Tony "blame it on the Nam":

> "Here's the lay of the land, Tony," I said. "I think you've got a big Purple Heart nailed up in the middle of our forehead. Everybody is supposed to feel you're the only guy who did bad time in Vietnam. You also give me the impression that somebody else is responsible for your addiction and getting you out of it. But the bottom line is you sell dope to people and they fuck up their lives with it." (311)

Yet for all the pretty speechmaking, Tony's story has struck Robicheaux to the quick. They are like feuding brothers. He lets Tony escape, making up some version of what happened that Minos Dautrieve doesn't really believe but can't counter. Robicheaux has, to some extent, let both himself and Tony blame it on the Nam. Underneath his hatred of whining, of people who don't take responsibility for their actions, is a sympathetic bond—a heart. Much later, Robicheaux receives a note from Tony that suggests he has beat off the tiger of addiction. It concludes with these words: "Face it, you dug being in the life. Even Jess thought you were one of us. That'd worry me" (316). It worries Robicheaux, too; crossing the line is too easy. He leaves law enforcement, "at least for the time being" (318).

In *A Stained White Radiance* (1992), Burke complicates Robicheaux's life with a threat against a member of the Sonnier family. The Sonniers, with whom Robicheaux grew up, were a highly dysfunctional clan in which the children were abused. One, Weldon, has become a successful businessman (mostly in oil), but is now in trouble with a New Orleans mobster (Joey Gouza). Weldon's wife is the sister of a former Klansman now running for the U.S. Senate on gang money as well as Aryan Brotherhood support. With the introduction of the Aryan Brotherhood, Burke once again identifies the growing power of right-wing paramilitary groups. Weldon owes money on a drugs-for-guns deal he piloted when his business was in trouble. During Vietnam, Weldon flew observation planes from carriers; he later did Air America flights out of Laos under CIA auspices (10). Thus, his special talents, his trafficking in illicit cargo, began as a government operation in which drug lords received cooperation from CIA operatives. Once again, Burke connects moral line-crossing with government activity and present dangers.

Weldon further links his Vietnam past to his present situations. He'd been tortured in Laos by a warlord, Colonel Liu, for refusing to load dope. Later he was ransomed back to the CIA. In the present, Weldon has ripped off drug traffickers for $180,000 by taking their money and not completing deliveries (202). Weldon thinks he can protect himself with his videotapes of action in Honduras and Colombia that implicate others (222–23). However, Robicheaux points out that the tapes provide no leverage at all. The footage on Weldon's tapes remind Robicheaux of events he'd seen in Vietnam, and readers are reminded of Alafair's background in El Salvador. A story like Weldon's might make for a special issue of *Soldier of Fortune* magazine, a central text of the paramilitary culture examined by Gibson.

Lyle Sonnier, now a fundamentalist preacher, was under Robicheaux's command in Vietnam. A tunnel rat at eighteen, Lyle snapped a trip wire going into a Vietcong tunnel, the explosion costing him two fingers and possibly his sanity and moral vision (11). He's seen it all and done it all, even began preaching as a fraud—but now claims to be (and seems to be) on the up and up. At one point, Lyle tells Robicheaux of killing a nun in Vietnam. Robicheaux and Lyle frequently exchange advice about dealing with guilt and denial (97–100). Elsewhere in the story, as elsewhere in the series, Robicheaux claims to have left his Vietnam guilt behind, but the reader doubts that claim.

Drew, sister of Weldon and Lyle, was once Robicheaux's girlfriend. She's something of a nutcase. There are well-founded rumors of sibling incest in the Sonnier family. The father, who was thought killed in a chemical explosion, returns to haunt their lives.

The attempted assassination of Weldon followed by the killing of the investigating sheriff's deputy draws Robicheaux into the case. Eventually, the mobster is set up by Robicheaux, and his hired hands are killed, but along the way Alafair and Bootsie are threatened. The Sonniers' father is later arrested trying to kill Weldon.

Robicheaux's struggle to keep sober and his friendship with Cletus Purcel are once again in play. And, once again, there is a rehearsal of Robicheaux's scars from pungi stick and Bouncing Betty (52). The reader also shares another telling of Robicheaux's Vietnam dream of an artillery barrage. Additionally, Robicheaux remembers "Vietnamese civilians who had survived B-52 raids. They were beyond speech; they trembled all over and made mewing and keening sounds that you did not want to take with you" (141). Incrementally, as novel builds on novel, Burke provides enough repeated and fresh detail to make, if it were extracted and rearranged, a novel of Robicheaux's time in Vietnam.

Sometimes the passages that fill in the world of war belong to other characters, and sometimes they are parts of stories only overheard and repeated. In *A Stained White Radiance*, for example, Weldon tells a story of a man named Ed

McGovern who flew supply drops for the French at Dien Bien Phu. McGovern, after many successful runs that earned him a legendary reputation as being inde- structible, flipped and burned while trying to set down on the highway leading to Hanoi (45). For Weldon, the death of this legendary figure is a sign of karma: "Highway One outside of Hanoi is waiting for us. It's all part of a piece" (45).

Midway through the novel, Lyle compares Weldon and Robicheaux in a way that underscores Robicheaux's freelance style and his abhorrence of regulations and authority: "You were both officers in the war. Neither one of you likes rules or people telling you what to do. Both of you have electric sparks leaking off your terminals" (164). Burke leaves it to Clete Purcel to make even more emphatic the characteristic disdain and distrust of bureaucrats and their regulations: "I learned in the corps you don't mess with the pencil pushers. You stay invisible. You piss off some corporal in personnel and two weeks later you're humping it with an ambush patrol outside of Chu Lai" (233).

At the end, Robicheaux takes leave from the sheriff's office. He is forever leav- ing and coming back.

In the Electric Mist with Confederate Dead (1993) is one of the best James Lee Burke novels. Unlike most in the Dave Robicheaux series, this one has few spe- cific Vietnam references, but many about the general nature of war. While Robicheaux investigates a serial killing, an actress who had borrowed a shirt with Robicheaux's name stenciled on the back is mistaken for him and shot; she is part of a movie crew filming a Civil War novel in Robicheaux's area. The movie is backed by mobster Julie "Baby Feet" Balboni who knew Robicheaux in school. Robicheaux, who has been slipped LSD in order to discredit him through making him appear to have fallen back into alcoholism, has hallucinations of Civil War battlefield scenes. These involve long talks with John Bell Hood, the valiant southern general, during which they compare war experiences. Late in the novel, Robicheaux uncovers the truth about a thirty-five-year-old murder he had wit- nessed. His partner in this adventure is FBI agent Rosie Gomez, one of several characters in the series through whom Burke broadens the panorama of race and gender among law enforcement officers.

As in the other Robicheaux stories, additional Vietnam veterans populate the plot. This time it's the movie director, Mike Goldman, who is the designated secret sharer. Goldman is given an instance of the guilt refrain that echoes through several novels:

> "The guy next to you takes a round, and then maybe you start wondering if you aren't secretly glad it was him instead of you." (141)

When characters whom Robicheaux essentially dislikes utter his own sentiments, Robicheaux's own self-respect is tested.

Robicheaux's central interchanges are with the imagined General Hood and the very real Elwood Sykes, the alcoholic star of the movie whom Robicheaux pities and befriends, though he is appalled by Sykes's weakness.

The imaginary conversations with the general turn in part on the never-ending nature of wars, the endless ramifications. They agree that the war of each "goes on and on" (162) and that "we never quit paying dues" (212). Through these interchanges, Burke underscores his series-long theme of the presence of the past. Most often, it is the fatherly general who draws the lessons from the shared experiences of battle. Echoing the theme of *Heaven's Prisoners*, Hood says, "Then you know it's the innocent about whom we need to be most concerned" (236). The general acts as Dave's conscience, often by reference to his own experience:

"Like you, I grieve over what I can't change. . . . How many lives would have been spared had we not lent ourselves to the defense of a repellent cause like slavery?"
    "People don't get to choose their time in history, general." (317)

As part of his attempt to help the alcoholic Elrod Sykes, Dave retells the story of getting four of his men killed on a trail, then getting drunk over it. "I used them," he says, "I didn't respect them for the brave men they were" (250). With this confession, Robicheaux tries to take such excuses away from Sykes.

Like *In the Electric Mist with Confederate Dead*, the next Robicheaux novel, *Dixie City Jam* (1994), has less than the customary amount of Vietnam flashback and reference. This one concerns Robicheaux's involvement with rivals wishing to exploit the treasures of a sunken Nazi U-boat. Neo-Nazi fanatics, an activist Jew (Hippo Bimstine), and New Orleans mob figures (the Calluci family) collide, as Robicheaux fights his wife's growing alcoholism and other personal matters. Sidekick (and Vietnam War veteran) Clete Purcel plays a major role in this novel. There is a marvelous cast of new supporting characters, including black police-woman Lucinda Bergeron and her son Zoot, Tommy Lonigan (a good-hearted gang figure who served in the Korean War), and the Nazi weirdos Marie Guilbeaux and Will Buchalter. Through the enterprises of the latter pair, Burke once again reminds his readers of the threat from right-wing paramilitary forces. A telling connection of mind-set and background in this novel is the confusion of a Nazi sword symbol (a tattoo design) with the bayonet symbol of the 101st Airborne unit (240).

As we would expect, Burke records the usual Robicheaux Vietnam tags: the wounds and bad memories along with brief references to lessons learned. Late in the novel, when Robicheaux is being tortured with electric shock, he lapses into imaginatively reliving the obsessively haunting Vietnam dust-off episode (296–97).

More than in the other Robicheaux adventures, this one underscores the combination of patriotism and prejudice that feeds underworld and paramilitary appetites. Here, the mix complicates Tommy Lonigan's character. Here also, through Tommy and also (rather obliquely) through Robicheaux's boss—the head of the New Iberia Sheriff's Department—Burke connects the experiences of Korean and Vietnam War veterans. And once again, the language of war, learned by Robicheaux in Vietnam, serves to operate for contemporary struggles between the forces of corruption and justice: "When you create a free fire zone, it works both ways. We're not operating on the old rules here" (203). There is no longer a gentlemanly code of getting along between gangsters or between gangsters and police.

Dave Robicheaux is an introspective tough guy, and he often broods about the behavior that ruined his first marriage, an event that lies years in the past before the series opens. In this instance, Robicheaux says:

> I had always wanted to believe that I had brought the violence in my life with me when I came back from Vietnam. But one of the most violent moments in my life, or at least the most indefensible, came at the end of my first marriage and not because I was a police officer or a war veteran. (207)

The question of whether Vietnam, as historical moment and symbol of the American spirit, can be held up as the causal agent for present misery or malfunction is raised over and over again in Burke's Robicheaux canon. Robicheaux's attempt here to separate the strands of self and deny blaming a violent act on Nam is one swing of a pendulum that is always in motion.

Late in the novel, Robicheaux sarcastically intones the connection between individual acts of contemporary police (or vigilante) violence and the Vietnam-era mind-set that lies behind it:

> It was old and familiar logic. If you feel like a reviled and excoriated white sojourner in a slum area, break the bones of a drunk black motorist with steel batons. If you cannot deal with the indigenous population of a Third World country, turn their rain forests into smoking gray wasteland with napalm and Agent Orange. (272)

Echoing his philosophizing in *Heaven's Prisoners* and elsewhere regarding violence, Robicheaux tells his audience that "*death* is never abstract":

> Death is the smell that rises green and putrescent from a body bag popped open in a tropical mortuary; the luminescent pustules that cover the skin of VC disinterred from a nighttime bog of mud and excrement when the 105's come in short; the purple mushrooms that grow as thick and knotted as tumors among the gum trees, where the boys in butternut brown ran futilely with aching breasts under a rain of airbursts that painted their clothes with torn rose petals. (419)

To render the concreteness of violence and death is one of Burke's artistic ambitions: without making the reader awaken to the reality of suffering and the shock of witnessing, his vision of post-Vietnam America would lack one of its most important dimensions. In *Dixie City Jam*, violence and death are palpable, but so is the hunger for the kill.

After several novels with slimmed-down attention to Vietnam scenes and present-day paramilitary ventures, Burke amplifies these ingredients once again in *Burning Angel* (1995). The somewhat confusing exposition involves a fight over land that is contested by gentry and descendents of former slaves. The white owner and one of the black women are lovers, complicating the tensions in the story. Gang figures seem to be manipulating the genteel Bertrand family, and Sonny Boy Marsallus has some part in this. We learn later that the mobsters are interested in putting through a lucrative real estate deal for a high-pollution factory that has been having difficulty finding a home.

Sonny Boy was rumored to be a DEA plant in Central America, where drug operations were tied to American government initiatives that parallel CIA activities in Vietnam and Laos (140). The mobsters are after Sonny Boy's diary which connects events in Central America with people who had Vietnam/Laos experiences, a connection that is one cultural message of the entire Robicheaux series. Sonny Boy's diary establishes connections that made it a "death list" in the wrong hands. The cocaine trail, we learn, always leads back to guns (194–95). Sonny Boy has put a copy of the diary into Robicheaux's hands, making Robicheaux a target. And it is Sonny Boy who utters the post-Vietnam vision of self-interested, power-hungry operations that know no traditional loyalties:

> "Dave, take the scales off your eyes. We don't serve flags or nations anymore. It's all business today. The ethos of Robert E. Lee is as dead as the world we grew up in." (299–300)

These operations need their own soldiers. In *Burning Angel*, the many references to paramilitary operations in Central America involve the same figures who are behind the land deal. The henchmen, soldiers of fortune with Vietnam backgrounds, are attached both to the gangs and to government operations. During his investigation, which quickly becomes a personal matter, Robicheaux is on and off the sheriff's force, his family once again threatened.

Clete Purcel plays a major role in this novel. He had worked for Sonny Boy in Central America, and his memories of what he saw down there are as bad as anything he'd seen in Vietnam (45). Aside from Clete and Robicheaux, *Burning Angel* involves other Vietnam War veterans. One of these is the current head of the Bertrand family, Moleen, who had been an air force major toward the end of the war—an intelligence officer who had never seen combat (20, 137). His soft life as a southern aristocrat is paralleled by the nature of his service.

The story gains complication and confusion as the present opens up the past. During the course of his investigation, Robicheaux finds the dog tag of the chopper pilot who rescued him in Vietnam. After Burke reprises the dust-off flashback, the reader learns that this pilot, Roy Bumgartner, had disappeared in Laos and was written off as MIA or traitor. Someone obviously knows Dave's record and has had a connection with the pilot (57–59).

Robicheaux's investigation takes him into the world of paramilitary culture, the local center being Tommy Carrol's Gun and Surplus Shop. Burke's sketch of the culture's citizens reads (in substance though not in style) like a passage from Gibson's study:

> It's probably safe to say the majority of them are self-deluded, uneducated, fearful of women, and defective physically. Their political knowledge, usually gathered from paramilitary magazines, has the moral dimensions of comic books. Some of them have been kicked out of the service on bad conduct and dishonorable discharges; others have neither the physical nor mental capacity to successfully complete traditional

basic training in the U.S. Army. After they pay large sums of money to slap mosqui-
toes at a merc training camp in the piney woods of north Florida, they have themselves tattooed with death heads and grandiloquently toast one another, usually in
peckerwood accents, with the classic Legionnaire's paean to spiritual nihilism, *"Vive
la guerre, vive la mort."* (62)

But those that rise in paramilitary culture are strongly motivated and exception-
ally able, even if their moral dimensions remain simplistic.

The exemplary figure here, and archenemy, is Emile Pogue. Pogue is a veteran
soldier of fortune who is after Sonny Boy for having killed his brother and
another S.O.F. named Jack. He has been an instructor at an Israeli jump school
and is skilled in weapons and survival techniques (66–67). Pogue is the man who
had planted the dog tags for Robicheaux to find. Bumgartner may have been one
of the CIA operatives left behind in Laos because he knew too much about U.S.
complicity in the drug trade (86–87). Pogue, too, must have had some connection
with that Southeast Asian adventure. He also claims to have met Robicheaux
before and knows about his gun purchase in Saigon's Bring Cash Alley (158) and
about Robicheaux's wounds (162).

This novel is filled with memories, dreams, and dream summaries, as well as
incidental tales of other people's Vietnam experiences. Clete remembers the smell
of a tank burning with soldiers inside (294–95). At one point, Robicheaux tells of
a helicopter pilot he knew whose chopper was shot down while carrying ammunition and civilians:

> most of the civilians burned to death or drowned. He became psychotic after the war
> and used to weight and sink plastic statues of Jesus all over the waterways of south-
> ern Louisiana. (275)

The man eventually hung himself, and Robicheaux reads reports on his psychiatric history that refer to him hearing the voices of the drowned. Robicheaux's
experiences suggest to him that such voices are real, not signs of insanity (275).

Nor is it insanity to buy into Robicheaux's conspiracy theory of a world in
which Colombian drug lords and Mafia-controlled casino operators directly or
indirectly control newspapers and "literally employ the governor's children":

> Floating casino owners with state legislators on a pad work their shuck on morning
> television shows like good-natured Rotarians. (304)

In this twilight world that Burke paints for Robicheaux's social and psychic
domain, characters like Robicheaux and Emile Pogue walk a thin rope across a
moral abyss, sometimes keeping their balance, sometimes falling. Pogue has
done a great deal of damage in the world, but he tried twice to rescue
Robicheaux's chopper pilot friend. Robicheaux has done much good, but not in
Vietnam—and the way in which he lives his life more often brings the swift justice of violence rather than the tedious justice of law.

As the action winds down, the sheriff tells his war story, one he had kept bot-
tled up through the several years Robicheaux had known him. He had sent three

North Korean POWs off with a BAR man who "enjoyed what he did." He knew he was making a mistake with that assignment, and he has lived with the guilt ever since. Explaining the impact of the experience, he tells Robicheaux, "That's why I always sit on you, always try to keep the net over us . . . so we don't take people off behind a hill." But then he adds, "It's the rules get us killed sometimes. You got too many bad people circling you" (379).

Bad people circling him can be Robicheaux's justification, then, for his own rule-breaking. But Burke makes it clear that this moral bog has no exit.

In *Cadillac Jukebox* (1996), Burke once again minimizes attention to Robicheaux's Vietnam background. Moreover, Burke has Robicheaux insist that "spirits of villagers, their mouths wide with the concussion of airbursts, no longer whispered to me from under the brown currents of the Mekong" (8). However, even if Robicheaux is no longer haunted by his memories, they are not erased. And the character formed in part by those ten months is not significantly changed. In fact, in spite of this disclaimer, Robicheaux does have a dream in which a threatening Vietcong figure appears, but he understands the chaotic dream as a figuring of his present dilemma: "Even in my sleep I knew the dream was not about Vietnam" (71). Vietnam, then, is now more than ever a way for Robicheaux and Burke to talk about the present.

The present finds Robicheaux involved in a case in which Aaron Crown, the convicted murderer of black civil rights worker Ely Dixon, convinces Robicheaux that he may not have been guilty of the crime. The timing of this appeal coincides with the gubernatorial race of Buford LaRose. LaRose, heir to a wealthy family, is a well-known college professor and author. He has made his reputation through a book on Aaron Crown that sent Crown to prison. If Robicheaux's investigation of Crown's claims undermines LaRose's book, the governorship is likely to be lost. Not surprisingly in a Burke novel, bad things start happening around Robicheaux once he sticks his neck out. In this case, Robicheaux is both threatened and bribed. It seems that the powerful criminals have something on LaRose, and therefore want him in office. Robicheaux's investigation will eventually uncover the players and their motives. He will also discover that Crown had accidentally killed the brother of his real target, a man who has turned his daughter into a prostitute.

That man is Jimmy Ray Dixon, a local hoodlum with some legitimate businesses, who is also one of the Vietnam War veterans through whom Burke continues to make his case about the war's endless consequences. Jimmy Ray claims he lost his hand in the service of his country (clearing mines), but he actually lost it to his business partners, Chinese thieves with whom he worked "selling stolen PX liquor on the Saigon black market" (211). In this respect, he is part of an odd trinity that includes Jerry Joe Plum, who still scratches at his parachute tattoo, and Dock Green, "who claimed to have been kidnapped from a construction site near Hue by the Viet Cong and buried alive on the banks of the Perfume River" (114). These men all seem to have claims on the LaRoses, especially the latter two who quickly land construction contracts for hospitals and rehabilitation centers upon Buford's election.

We discover that Buford is less vulnerable than his wife, Karyn, who when in college used a test stolen by Persephone Giaconi, former Mafia princess and now Dock Green's wife. Karyn is only the most recent of several femmes fatales in the Robicheaux novels who try to manipulate Robicheaux through seduction. She is one of those "dangerous temptresses" described in Gibson's study "who have to be mastered, avoided, or terminated" (12).

In *Cadillac Jukebox*, the 1960s and 1970s are demonized in an additional way. Not only is this the Vietnam War era, but it is the hippie era. Burke invents a Timothy Leary stand-in, an aging psychedelic philosopher named Clay Mason who seems responsible for Buford LaRose's addiction, against whom Robicheaux can castigate the excesses of liberalism as much as he excoriates right-wing hate-mongers.

Robicheaux's Vietnam War background is a given (as is Burke's stature as a best-selling author), rather than a manifestly demonstrated feature in *Cadillac Jukebox*. A handful of memories, an erotic ceremonial cleaning of the Colt .45 bought in Saigon (138), and referential interchanges with old sidekick Clete Purcel do the work. When Robicheaux is down on himself for causing pain to others in his war against corruption Clete once again preaches a gospel that looks back to what they shared:

> "You're a police officer. You can't ignore what you see happening around you. If you fuck up, that's the breaks. In a firefight you stomp ass and take names and let somebody else add up the arithmetic. Get off your own case." (245)

Toward the end of the novel, Robicheaux contemplates turning in his badge and becoming a private eye, as he had done briefly several novels back in partnership with Clete. The question of whether he must work within the establishment or for himself permeates the whole series, making Robicheaux an outsider among law officers. By having Robicheaux wear a badge, Burke has been able to show the great disparity between the established forces for order and the "dark world" of well-armed and well-financed appetites for whom the law is rarely much more than a nuisance.

Most of Burke's Dave Robicheaux material parallels the Reagan-Bush era, an era which James William Gibson describes as having "paramilitarism as state policy" (265). The real life story of Oliver North, for example, is part and parcel of the world Burke envisions. The interest, in both policy and male fantasy, in special forces without a clear chain of command or accountability makes a character like North heroic and makes Burke's stories of government/gangster collusion credible. We don't flinch when we learn in *Burning Angel* that the bad guys have access to requests that go through FBI and CIA computers and fax machines, like Robicheaux's requests for information about Sonny Boy and Emile Pogue (82).

According to Gibson, events like the invasion of Panama and the arrest of Noriega revealed at once the psychic need for redemptive warrior engagement in the post-Vietnam era and habitual government collusion with drug traffickers. The romanticizing of seemingly independent Green Berets, SWAT teams, and SEALS creates the attraction to self-nominated militias. If Dave Robicheaux is sometimes a rogue cop, he is a cleaned-up version of a popular tradition, just as Oliver North is the hero as squared-away rogue soldier.

But Robicheaux is more than that. As Gibson describes the warrior-hero of the post-Vietnam era, he uncovers a diseased culture. He finds, for example, a lopsided notion of masculinity that allows no nurturing role for fathers. Robicheaux is born in part from the death of his first marriage and his chronic alcoholism, and then reborn in the violent death of his second. wife. In this sense, it takes the death of family to spring the isolated, independent warrior who in most instances will devalue women (304). Burke, however, is clear about Dave Robicheaux's conscious desire to be integrated into a family unit.

After he rescues and adopts Alafair, he becomes a caring, attentive, nurturing father. Alafair's well-being is never far from his thoughts over the decade of her growing up. Burke allows Robicheaux a certain domesticity at home with Bootsie, Alafair, and Batiste, the black man who works the boat rental and bait shop business with Robicheaux and serves as his surrogate father. Though black-widow women come into play in several novels, Robicheaux finds himself mated with women whom he respects, and he truly shares as much as he can with them. His obsessions with his cases and with Vietnam strain his relationship with Bootsie, but both of them fight together to gain a healthy perspective on who they are. Burke also pairs Robicheaux on the job with a series of women with whom he can truly partner. Though they have disagreements, Robicheaux is not guilty of sexist patronizing. Burke's portrait, over the last few novels, of Robicheaux's relationship with Helen Soileau is the most intriguing of several working relationships in the series.

Dave Robicheaux is, then, the post-Vietnam New War hero in the process of turning the corner. His dreams no longer poisoning him with guilt or feelings of inadequacy, he is more and more grounded in the so-called simple pleasures. As do many of the Robicheaux novels, *Cadillac Jukebox* ends with an idyllic portrait of family life. He and Alafair ride her Appaloosa "and put up a kite in the wind. The kite was a big one, the paper emblazoned with an American flag, and it rose quickly into the sky, higher and higher, until it was only a distant speck above the sugarcane fields to the north" (297). Then Bootsie and Alafair and Dave dance together to Cajun classics as the wind accompanying a storm blows the cane and wisteria so that "shadows and protean shapes formed and reformed themselves, like Greek players on an outdoor stage beckoning to us, luring us from pastoral chores into an amphitheater by the sea, where we would witness once again the unfinished story of ourselves" (297). With this transcendent vision following the dance of family, Burke suggests the possibility of renouncing the warrior myth as the exclusive hero story. He seems to echo Gibson's call, agreeing that "transforming warrior culture is not about men becoming something less than they are, but rather, something more" (309).[3]

NOTES

1. Gibson has a long passage on the history and mythos of the semiautomatic Colt .45, first adopted by the U.S. Army in 1911. In his chapter on "The Hero's Magic Weapons," he observes, "To own and shoot a Colt .45 automatic opens a tremendous historical domain for an imaginary traveler." The weapon has "mythic status" as a tough reliable killing machine with which the warrior can bond. See pp. 85–86. For Robicheaux, this particular weapon is clearly talismanic.

2. An offstage character in *Dixie City Jam*, the son of Reverend Oswald Flat, also became an addict in Vietnam. He could never shake the addiction, drugs being so plentiful on the street. Finally, he died from an overdose. (229)

3. The next Robicheaux novel, *Sunset Limited* (1998), does not continue this thread of idealized domesticity. In this regard, it seems to break the direction the sequence has developed for its hero's transformation.

Chapter Nine

Vietnam War Themes
in Korean War Fiction

Here is a quotation from a critically successful war novel: "If the soldiers from the North did not burn the village, the big machines of the foreigners certainly crushed it" (161).

The Vietnam War again? Another liberal diatribe on how we manage to bring destruction to those we insist upon helping? Here is more: "They come with their machines and their iron hearts, the foreigners, and change the face of the world" (205). The quotations are from Chaim Potok's *I Am the Clay* (1992), a searingly poetic novel about South Korean refugees during the loss and regaining of Seoul.

In the popular view, the war in Vietnam waged by the United States and its allies was a unique enterprise. This mystique of difference suggests discontinuities with past military ventures, especially discontinuities in national purpose and in the nature of the warriors' experiences. Moreover, this supposedly aberrant character of American involvement in Vietnam is left to serve as partial explanation for an unsatisfactory outcome. Vietnam War representation, particularly in fiction, underscores and reflects this view, imaging the "unique" war on many levels. However, an examination of Korean War fiction goes a long way towards demythologizing the uniqueness of Vietnam by offering striking parallels and by placing the Vietnam experience in a larger context of Asian misadventure.

Unfortunately, the imaginative literature of the Korean War has been little known, hard to find, and barely scrutinized.[1] Nonetheless, dozens of novels were published during the Korean War and the Cold War years embodying a wide range of perspectives on that conflict. Criticism has taken a long time to catch up. In his 1970 study, *An Armed America: Its Face in Fiction*, Wayne Charles Miller asserts that the Korean conflict "seems an event that the United States is anxious to forget; for the most part," he continues, "the fiction that emerges from that war will not prohibit the processes" (245). Briefly reviewing five titles in less than four pages of a monograph with 270 pages of text, Miller does little to support his proposition. He, too, wants to forget Korea. Moreover, he insists that Korean War novels "have followed in the paths established by their immediate predecessors" (248) while Cold War novels contemplating the nuclear age have been the works which break new ground.

In his 1975 study *The American Soldier in Fiction, 1880–1963*, Peter Aichinger devotes a four-page chapter to the literature of the Korean War, treating only two war novels plus William Styron's *The Long March*. Whatever his arguments are, they can be dismissed as based on insufficient evidence. Jeffrey Walsh's *American War Literature 1914 to Vietnam*, published in 1982, is even more disappointing, with six brief index references to Korea and no discussion of the literature at all. A fleeting reference to *M*A*S*H* places it as a Vietnam War novel.

Also writing in 1982, David I. Steinberg asks,

> Where are the American novels of the Korean War, or even the American movies on it? There are a few, but they are singularly lacking, in abiding interest, and it would be unusual to find today an American who can name a novel or movie that centered on the Korean "police action." (9)

But Steinberg, like the others, did not look very closely.

Only Arne Axelsson's *Restrained Response: American Novels of the Cold War and Korea, 1945–1962* (1990) gives significant attention to the literature of the Korean War. Part 2 of Axelsson's book, called "The Korean Corpus," provides a chapter each on POW novels, novels of the sea and air war, and novels of ground fighting (divided into Marine and Army representations). Axelsson's chapters are supplemented by brief summaries of novels not treated in his main text.

While there are many things to be observed about this body of literature, my principal concern is to maintain that many of these works anticipate or echo the themes of Vietnam War literature and include features that have been singled out by Vietnam literature scholars—myself included—as the unique, distinguishing characteristics of that war, at least as represented in literature.

A convenient summary of these distinctions is found in Tobey C. Herzog's *Vietnam War Stories: Innocence Lost* (1992). After reminding readers that several historians had found numerous parallels between the wars in Korea and Vietnam, Herzog lists the supposedly unique factors of the Vietnam experience—especially those developed in memoir and fictional representation. They are:

> (1) a soldier's individual entrance and exit from the war rather than in a military unit; (2) the widespread opposition at home to the war, especially after 1968; (3) Vietnam as a "contained conflict" without distinct battle lines; (4) the emphasis on body-counts as an indication of battlefield success; (5) a limited tour of duty for American soldiers; (6) a brief post-combat transition period for the returning soldier from the battlefield to the United States; and (7) an unusually high incidence of delayed psychiatric casualties. (47–48)

Elsewhere, Herzog summarizes other features that supposedly separate the Vietnam War from others, features that are repeated over and over again in Vietnam War representations. The war was "waged against the elements" and as well as against a frequently invisible foe who could be readily confused with the ally. In this confusion, innocent civilians might be killed, as might unsuspecting American soldiers (52). As we shall see, many of these features find representation in the literature of the Korean War, as do a number of others that don't make Herzog's inventory.

One of the clichés of the Vietnam confrontation is that the enemy ruled the night. No matter what objectives American and South Vietnamese forces achieved by daylight, the Vietcong and North Vietnamese were able to retake them once darkness set in. This day/night pulse figures as a unique characteristic of the Vietnam War in such popular representations as Billy Joel's song "Goodnight, Saigon." However, novels of the Korean conflict present identical observations. In Con Sellers *Brothers in Battle* (1989), we learn: "The nights belonged to the North Koreans, and the little bastards were probably infiltrating at this moment" (77). Communist forces also own the night in Michael Lynch's *An American Soldier* (1969), while James Hickey's *Chrysanthemum in the Snow: The Novel of the Korean War* (1990) supports this same understanding, though much less forcefully. In Pat Frank's *Hold Back the Night* (1952), one of the earliest and best novels of the Korean War, we discover that "the night crawled with life and movement. . . . The enemy dared not use the roads by day, for fear of American planes, but the night was his" (90).

Another motif of Vietnam War representation involves the United States' misdirected pride in its vastly superior technological capacity. Here too, Korean War representations provide parallel insights. Such a faith in superior technology against backward natives is rehearsed, in Walt Sheldon's *Troubling of a Star* (1953), by a civilian in Air Force technical support named Johnny Pendermeyer. And in Frank's *Hold Back the Night*, the success of the technologically backward enemy, a force including Mongolian cavalry patrols, is accounted for by its skill, its numbers, its commitment, and its invisibility. In representations of both wars, our technological superiority is not always relevant or decisive, and our faith in it is viewed as a blinding limitation. Writing directly about the Korean War rather than its representations, David Halberstam observes (in his monumental *The Fifties*, 1993) that America entered the war with an "arrogance born of racial prejudice" (71), tragically underestimating North Korean military skill and weaponry. Such a notion, too, can be found in many of the literary representations, but more often the emphasis is on the compensatory skills of the North Koreans and their Chinese allies. Our superior armaments did not make us a superior force under the political, geographical, and climatic conditions of the war.

Many novels of the Vietnam War describe the Vietnamese jungles and the extreme heat as being more of a threat to U.S. forces than the enemy. Confrontation on this foreign soil was quite a different matter from battle in the European theater of World War II, while Pacific theater representation does not insistently image the climate as a virtual foe. However, Korean War fiction invariably does just this. Most often, it is the cold with which American and other United Nations forces battle. Frank's *Hold Back the Night* stresses extreme hardship caused not only by an unusual enemy force but also by difficult terrain and climatic conditions: "This wind that had crossed the frozen steppes of Asia screamed like a live and fanatic enemy" (203). Hickey's *Chrysanthemum in the Snow* paints the extremes of both heat and cold as well as the difficulty of uphill fighting in mountainous country. Arduous mountain fighting is also effectively portrayed in *Unit Pride* (1981), by John McAleer and Billy Dickson, a novel that provides descriptions of North Korean tunnel networks rivaling anything represented in Vietnam War writings.

In much Vietnam War literature, we read about the lack of preparedness and lack of will on the part of our South Vietnam ally's military forces. Americans are perplexed by their call to a commitment that seems inadequately shared by the very people we are trying to help. Such representations of the indigenous ally are also a feature of Korean War fiction. The inadequacy of the allied force (ROK army) is represented in Lynch's *An American Soldier* in a manner that echoes the complaints about the poor fighting skills of the South Vietnamese:

— These R.O.K. troops are worth shit, Spina said.
— They're gooks, what do you expect? Cernak said. (124)

Sellers' *Brothers in Battle* (1989) however, takes a mixed view and presents major characters who are valiant South Korean warriors.

Negative attitudes toward those we are supposedly helping are based, according to several Vietnam portraits, on misunderstanding due to cultural difference. David Halberstam's *One Very Hot Day* (1967) is a key novel in this regard, juxtaposing the perceptions of American and South Vietnamese officers. Among Korean War novels, this concern is central to Hickey's *Chrysanthemum in the Snow*. An intriguing feature of Hickey's novel is that two of the members of the squad are South Koreans. One of them, Choi, who speaks English fairly well, is able to provide insights about contrasts between American and Korean values that lead to misunderstandings. American arrogance and an ignorant, abusive sense of superiority is frequently underscored. Choi meditates on his American friends:

As he understood them, they had come to Korea armored in their own superiority to correct the political situation of a nation older than their own god. This amused, rather than angered, although it did anger that so many of the Americans regarded him and his countrymen as barbaric subhumans. The Tungusic Koreans, a people who had invented movable type and the phonetic alphabet, who had devised the suspension bridge and astronomical instruments to fix the stars in their courses, and the compass and the armored ship. Barbarians? Ha. (176)

Vietnam War literature often concerns itself with racist attitudes toward both enemies and friends. Cruelties toward South Vietnamese abound, as do representations of the impossibility of distinguishing friend from enemy in an absurd war. So, too, in Korean War narratives. In the words of Dr. Benjamin Beer, hero and narrator of Stephen Becker's *Dog Tags* (1973), "By now no one knew for sure who the enemy was" (75). The concern with distinguishing friendly and enemy Koreans and the inherent frustration in this situation also shows up in Thomas Anderson's *Your Own Beloved Sons* (1956), one of the most skillful of the Korean

War novels. It includes a questionable shooting of Koreans who might be ROK allies (though they were found in a hut in which Russian automatic rifles were hidden) and who at any rate could have easily been taken prisoner. "What's two goddam Gooks?" (145) is the rationale. On another occasion, a Korean is shot by an American who had been ordered only to fire a warning above his head.

Thus, the "gook syndrome" of the Vietnam era ("the only good gook is a dead gook") is only an extension of attitudes formed in the Korean conflict. The term itself was probably applied to Vietnamese—all Asians, finally—by Korean War veterans who later served in Vietnam. William Crawford's *Gresham's War* (1968) portrays American hostility and violence toward South Korean civilian allies (and even a ROK who is part of the American squad) as well as many other evidences of blatant racism (nicknames here are "shambos" as well as gooks).

Elsewhere in Anderson's novel, we read, "All them civilian Gooks are more trouble than the real soldiers; they know there's a war going on and still stick around and get their ass in the way" (129). There is also the accidental killing of a young boy by Americans firing into a haystack in a Korean village in which a sniper had been operating (130 ff).

Through one of the sergeants in *Brothers in Battle*, Con Sellers makes the point about how Americans tend to lump all Asians together, applying one set of prejudices to all. Conditioned to hate the Japanese during his World War II experience, the sergeant can only imagine Japanese horrors when he sees friendly Korean faces.

Commitment and clarity of purpose characterize the North Vietnamese and Vietcong forces in literary representation. While Americans fight valiantly, they often question the reason for U.S. involvement or simply don't understand it. Moreover, they frequently sense that the folks back home aren't behind them. These same attitudes can be found in representations of the Korean War. In Frank's *Hold Back the Night*, the enemy is committed and sure of its purpose, while the American soldiers are not uniformly convinced of the stakes. They wonder why it is important that they must risk their lives fighting Chinese in Korea. Even in James Michener's flag-waving *The Bridges at Toko-Ri* (1953), the war is sometimes seen as destiny rather than as militarily and politically rational. And in *Gresham's War* (1968), Crawford represents the American soldiers' sense of fighting for U.S. citizens who don't care about or value their sacrifices. In an earlier Crawford novel, *Give Me Tomorrow* (1962), a soldier complains about the contrast between Korea and the Big War in a way that anticipates Vietnam: "At least the people back home were with us" (92).

Though it seems paradoxical, communist Vietnamese saw themselves first and foremost as nationalists determined to rid their country of outsiders. For many, including those fictive ones whose concerns are the stuff of novels, the fight was for a unified Vietnam governed by Vietnamese. A history of invasion and occupation lay behind the ferocity of their fighting. They were in it for the long run. Similarly, in Con Sellers's novel of Korea, communist North Koreans find in communism a means to a nationalistic end. Sellers portrays a diehard North Korean colonel who wants his country cleansed and decontaminated, even if that means wiping out the weak-willed southerners who invite the dilution of Korean identity. This warrior seems to believe that he can deal with the Chinese later, after using them to throw out even more unholy occupants.

In the popular imagination as reinforced by representations of that conflict, the Vietnam War is considered unique in its commanders' calls for enemy body counts as measures of progress. Indeed, William Turner Huggett took the phrase for his characterizing title (*Body Count*, 1973), and it is also the title of the long, central section of Gustav Hasford's *The Short-Timers* (1979). However, Korean War fiction once again portrays this mind-set. In Sheldon's *Troubling of a Star*, Col. Straker develops a plan to deploy air units against the kind of targets that they are proven most successful against, and for his command he wishes to further the commitment of air power against ground troops. For Straker, the enemy body count is an essential measure of success, a success he hopes to turn into a promotion to general. (Jesse C. Gatlin's treatment of careerism and other moral issues in Sheldon's novel is worthy of note.) Frank's *Hold Back the Night* also imagines the conflict as a war of attrition in which body count is a register of performance.

Several other characteristics of the Vietnam War as defined in fiction find their reflections in earlier or later literary responses to the Korean conflict. These include drug problems, detailed in Lynch's *An American Soldier*, in which both drug use and drug trafficking are described. Lynch has a character observe, ". . . whisky, heroin, opium. You name it. If the driver doesn't have it, he'll get it for you" (265). The constant, sometimes intrusive presence of media—a theme familiar to readers of Vietnam War literature, is turned to comic purposes in Coon's Korean War novel, *Meanwhile, Back at the Front* (1961); and the influence of media coverage on public opinion, a prominent concern in several Vietnam War texts, is of concern also in Frank G. Slaughter's *Sword and Scalpel* (1957). Sheldon also pays attention to the press establishment and the public relations front of the Korean effort. And the Vietnam War theme of official misrepresentations of the war's progress is anticipated by Michener: "In this special war there were special rules to keep the people back in American from becoming worried" (50). The issue here is that we were fighting Russian equipment and Russian-manned radar installations, but not admitting it. More intriguing than these parallels, however, are those evoking the frustrations of limited warfare and the horror of napalm.

"Dow shalt not kill" was one of the well-known slogans of antiwar protesters who condemned the use of napalm in Vietnam. "Crispy-critters" is the slang term for the burned corpses found after a napalm (or flamethrower) attack, a term familiar from Vietnam War literature and film. The iconography of napalm in Vietnam War representations is so strong that it has distorted our sense of history about that horrible weapon. Herzog reminds us that the image of the napalm victim is one of a handful of key images that defined the war in American's imaginations: "a young Vietnamese girl, arms outstretched, her clothes burned off, screaming as she flees a napalm attack" (49).

But napalm was nothing new.

Invented in 1943, napalm had extensive use in the later stages of World War II. It was a staple of America's arsenal in Korea at the same time that the French were using it as an antipersonnel weapon in Indo-China. So-called UN "interdiction" efforts often involved the use of napalm in ways that brought tragedy to the civilian population. Though newspaper reports made mention of "jellied gasoline bombs," there seems to have been little reportorial witness, and television coverage of the war was minuscule (Stockholm 39–55). The American public had little, if any, awareness of the consequences of napalm bombing during the Korean War, while during the Vietnam War photojournalism and film reports brought home its devastating effects. In the public consciousness, as informed by the media and literary endeavor, Vietnam is the Napalm War, and Bruce Weigl's poem "Song of Napalm" is one of its anthems.

Nonetheless, the largely unread novelists of the Korean War wrote of napalm and its horrors. In Walt Sheldon's *Troubling of a Star*, one of the officers, Captain Tindle, questions his ability to fly a bombing mission again after witnessing the results of napalm bombing at the close range of forward air controller, a duty he performed for sixty days. Questioned about the utility of air strikes for antipersonnel actions, Tindle nervously answers, "When it comes to troops, napalm can't be beat. I've—I've watched it hit at close range," he stutters (20). The narration continues: "As he talked he could again smell the hot smell and hear the screams and see the human beings blacken and shrivel" (31). In a later scene, Sheldon describes another napalm attack: "One man near the whooshing curled and became black and then shrank, like overcooked bacon, into virtual nothingness. Now, mingled with the oil and gunpowder smell, Straker could detect the awful stink of charred flesh" (256).

Perhaps the best known parallel between the two wars is the frustrating effect of "limited war" policies. Vietnam War literature raised the consciousness of readers about what it meant to fight a war with one's hands tied or with unsure objectives. Moreover, any objective short of decisive victory, we discover in Vietnam War representations, brings a sense of despair and victimization to one's own troops. Something like this despair permeates Rolando Hinojosa's fine, diary-style novel of Korean War action, *The Useless Servants* (1993). In Lynch's *An American Soldier*, we have a sensitive portrait of the psychological strain that accompanied such circumstances in Korea. How does the mourning soldier cope with the deaths of his fallen friends? How does one redeem their deaths when war is kept short of victory? Political limitations on military actions are given careful attention in this novel, along with their demoralizing consequences.

Sheldon's *Troubling of a Star* also develops the theme of political constraints on military actions. Here, we follow the pilots' frustration at not being able to bomb targets in China and Russia in order to cripple the North Korean war effort. In the Korean conflict, as Sheldon makes clear, even an air strike behind the lines was not customary during the first year or so of the war. In both of his Korean War novels, William Crawford underscores this theme: "the United Nations does not want to win this war, only to fight it" (*Give Me Tomorrow*, 200); "They ain't gonna let us win, goddamnit, don't you see?" (*Gresham's War*, 56); "We are fighting it all wrong and we aren't trying to win. . . . They [the people back home] know we are losing and claim they don't like it but no one is doing a damned thing about it" (*Gresham's War*, 95).

Both the literature of the Vietnam War and that of the Korean conflict provide a great many narratives, fictional and otherwise, of the POW experience. Because these works belong to a fairly specialized subgenre needing separate treatment, I consider them outside the scope of the present discussion.

Though Axelsson suggests that the Vietnam War influences the presentation of Korean stories published in the 1965–1969 period (171), and while it is possible to discern an influence of the Vietnam War and its literature in the second wave of Korean War novels (especially *Gresham's War*, which provides the first instance I have discovered of the Vietnam-era term "Indian Country"), many of the issues that critics have made hallmark features of Vietnam War fiction are found in the earliest Korean War representations. These include such works of the 1950s as Sheldon's *Troubling of a Star*, Anderson's *Your Own Beloved Sons*, and Frank's *Hold Back the Night* as well as several titles of the early 1960s. That is the surprise. Cultural critiques bemoan our amnesia regarding Vietnam; however, with regard to the fighting in Korea, the American public never paid enough attention in the first place to slip into amnesia.

Attending to the history of Vietnam War writing, Andrew Martin notes "a whole range of cultural institutions that were working to marginalize the Vietnam experience":

> Even when some elements of this ideological gatekeeping and cultural selection could agree on the worthiness of a piece of Vietnam writing, the uncertainty of popular reception remained beyond the influence of the institutions of literary production. The struggle to establish a language of the Vietnam experience, then, came to pass within a contested process in which the possibilities and difficulties of literary production and reception formed part of a wider array of cultural negotiations taking place in the aftermath of Vietnam. (77)

But such gatekeeping and cultural negotiations have had a far less systematic review and a far more perplexing history in the aftermath of Korea—perhaps both because we did not let it touch us and because we never quite finished with it, as recent events in Korea make tragically evident and as a novel like William Roskey's *Muffled Shots: A Year on the DMZ* (1988), a tale of combat in 1967 with North Korean line-crossers, underscores.

Riding, perhaps, on the success of Vietnam War literature in the marketplace, writers and publishers have released a good number of Korean War titles in recent years. These include Brian Kelleher's *The Gathering Storm* (1989), Ed Ruggero's *38 North Yankee* (1990), D. J. Meador's *Unforgotten: A Novel of the Korean War* (1999), and the titles discussed earlier by Hickey, Hinojosa, Potok, and Sellers. Perhaps the normalization of a cultural dislocation is signaled by its adoption by romance writers. At least one such signal, Lindsay McKenna's *Dawn of Valor* (1991), has followed in the wake of several romances of the Vietnam War: "Korea in 1950 was no place for a woman!" Older historical and analytical studies of the

Korean War have been reissued and new ones have been produced. Several historians of the Vietnam War agree with Marilyn B. Young in seeing Vietnam as a natural outgrowth of the same American Cold War foreign policy that contributed to the making of but could not resolve the Korean conflict: "The end of fighting in Korea, then, could only mean a pause between wars, a truce rather than a peace. There could be no full demobilization in the face of such an enemy" (Young 28). Slowly, quietly, we are beginning to pay attention to momentous events of almost fifty years ago that went largely unnoticed by the American public at the time.[2] It took Vietnam and its long shadow to get us there, but it took Korea—or our unwillingness to learn from it—to bring us to Vietnam.

NOTES

1. With the fiftieth anniversary of the war at hand, these unfortunate decades of neglect are likely to end. See the recent *Retrieving Bones: Stories and Poems of the Korean War,* edited by W. D. Ehrhart and Philip K. Jason.

2. The 1997 publication of a revised edition of *The Hunters,* James Salter's classic 1956 novel of the air war, may have been a harbinger of renewed interest. The various fiftieth anniversary projects, including the establishment of a Korean War Veterans National Museum and Library in Tuscola, Illinois, will help awaken further interest.

Chapter Ten

Going Back to Go Forward

In his concluding chapter, or "Afterword," to *Walking Point* (1988), Thomas Myers conjectures that "the return to Vietnam of Ward Just's narrator in *The American Blues* is only a prefatory gesture in a larger collective rite, one that begins with the recognition that the Vietnam War will remain a permanent feature within the American cultural landscape." Myers continues, "Grafted together in the most tragic way, Vietnam and the United States are now like one of Stephen Wright's botanical metaphors, a hybrid cultural organism whose growth patterns cannot be prophesied" (222). Twelve years later, Myers comments seem prophetic enough, though the growth patterns are less uncertain. The brief return of Just's protagonist in his 1984 novel has indeed been a "prefatory gesture" anticipating the later lives and works of veterans and veteran writers. Like Just's correspondent, they have had to go back to go forward. Unlike him, they may achieve closure. At the outset of the twenty-first century, the grafting seems less tragic.

Among the few inspiring outcomes of the Vietnam War are the efforts of many veterans, and especially veteran writers, to resolve issues of conflict and to create peace with understanding between the people of the United States and those of Vietnam.

As early as December 1981, members of the Vietnam Veterans of America Board of Directors had traveled to Vietnam to establish a dialogue on such issues as Americans missing in action (an issue raised by the returnee in Just's novel), Agent Orange, and American-Vietnamese children who had been raised in Vietnam since the war. About six months later, a follow-up contingent came that included Lynda Van Devanter, who would attach an "Epilogue: Going Back" to *Home Before Morning*—her memoir of the war years, a memoir begun in 1979, she tells readers, as therapy. Though her visit in May 1982 was short, and the

131

record of it in her book only a dozen pages, one of her observations sets the tone for the wide range of reconciliation efforts:

> I began to grasp a feeling for the people and the country that had never been available to me before. War destroys so many things, and one of the first to go is the ability to think of the enemy as human beings with a history and a future. . . . We were now finally having the opportunity to see each other as humans. It was an important step for me. (312)

As this visit ends, Van Devanter is able to lay to rest demons that had troubled her for twelve years: "The tears came washing over me, this time, finally, in relief. It was over. The war was over for me" (314).

The most notable and influential gathering of authors who had served in Vietnam took place three years after Van Devanter's visit under the auspices of The Asia Society. Its theme was "The Vietnam Experience in American Literature," though its sponsoring organization suggested a larger frame of reference. The Asia Society knew that the images of nations and events fostered by literary efforts become, in time, collective memory. The Asia Society context created an undercurrent, occasionally expressed, of how a full understanding was compromised by "the lack of an Asian dimension to the literature on the Vietnam War" (Lomperis 63).

This observation carried a double weight. It first recognized that American writers had not reflected Vietnamese perspectives, that most American literature of the war furthered the cultural narcissism of the war's very conduct. Second, and more important, it recognized an urgent need to hear from Vietnamese writers. Arnold Isaacs observed that "the Vietnamese are absent from the history of American policy formation, just as much as they are absent from most of these novels. They were in the scenery, but they were not anything we were really looking at" (Lomperis 74). Perhaps only Vietnamese writers could help us see what American writers would, of necessity, leave out. Can we learn from history if we read only a small slice of it? Can we gain meaningful insights on historical conflicts if we, at the outset, eliminate half of the perspective we need? Can we make peace without ever really looking at and listening to one another?

Veteran writers, understanding their own limitations, knew what had to be done. They needed to return to Vietnam, as Van Devanter and other veterans had, to see the people as people. They needed to foster a dialogue with their Vietnamese counterparts and promote access to writings by Vietnamese. In the process, they needed to bring Vietnamese writers to the United States. Ultimately, Americans and Vietnamese had to work together, and their war-veteran writers could lead the way.

Before going further, we should note that the mid-eighties brought other programs of healing to maturity. The business of healing at home, healing the wounds among U.S. citizens on all sides of the political spectrum, required some measure of progress before the healing between the peoples of two nations could hope for much success. The writer's conference at The Asia Center can be seen, in part, in that light, as veteran writers with different perspectives on the justice and conduct of the war interacted. Among other efforts toward national reconciliation was the anthology *Unwinding the Vietnam War: From War into Peace* (1987), a collection of voices and images published in conjunction with the Washington Project for the Arts. Editor Reese Williams asked the collection's rhetorical question: "What would happen if we let our memories of the war become instruments of peace?" (5). Unfortunately, the book includes only one Vietnamese voice, and that voice is of an immigrant to the United States.

Poets John Balaban, W. D. Ehrhart, and Bruce Weigl were among those who attended The Asia Center conference in May 1985. In December, the three men were in Vietnam. Their sponsor, ironically, was General Tran Kinh Chi, vice president of Vietnam's War Crimes Commission. Ehrhart's record of that two-week visit takes us into the center of the emotional and spiritual dynamic of reconciliation, but it is neither sentimental nor naïve. Ehrhart found neither a communist utopia nor a time-frozen battlefield, but rather a people earnestly going about the business of rebuilding while healing their own inner divisions. He finds appalling bureaucracy. He finds stereotypical assumptions about Americans. It is difficult to get underneath the official gestures and meet his Vietnamese hosts, guides, and translators person-to-person.

Their hosts have an itinerary for the visiting poets that promotes a political agenda. How could it be otherwise? But this trio of Americans doesn't need the packaged history lessons, at least not as a steady diet. Ehrhart chafes: hasn't he already spent a good part of his adult life carefully studying the causes and consequences of this war? He is no longer a schoolboy and doesn't wish to be treated like one; he is not the naïve, idealistic youth who unquestioningly answered his country's call. Ehrhart and the others push for the individual revelations, not the safe, tedious blather of officialdom. In bits and pieces the masks disintegrate, revealing the human faces the American visitors (revisitors) sought. This is the small but all-important victory won from an invitation shaped by suspicion and policy. A cautious experiment, the visit turns into something more profound.

As he says his goodbye, Ehrhart contemplates his host:

> He is a communist general, a former enemy, a man whose political philosophy does not sit well with me. But in the past 16 days, he has been a kind host and solicitous companion, full of humor and grace, and I have grown genuinely fond of him. Perhaps a day will come when I will not have to feel the need to justify my affection for this man who was once my adversary. I extend my hand, but the general brushes it aside and embraces me with both arms, giving me a kiss on each cheek. And then he turns and is gone. (*Going Back* 175)

Before the trip ever began, Ehrhart imagined himself visiting the region where he had fought, the central highlands and the city of Hue. Near the beginning of the visit, it becomes clear that this won't happen: such a trip is not in his host's plans, and the plans cannot be changed to accommodate Ehrhart's wish to make a private peace where in 1967 he once made war. However, he does get to visit some areas that resemble what he remembers and others that have the glow of tranquility. In the end, that is good enough:

> Now when I think of Vietnam, I will not see in my mind's eye the barbed wire and the grim patrols and the violent death that always exploded with no warning. Now I will see those graceful fishing boats gliding out of the late afternoon sun across the South China Sea toward safe harbor at Vung Tau, and the buffalo boys riding the backs of those great gray beasts in the fields along the road to Tay Ninh. Now I will not hear the guns, but rather the gentle rhythmic beat of rice stalks striking the threshing mats. (180)

More than likely, his thoughts will bring up both sets of images, the old as well as the new.

Of course, Ehrhart's experience was a personal one. However, as a writer he was compelled to share it. As we look over his shoulder, we can make a journey with him that brings the possibility of peace closer and that relaxes the strings of tension and suspicion that can lead to war. While his narrative has a special, prominent place in the literature of return, Ehrhart has also written several poems about this trip. One, "Second Thoughts," which appears in *Just for Laughs* (1990), tells of his encounter with Nguyen Van Hung in Hanoi. The Vietnamese veteran cannot, like the speaker, roll a cigarette "because it takes two hands / and you have only one, the other / lost years ago somewhere near Laos." The two men discover shared experiences; the poet calls them "partners / in that ugly dance of men / who do the killing and the dying / and survive." Contemplating his counterpart and himself, Ehrhart concludes:

> Now you run a factory, I teach and write.
> You lost your arm, but have no
> second thoughts about the war you fought.
> I lost a piece of my humanity,
> its absence heavy as a severed arm—
>
> but there I go again; those second thoughts
> I carry always like an empty sleeve
> when you are happy just to share
> a cigarette and *Lua Moi*, the simple joy
> of being with an old friend. (27–8)

Other poems from this experience include "For Mrs. Na," "Twice Betrayed," and "Last Flight Out from the War Zone," dedicated to Bruce Weigl.

As might be expected, Weigl and John Balaban have also written poems about this 1985 visit. Weigl's "Dialectical Materialism" recounts a walk through Hanoi that December, apparently with his fellow poets. His images set the ongoing city life against the destruction of the war, some of its traces still present, some of them in the poet's memory. They meet a man filling water buckets at the river:

> When we ask our questions
> he points to a stone and stick

house beyond the dikes
one thousand meters from the bridge
our great planes
could not finally knock down.
He doesn't say
how he must have huddled
those nights with his family,
how he must have spread himself
over them
until the village bell
called them back to their beds.
These are questions which
people who have everything
ask people who have nothing
and they do not understand.
(*Song of Napalm* 66–67)

Add to this literature of return Balaban's "Mr. Giai's Poem," which has for its subject a man who figures prominently in Ehrhart's narrative. Mr. Giai and his American guests are telling war stories, Giai's about when the French were shelling Haiphong harbor, sending Giai and two friends to seek out his unit as women and children streamed by them to the imagined safety of Hanoi. The soldiers stop at a deserted inn for coffee, a cigarette, and whiskey—all miraculously available. Then they leave to fight. Giai had written a poem about that experience that was published in the Army paper, and now he relates the story of the poem's genesis to the visiting poets. Balaban writes:

Forty years of combat now behind him
—Japanese, Americans, and the French.
Wounded twice, deployed in jungles for nine years,
his son just killed in Cambodia,
Giai tells this tale to three Americans
each young enough to be his son:
an ex-Marine once rocketed in Hue,
an Army grunt, mortared at Bong Son,
a CO hit by a stray of shrapnel.

All four now silent in the floating restaurant
rocking on moorlines in the Saigon river.
Crabshells and beer bottles litter their table.
A rat runs a rafter overhead. A wave slaps by.
"That moment," Giai adds, "was a little like now."
They raise their glasses to the river's amber light,
all four as quiet as if carved in ivory.
(*Locusts at the End of Summer* 129–30)

That picture of raised glasses, of astonished, transforming silence, evokes the kind of human bond that can blunt weapons and assuage the hatreds that employ them.

While Ehrhart, Weigl, and Balaban were making their trip to Vietnam in late 1985, back in the United States a most valuable institution was making its own journey from a fledgling organization focused primarily on veterans' issues to a multifaceted engine of international good will.

The William Joiner Center for the Study of War and Social Consequences was founded in October 1982 as a voice for veterans and a home for scholarship on the Vietnam War and its aftermath. Housed at the University of Massachusetts, the Center soon developed major holdings and special research collections, including the documents that supported the PBS thirteen-part series, "Vietnam: A Television History." The Center also developed educational and humanitarian exchanges and veteran-to-veteran contacts between Vietnam and the United States. Before long, many of the Vietnam veteran writers became regular participants in Joiner Center programs.

In 1988 the Joiner Center hosted its first writing workshop in conjunction with the University of Massachusetts at Boston Creative Writing Program. Novelist Le Luu and short story writer Nguy Ngu worked alongside American Vietnam veteran writers. Of course, these Vietnamese writers needed their government's permission to travel here, as well as the U.S. government's permission to visit. The December 1988 issue of the *Joiner Center Newsletter* summarizes a talk by Le Luu in which he "stressed the mutual bonds and experiences that veterans share and noted the role of literature in establishing friendship and understanding" (1). American writers Tim O'Brien, Larry Rottman, Lamont Steptoe, Bruce Weigl, John Balaban, and W. D. Ehrhart participated in this first workshop-conference, as did essayist Leo Cawley of *The Nation*.

This dimension of the Joiner Center no doubt has something to do with the interests of its director, Kevin Bowen, a Vietnam veteran who is also an English professor and poet. Bowen became codirector of the Center in 1984 and director in 1993. In 1987, he made the first of many trips to Vietnam on behalf of the Center's programs. Several of the poems in his *Playing Basketball with the Viet Cong* (1994) convey his feelings as a veteran who went back. In fact, these trips to Vietnam seem to inform Bowen's handling of poems that go back to the time of his tour of duty. It is as if the impact of return has energized his perception and provided a fertile perspective that allows his later-blooming art to flourish in strikingly original ways.

The second writer's workshop had several repeat faculty, but also new "veteran writers" including Philip Caputo, Robert Mason, Wayne Karlin, and Marilyn McMahon. Le Luu returned from Vietnam, and with him were two other Vietnamese writers. In spring 1990, W. D. Ehrhart took up residence as Visiting Professor of War and Social Consequences, underscoring by his very presence the centrality of veteran writers to the Center's educational and humanitarian concerns. Meanwhile, from year to year, the summer writer's workshop continued to blend old and new participants, gaining the insights and talent of such key American writers as Gloria Emerson, Yusef Komunyakaa, and Larry Heinemann as well as more and more Vietnamese participants.

The dynamic personal and professional interaction of veteran writers from the two nations gave rise to a series of publishing projects at the University of Massachusetts Press. One of these projects grew out of the Joiner Center's "Captured Document Collection." It is a good example of various Joiner Center interests coming together. *Poems from Captured Documents* (1994) is a bilingual collection of transcriptions and translations made from poems found in the captured journals and notebooks of common soldiers who had been the enemy of American forces in Vietnam. Though found among papers gathered for military intelligence purposes, these poems provide intelligence of a higher order than expected: intelligence of the borderless boundaries of the human heart. Many of them are poems of love, longing, bewilderment, and homesickness: the very themes found in the journals (and compilations of letters home) written by American servicemen. Duc Thanh's "Remembering Past Love" is such a poem:

> On a cold and windy evening I went away.
> Please wait for me, Hong.
> The swallows return to this place of wind and mist
> So I remember our love these past three years.
>
> I remember the path we walked to the river
> Where we came together and talked.
> We walked that path so often
> Our feet carried the river's sand into our village.
>
> Endless and indifferent, the green river flows.
> I hope you will wait for me.
> I long for the day of my dreams
> When North and South are one. (55)

Like the stories in Robert Olen Butler's *A Good Scent from a Strange Mountain*, these poems compellingly voice the essential humanity of the Vietnamese—but in this case the "other" is also the enemy.

The voices, translator Bruce Weigl reminds us, are the work of people not primarily defined as writers. In his introduction, Weigl puts it this way: "Although not professional poets, like most Vietnamese, these soldiers wrote poetry. For anyone growing up in Vietnam, hearing, reading, singing, or writing poetry in either the written or oral tradition is as natural as breathing and practically as essential" (ix). For American readers, particularly students, this fact of Vietnamese culture carries a powerful insight.

As we have already noted, Bruce Weigl was one of those Vietnam veteran writers who had long associated himself with postwar interaction with the Vietnamese. As one of the translators, he brought his credentials as an accomplished American poet who had served during the war, had returned to learn more about the Vietnamese people, and had worked with Vietnamese writers at Joiner Center workshops. In fact, his participation in Joiner Center activities had brought him into contact with Thanh T. Nguyen, a research associate who is a native speaker of Vietnamese and an accomplished scholar. She became his coworker in the translation enterprise that, according to Weigl, "changed both of our lives significantly" (xi).

The description of their methodology conveys the process of Weigl's advanced education in Vietnamese culture. In making these translations, he worked on each jointly produced English draft "as if it were my own and I was revising" (xii). Then Ms. Nguyen would check it against the original and further revisions would follow. Finally, Weigl went to Hanoi to engage the assistance of Vietnamese translators skilled in their nation's poetry. In his own way, then, Weigl became "the other" whom he first met on the battlefield. The success of these translations comes from his respect for the individuals who wrote them, the shared experience of the war itself, and Weigl's immersion in Vietnamese culture and its poetics. He has given his former adversaries, most long since dead, an American tongue that is simultaneously his own.

FLASHBACK: BRUCE WEIGL'S *SONG OF NAPALM*

Of all the literature to have come out of the Vietnam War, only a small percentage will be read in the next century. Curiosity about the war has led to the publication of hundreds of memoirs and novels, several collections of short stories and poems, a handful of plays and miscellaneous anthologies, and a growing number of critical studies. While more are coming out every year, only a modest number of these books will transcend the fashionable interest in the war to become permanent parts of our literary culture. *Song of Napalm* is one of those few. The time will come when it will be valued as a powerful achievement in American poetry that just happens to be about the Vietnam War. The permanence of many of these poems will shape our understanding of what war is and what man is. Weigl's achievement is to have found a language that is deeply personal without being neurotically private. The vision released by that language is not only filled with horror and loathing, fear and trembling, innocence and guilt, it is also—with the gentlest and sweetest of surprising ironies—filled with love and beauty, too. These poems sting and sear, but they also insist that there is hope—that there is more to us than the ugliness let loose in war's insanity. Not many of them assert this hope directly, but the hope is implicit in the poet's care, in the loving-kindness of making and sharing.

Song of Napalm is a new orchestration of poems that appeared in Weigl's earlier books, with several new pieces (like "Dialectical Materialism") collected for the first time. In *A Romance* (1979) and *The Monkey Wars* (1985), Weigl's Vietnam poems alternated with poems of domestic life. Though the Vietnam experience focused those collections, it was subordinated to a larger vision of contemporary American experience. The questions of what we do with our love and our cruelty, of how we become responsibly engaged with others in a world whose beauty is agonizingly real and constantly threatened, of who we are as agents and victims of a nation's destiny, linked the persona's wartime and peacetime sensibility.

In bringing the Vietnam poems together in one book, Weigl has stripped them of a special power and relevance that grew out of their former contexts. Yet there are obvious gains, too. The cumulative impact of his protagonist's Vietnam story and memory is available only here, and that impact is almost overwhelming. Weigl's art survives this narrowing of scope, even thrives on it, as the intensity of vision builds from section to section, poem to poem.

Weigl's poems remind us of simple truths: that the Vietnamese people, like all people, like ourselves, are miracles of creation. So is their land. Whether enemy or compromised friend, each shares in the beauty of humankind that moves us to love and, strangely, to the utmost violence. In "The Girl at the Chu Lai Laundry," the war is almost put on hold for the laundry girl's insistence that the soldier cannot have his clothes because they aren't dry yet. Though his platoon is moving out, the girl's practical pride in the perfection of her task contends with the immense momentum of the war. Weigl tells us that she is "beautiful with her facts"—and she is, as she twists "the black rope of her hair in the sun." What does a war have to do with this innocence and charm? A few pages further on, in "Surrounding Blues on the Way Down," an older soldier who "did not hate the war" brakes his jeep and backs up to "a mama san / bent over from her stuffed sack of flowers." Before the eyes of the eighteen year old narrator who "was barely in country," he slams the woman to her knees, "the plastic butt of his M16 / crashing down on her." For this soldier, the war has fed an appetite and in the process increased it. For the speaker, the moment has become a turning point, at least in memory: up until then he "did not hate the beautiful war."

"The Last Lie" tells a similar story, this time of a soldier hurling C-ration cans at the heads of children begging for food: the final betrayal of the newsreel image of benevolence. But this is not a narrow political sequence, another instance of American misconduct. It is the age-old tale of how humans can find themselves turned inside out. Where did this man's rage come from?

The design of *Song of Napalm* suggests answers. One such suggestion is in "Snowy Egret," a poem about a boy who shoots at the beautiful bird only to "flush it from the shadows . . . to watch it fly." Or so he tells the speaker, whose wife has wakened him upon hearing the shot. The boy is truly sorry; he is trying to bury the blood-spattered egret because if his father finds out he "will kill him." But the speaker, a neighbor, knows that there is a lie in the boy's protestations and that there is something in all of our lives that, like the boy's father's history of excessive punishments, leads us to violence. This is the something "that can make a good boy steal away, / wiping out from the blue face of the pond / what he hadn't even known he loved, / blasting such beauty into nothing." How far is it from a young boy taking aim and shooting a beautiful egret to a young man finding a mysterious, secret pleasure in killing other human beings—especially if they look just like those labeled "enemy"?

Alongside of Weigl's awareness of the violence hidden in everyone is another, more romantic perception. In desperate moments, even anonymous, transient sexual giving is part of a larger coming together—a sheltering recognition of mutual suffering. "The Way of Tet" provides a memory of a young American soldier making love to a Vietnamese bar girl. Some hints are given that they have met before, that some kind of relationship has begun. Still, there is nothing to define it or grant it a future. There is nothing between them: not language, certainly not culture or sense of purpose. Amidst the deaths of Tet, at his touch, in the reflected glow of illumination rounds on her skin, "the automatic shape of love unfolds."

Less obviously, this same motif runs through a companion poem, "Song for the Lost Private." Even though the speaker is drunk (we imagine either that his buddy has just been killed in action or that the speaker's own innocence has been lost) and has haggled with the bar girl over money; even though he cannot perform and is embarrassed by the girl trying to give the money back; even though he tries again and is paralyzed by his reflection in the mirror; even though this is a poem of exploitation and smallness, it resolves in a gentle moment of grace: "I couldn't sleep so I touched her / small shoulders, traced the curve on her spine, / traced the scars, the miles / we were from home." In poems like these, the war's agony brings people together in selfish intimacies that, because they are so desperately needed, transcend the decadence of the situation. Between the poems of violence and the poems of gentleness runs Weigl's dialectic of feeling, the story of the narrow distance between love and violence and the duality in our nature.

Weigl insists that the violence does not begin out there in the war, but in the warrior. He also insists, as in "The Soldier's Brief Epistle," that the warrior is in all of us. The particular things this poet has to tell us about the Vietnam War are, finally, less important than what he has to tell us about ourselves. "You think you're far away from me / but you're right here in my pants" he tells the snug statesiders who don't wear the killer taint of war. With terrifying understatement, the speaker answers the omnipresent what's-it-like question: "It's like / a bad habit, pulling the trigger, / like a dream come true." (Remember the boy in "Snowy Egret" and the boy's father.) The utter triteness of the response levels all the wished-for distinctions, withers our safe righteousness.

Weigl's poems explore human conduct in the war environment as if it were a laboratory for the soul. He conjures dreams that blend fragile beauty with pain— perhaps the dreams of painkilling drugs or self-protecting denial. Poems like "Sailing to Bien Hoa" and "Amnesia" involve images of flight in which both the wish to escape and the reasons for the wish are delicately suggested. In a related poem, "Him, On the Bicycle," the speaker imagines himself transported from the circling helicopter to the man below fleeing on his bicycle. The soldier first rides behind the cyclist, then jumps off and pushes. The man "lifts his feet, / we don't waste a stroke. / His hat flies off, / I catch it behind my back, / put it on, I want to live forever!" In "LZ Nowhere," the soldier strokes the blades and moves the rudder and flaps of the liftship "so it felt like legs parting / or someone's arms opening to me." The dream of sexual embrace is every lonely, scared soldier's dream; and, as we have seen, the mind's transformation of prostitutes into lovers is a necessity.

The "Vietnam experience" as Weigl has recorded it in these poems is not one color, one tone, one emotion. While many poems interact to deepen themes such as loneliness, guilt, and lost innocence, others sound single notes. One of the most finely crafted poems is "Temple Near Quang Tri, Not on the Map." A brief narrative with lyric intensity, it tells of a squad's twilight entry to search this sacred space. Its cleanliness, beauty, and atmosphere of peace are all focused on the small Vietnamese man sitting bent over against a wall and speaking something barely audible. The CO fires into the wall to check for enemy rice stores. Finding nothing, he signals the squad to leave. One soldier approaches and begins to straighten the man up only to find that he is wired to an explosive device: he cannot move further without setting it off.

We aren't told exactly what happens next—or when. With consummate skill, Weigl redirects our vision: "The sparrows / burst off the walls into the jungle." Louder than any explosion is this eerie mixture of anticipation and imagined climax. The decorum of the poem is so exquisite; the truth of dismembered bodies a horror of greater, unspeakable magnitude. The sudden awareness of death's proximity hits with heart-stopping power.

The overwhelming, all-encompassing, sickening foulness of the war is expressed in "Burning Shit at An Khe," a story of a familiar duty from which the speaker tries to flee. But the latrine pit is a metaphor for the larger condition from which flight is impossible. Recognizing this, the speaker lays down in it and finger-paints "the words of who I am / across my chest / until I'm covered and there's only one smell, / one word." "Monkey" describes the addictiveness of war that affects both the veteran's habits and the habits of those who try to relate to him. The frantic rounds of repeated behavior, the intensity of those experiences, remakes the individual by etching new habits into his nervous system in a relatively short period of time. The monkey in the poem is at once the enemy without, the enemy within, and the drug slang "monkey on one's back." Weigl acknowledges the epidemic of drug use by servicemen in Vietnam, making it into a metaphor of personal and national blood lust. The monkey in each of us is the near-human animal—the thing that "apes" our human gestures but is driven only by appetite and survival instinct. It also represents our racist attitude toward the enemy, seen as little more than monkey by those conditioned to take lives.

There is anguish and pity in these poems, and there is love. There is courage. But there is not glory. Hope stands in its place. *Song of Napalm* is a book of redemption, or at least of possible redemption. Of all the soldier-poets who have treated the Vietnam War, Bruce Weigl is the one most polished in his craft and perhaps the one with the most comprehensive vision of what war tells us about ourselves. The Vietnam War is Weigl's vehicle. Through it, he reminds us not only of how far we can fall from our better selves, but also that our better selves are real and that we can become worthy in spite of our past deeds.

While we may have no confidence that Weigl's acts of healing, whether in his original poetry or in his translations of the work of Vietnamese soldier-poets, can make the kind of difference that lessens the likelihood of war, we must behave as if they can. After all, any reader can become one with the unknown author of the following lines from a poem called "Tenth Night of the Moon":

Although mountains and rivers separate us,
Our love blossoms inside me.

But in the cold winter rain
Our burning hearts die.
Was it a dream,
Or did I lose my way in an angel's garden
And see your lips open into a smile? (39)

Once we are one with "the other," how can we deny his humanity? His life?

Poems from Captured Documents is one of many titles from the University of Massachusetts Press that brought Joiner Center initiatives into print. Other translation projects include Nguyen Quang Thieu's *The Women Carry River Water* (1997), a collection of poems translated by the author and Martha Collins, and Le Luu's novel, *A Time Far Past* (1997), translated by Ngo Vinh Hai, Nguyen Vinh Hai, Kevin Bowen, and David Hunt. The work of bringing important Vietnamese writers to English language (and particularly American) audiences became a significant and distinctive portion of the press's activities. In 1998, the press brought out *Mountain River: Vietnamese Poetry from the Wars, 1948–1993*, edited by Bowen, Weigl, and Nguyn Ba Chung. This anthology offers a rich body of material to set against copious anthologizing of American veteran poets of our Vietnam War while at the same time showing Vietnamese war poetry in a somewhat broader historical context. As with other bilingual efforts, the publication of this text required the cooperation of the Vietnamese Writers' Association.

More directly an outgrowth of the Joiner Center mission is the 1997 *Writing between the Lines: An Anthology on War and Its Social Consequences.* Edited by Bowen and Weigl, this effort interweaves war-related works from Vietnam, the United States, and Central America. The collection counters the easy ethnocentricity of a purely American perspective on the late twentieth-century wars in which we have been involved. It includes poems, stories, and memoirs. Significantly, it includes a small subsection titled "Going Back" that recognizes this late and important phase of the enormous body of literature growing out of the Vietnam War. This section includes work by Bowen, Weigl, Komunyakaa, Grace Paley, and Lady Borton, as well as the chapter from Lynda Van Devanter's memoir addressed at the beginning of this chapter. In a single volume, works from various cultures, cultures once in deadly conflict, speak to one another.

The publishing commitment to this healing enterprise has not been left solely to the efforts of the University of Massachusetts Press. Another important venture from New England, Curbstone Press, has added to its list several similar titles, extending the possibility of educating the public through socially conscious literary art. During the summer of 1993, Wayne Karlin was one of the guest writers at the Joiner Center. He formed deep friendships with the Vietnamese writers he met there. They all came to realize, as Karlin puts it, "how terrible it would have been if we'd succeeded in killing each other" (xi). Anticipating the upcoming twentieth anniversary of the war's end, and recalling that it was already the twentieth anniversary of a trailblazing Vietnam War anthology of fiction—*Free Fire Zone* (1973)—which he had co-edited, Karlin proposed a new fiction anthology including writers from both the United States and Vietnam. Le Minh Khue, whom

Karlin became close to that summer, agreed to collaborate in the venture, and the Vietnam Writers' Association approved her participation. Later that summer, Karlin met Truong Hong Son (Truong Vu), a writer and literary scholar who had immigrated to the United States. He became the third member of the editorial team that produced *The Other Side of Heaven: Post-War Fiction by Vietnamese and American Writers* (1995).

In the process of preparing this anthology, Karlin made his first trip to Vietnam since the war. He writes of that brief December 1994 trip: "During my stay I was able to see the country the way I had come to see my friends from Vietnam: it shifted out of the morass of association, memory and imagination and became real to me, a country and a people rather than a war" (xiv). In organizing the anthology, Karlin has found thematic groupings, like chapters of a novel, that allow Vietnamese and American perspectives to interact. A chapter of Karlin's own novel, the 1998 *Prisoners*, refashions this 1994 trip into the experience of his protagonist. The process of return now has a life in fiction as well as in poetry and memoir.[1]

A fuller remembrance of Karlin's important 1993 meeting with Le Minh Khue is found in his memoir, *Rumors and Stones: A Journey* (1996). The chapter, "As If from Leaves, As If from Sky," is one in which these strangers reveal their wartime pasts. At fifteen, Khue had joined the North Vietnamese Army, along with many of her school friends. She worked in a sapper group, defusing or exploding American bombs while living under constant attack, often from helicopters. Karlin had been in a helicopter crew that had flown over the Khe Sanh area, and his year "intersected with one of the years she'd been there and so more than likely we'd been very near each other at times during the war" (69). After a moment of silence, Khue rests a hand on Karlin's arm, "a gesture of comfort and connection," opening a floodgate of piercing memory (70).

Karlin has also made a poem of this meeting:

MEETING

For Le Minh Khue
At fifteen
she'd run away to
join the army
to fight you, she said
she'd never been this close
to an American before
I was nineteen, I said

Once, she said
she'd spied on the G.I.'s
bathing at Khe Sanh
but they were too far away
she couldn't see anything
You were ghosts to us, I said

The helicopters scared her
the most, she said
They came down
I know, I said

and thought of
her crouching under
jungle canopy
the downward arc
the red flashes of my tracers
the strangeness of connection

Twenty and more years before
I'd searched for her
on the ground
as she'd searched for me
in the air
our eyes aching with fear
and the need to see

but I didn't see her
beneath the green canopy
the smoke twisting
like ghosts
against dark mountains

and she didn't see me
in the stir of treetops
the light shivering
like panic
through the branches

until now
as simply as forgetting
a dream
we looked
and our faces emerged
as if from leaves
as if from sky
(*Poet Lore* 89.1, Spring 1994)

Wayne Karlin's work with Curbstone Press includes the editorship of a translation series of books by prominent Vietnamese writers. The first of these volumes is by his friend Le Minh Khue, who is chief fiction editor at the Vietnam
Writers' Publishing House in Hanoi. Her *The Stars, the Earth, the River* (1997) is
a collection of short stories focused primarily on the internal struggles of postwar
Vietnam. *Behind the Red Mist* (1998), the short fiction of Ho Anh Thai, brings
another important writer of postwar Vietnam to an American audience. More such

volumes are in progress. Karlin has also co-edited a volume of contemporary American short stories that is the first collection of American literary fiction published in Vietnam since before the war.

One of the most striking stories of return is that told at the end of John Balaban's memoir, *Remembering Heaven's Face*. In it, Balaban records his 1989 return in an attempt to find the children he helped give medical care during his time as a conscientious objector working for the Committee of Responsibility to Save War-Burned and War-Injured Children. Successful in part, Balaban's emotion-charged reunions cannot be separated from the larger story.

FLASHBACK: JOHN BALABAN'S *REMEMBERING HEAVEN'S FACE*

This memoir of John Balaban's years in war-ravaged Vietnam is one of that war's few legacies of beauty. If anyone doubts that tragedy can be turned to hope, that suffering can be turned to hope, let that person read *Remembering Heaven's Face*. Like Weigl's *Song of Napalm*, it is, on many levels, a love story.

Because Balaban performed alternative service in Vietnam as a conscientious objector, his experiences and perspectives on the war are quite different from the more familiar ones of the combat veteran or the journalist. Because he was drawn to learn about the people—their customs and language—he provides insights that transcend the tourist variety. Because his mission was largely personal, his account owes nothing to institutional purposes. Because he is a gifted and painstaking wordsmith, his memoir ranks among the finest pieces of writing to come out of the war. In fact, it ranks right up there with his own earlier efforts. These include three volumes of poetry in which Balaban's reflections on the war are found among poems on a wide range of topics: *After Our War*, 1974; *Blue Mountain*, 1982; and *Words for My Daughter*, 1991. His *Coming Down Again* (1985), a novel set in Southeast Asia at the war's end, parallels, in its spellbinding descriptive power, many of the evocations of place and the narrative assurance of *Remembering Heaven's Face*. Balaban's text for a collection of photographs of Vietnam (Geoffrey Clifford's *Vietnam: The Land We Never Knew*, 1989) marks again his acceptance of the truth uttered late in the memoir: "As the years have passed since the end of the war, much of my life has been threaded through the needle of Vietnam." Mostly, however, the power of Balaban's story, a story told at a distance of twenty years, is the power of his compassion, the power of his generous heart.

Some of the themes found in *Remembering Heaven's Face* are already well known. Balaban introduces us to self-serving bureaucracies (both American and Vietnamese) that reduce human issues to statistics and arcane ceremonies of paperwork. Such matters are depressing enough in the context of requisitioning military supplies or assessing the progress of the war (body counts)—the usual stuff of Vietnam narratives. However, when one is trying to save the lives of innocent children, as Balaban was, the absurdities of abstraction and procedure become tragic.

Balaban performed his compensatory service for two private organizations whose activities were sanctioned (though not always supported) by the U.S. government. During his first tour, for International Voluntary Services (IVS), he taught linguistics at a Vietnamese university in Can Tho. His housing arrangements, travels, and work brought him into contact with various U.S. officials and, more important, with the Vietnamese. Always ready to go beyond the narrow range of prescribed duties, Balaban let his curiosity and his desire to help pull him further and further into the lives of ordinary people. He quickly discovered that there was no shortage of pain to be relieved. Sadly, he also discovered that his work for IVS could be counterproductive. To the extent that such organizations served American propaganda purposes, they indirectly supported the U.S. war effort. Balaban, along with other IVS personnel, protested.

Less susceptible to such manipulation were the endeavors of the newly-formed Committee of Responsibility to Save War-Burned and War-Injured Children, a group that Balaban joined next in order to complete his Selective Service obligation in a less compromised situation.

His work for COR is the heart of the book. Balaban's remembrance of intimate connection with the maimed and burned innocents of the war is recorded with such moving intensity that no reader is likely to forget it. As we make the rounds of the first group of children designated for transport to U.S. hospitals, we enter a world on the fringe of combat, exploding with all the emotions that war accelerates. We meet not only the horribly damaged children, but also their confused, suffering families. We meet Balaban's COR associates, the personnel of various Vietnamese hospitals, and the hierarchy of approval-givers (or refusers). We encounter, as Balaban did, the extremes of self-interest and generosity as the children temporarily become hostages to the politics of war.[1]

Balaban's "moral witness" is nowhere more striking than in his account of these children, though it is equaled perhaps by that of his search, twenty years later, into what had become of them. Among the victims is "Dao Thi Thai, a fifteen-year-old girl, scalped by boat propeller blades after tumbling into the water during a mortar attack. The incident left her with an exposed skull cap as well as a fractured humerus in her left arm." Most of the children, of course, were injured directly by either enemy or "friendly" fire.

Working against deadlines, Balaban and his associates processed dozens of forms requiring permissions from reluctant officials in order to place the children on Air Force hospital planes carrying American wounded out of Vietnam. The children could fly only on a "space-available basis"; no special flights were authorized. Balaban concluded that although the American and South Vietnamese officials felt obligated to allow COR to work in Vietnam, they "had no serious interest in letting us take these rather bad advertisements for the war out of the country." Nevertheless, the rescue efforts were largely successful.

One of the book's powerful ironies has to do with the return of these children after their treatment and recuperation in the United States. Money had to be found for commercial flights, since the U.S. government provided no funds for their return. Moreover, in mid-1969, bringing war-injured children to Vietnam was not a duty to fill one with optimism. Many had become fond of their American foster parents and of American comforts. Now they were plunged back into a world of deprivation and fear. Balaban was fully cognizant of these issues, but the children's medical situations were desperate; saving their lives came first.

Remembering Heaven's Face is more than the story of Balaban and these children. Along the way, Balaban tells the stories of others: exemplary figures like Dave Gitelson, the dedicated wanderer who brought agricultural expertise to Vietnamese farmers—but, more important, befriended them. He tells of talented but restless souls like Steve Erhart, a young writer whose motives for attachment to Southeast Asia were complex. He introduces other medical volunteers, such as John Clarke, a young surgeon on the British Pediatrics Team with whom Balaban caroused in Saigon. He also makes real the individual Vietnamese; Balaban brings them out from behind the cardboard stereotypes of American popular culture and allows the reader to know them as few other American writers have done. The vividly realized Vietnamese include Dr. Khoa, one of Balaban's few allies at the Can Tho hospital; Miss Khuy, who assisted COR personnel with the children; and the friendly Buu family, with whom Balaban resided.

Through his experiences, with varying degrees of conscious concern for the process, Balaban was becoming a student of Vietnamese history and culture. The eyes he writes through so many years later (but from notebooks kept at the time) are informed by much more than a brand-name American past and a secure western vision. Balaban's education, sometimes spontaneous and sometimes an act of labor, is artfully and lovingly shared. Throughout the book, his paragraphs are leavened by Vietnamese aphorisms and his own meditations upon them; these gradually adjust the reader's scales of judgment.

Balaban's descriptions of place—whether urban or rural, tranquil or action-filled—are indelible. Few have seen so well or been so receptive to Vietnam's range of sensations. The Mekong Delta, the Phoenix Island sanctuary of the "Coconut Monk," and the streets of Saigon are brilliantly etched. Not just the sights, but also the tastes, smells and sounds are vividly rendered. In these descriptions, Balaban reveals his love of Vietnam and of the appealingly different sense of self in the world that he found there. It is easy to understand why he returned so soon after his voluntary service commitments were over, as a young, married scholar, to capture the folk poetry of the land and bring it home with him—an offering for understanding, respect, and peace.

As Balaban tells of his preparations to return, the reader enters a second love story—the one between the author and the woman he marries. The humanist and translator, accompanied by his young wife, reentered the world of pain to recover the essence of the ever-enduring Vietnamese. The major fruit of that endeavor, *Cao Dao Vietnam: A Bilingual Anthology of Vietnamese Folk Poetry* (1980), is one of Balaban's many acts of obedience to his fate, a fate that brought him first as a witness and transformed him into a healer.

John Balaban is able to bring to American readers a simple truth that is so often obscured by the writings of other Americans who participated in or witnessed the Vietnam War: Vietnam, though a place of frequent conflict, has an existence far apart from its ten-year role as an American battlefield. Even while the enormous enterprise dominated the visible texture of life there, there was something always larger, steadier, and more profound that Balaban was prepared and allowed to glimpse. While others knew and spoke of this truth intellectually, sometimes from the disengaged perspective of a brainy relativism, Balaban came to know it in his poet's soul.

John Balaban is one of a number of writers whose experience in Vietnam was transforming and who was compelled, in part because of that experience, to become engaged in the writing life. More than most, Balaban's background in literature prepared him to tap traditions and bend them to his needs. He is one of the most literary of the generation of Vietnam War witnesses, his work outside the mainstream of "grunt" writing that has gained favor with those who find the untutored and often unpolished energies of lesser writers somehow more authentic.

As Balaban continues what Philip D. Beidler calls "the enterprise of post-Vietnam poetic-cultural mythmaking" (in *Re-Writing America: Vietnam Authors in Their Generation*, 1991), his mastery of the common literary inheritance provides a richness of esthetic texture and shape that allows his unique vision canonical stature. This is a vision broadened not only by facing the dangers of a horrible war (Balaban was under fire more often than many a uniformed conscript or volunteer), but also by his sympathetic understanding of that other culture in which Americans found and often misperceived their allies and enemies. Balaban has remade himself into a citizen of a larger world of potentially harmonious values and purposes, and in so doing he points to a new vision of America's future.

Remembering Heaven's Face, then, is a poet's story. Though Balaban makes only passing reference to the poems he was writing during the years remembered here, everything else about the book reflects the poet's growth in sensibility and selfhood. Balaban's memoir has the elegance of Philip Caputo's *A Rumor of War* (1977), the rage of Ron Kovic's *Born on the Fourth of July* (1976), the artfulness of Michael Herr's *Dispatches* (1977), and the healing power of Linda Van Devanter's *Home Before Morning* (1983). It has also, however, a rare wisdom and beauty—or perhaps the beauty is the wisdom.

It was the happiest of accidents, if an accident at all, that *Remembering Heaven's Face* found its way into print during the same year that the movement toward official U.S. diplomatic relations with Vietnam hit full stride. Balaban's own return to Vietnam late in 1989 convinced him that the Vietnamese were forgetting the war and that the land itself had almost forgotten it. Balaban considers the U.S. policy of trade and diplomatic embargoes "self-punishing and miserly in American spirit." It is time, says everything in this book, to help and to heal.

Balaban's stature as a poet has grown with each new volume. His *Locusts at the Edge of Summer: New and Selected Poems* (1997) received uniform acclaim and was a finalist for the National Book Award. In poems like the previously uncollected "Collateral Damage," he continues to be a moral witness to America's Vietnam enterprise. And, like so many of his contemporaries who have seen the horrors of this war, learned to love the people, and returned, Balaban has made his special offerings to a reconciled, friendly future. Along with Nguyen

Qui Duc, he has edited *Vietnam: A Traveler's Literary Companion* (1996), one more important effort to bring Vietnam voices to American readers.[2] In this case, the works were selected to present Vietnam today—its landscapes, neighborhoods, and culture. Significantly, it is a book without war stories.

Closing her fascinating chapter on W. D. Ehrhart (in *Worlds of Hurt*), Kali Tal writes of those few who "take as their responsibility the impossible task of bearing witness both to what we are, and to what we could be" (114). Like Ehrhart, many of these others—including Balaban, Bowen, Karlin, Van Devanter, and Weigl—have found it necessary to go back in order to go forward.

NOTES

1. The most probing treatment of the spiritual dynamics of return runs through several works by Robert Olen Butler, beginning with the 1975 return of Thomas Fleming in *On Distant Ground* (1985). Butler's 1997 *The Deep Green Sea* is fully focused on such a search for closure and peace. His protagonist, Ben, who had served in 1966–67, returns in 1994 only to fall in love with Tien, a child of the "new Vietnam" who is young enough to be his daughter. Indeed, her father was an American soldier who, so she believes, was killed before she was born, and Ben had had an affair with a bar girl much like his young lover's mother. In Ben's narrative, he muses "I was in Vietnam because of a desire just like that one you can have about sex, the desire for things to be whole. And I know now how that desire got stuck over here, how it failed to make it onto the plane back home in 1967" (54).

2. Other related projects include Balaban's cofounding of the Vietnamese Nôm Preservation Foundation, dedicated to rescuing one thousand years of Vietnamese literature recorded in a virtually forgotten ideographic script. His *Spring Essence: The Poetry of Ho Xuan Huong* (scheduled for publication in 2000), a translation of the work of a major Vietnamese poet, is one step in bringing back to the Vietnamese and making available to western readers important work scripted in the nôm writing system.

Coda:
Teaching
War Literature

Coda: Part One

Teaching the Literature of the War

or *Teaching the War through Literature*

At the United States Naval Academy, when I taught two sections of a literature of the Vietnam War course during the winter-spring semester of 1991, cable lines were piping CNN coverage of "The War in the Gulf" into the classroom. For weeks, each class session was framed by urgent, repetitive news and analysis of this latest national and military enterprise that put American lives at risk. My students, young men and women who would soon be junior officers in the U.S. Navy and the Marine Corps, had their imaginations whipped from one war to another as they thought about their futures. As we turned off the television and began to examine David Halberstam's *One Very Hot Day*, were we studying war through literature?—or literature through a war novel?

Those who, as members of English or literature departments, teach Vietnam War literature confront the dilemma of whether to teach the *literature* or the *war* through the literature.

Teaching the literature involves, as always, addressing the conventions of genre and invoking standards for esthetic judgment. Formalists would like to leave it at that, but it can't be done. Once one has decided to select a body of work defined by subject matter, one can't simply ignore the "matter." Even if one chooses to emphasize *how* various issues are addressed—fear, leadership, racism, military strategy—one needs to develop some context outside of the imaginative literature itself. One is forced to "teach the war" to some extent. Nonetheless, one can provide students with tools for literary analysis and evaluation within the confines of a subject matter reading list. Indeed, the business of distinguishing the differences between the structures, styles, and conventions of various works can be handled with a special efficiency if the works themselves have common or overlapping content.

However, when teaching the war becomes the primary focus of a literature course, the criteria for selecting texts is quite different from what they are when selecting texts for their pedagogical serviceability as models for the standard con-

153

cerns of literary study. If one puts the literature in the service of an understanding of the war, the sought-after understanding drives a selection process that is likely to reveal a political agenda or at least certain political assumptions. Selection processes that attempt to be objective are likely to rest primarily on the frail criterion of authenticity as popularly understood. Many works that fail the tests of significant literary achievement demand attention as tools with which to teach the war.

What is important is to make the purposes and assumptions of the course and the reading list explicit both to the instructor and to the students.

What follows is a series of hypothetical courses with representative reading lists, most of which are given identifying names. I encourage instructors to note additional items for the lists I mention, additional bases for list-making, and comments about the dichotomous stance I begin with and the issues this stance raises for you. Initially, we might see ourselves as teaching the war through literature.

I. TEACHING THE WAR THROUGH LITERATURE

A. *Chronolist:* This follows the seven-part structure of John Clark Pratt's "Bibliographic Commentary" (found in Timothy J. Lomperis's *"Reading the Wind"*: *The Literature of the Vietnam War*). The seven parts are a prologue to 1955, five acts, and an epilogue (everything since 1975). Though this list organizes novels (by the years they cover, not when they were published), other genres could be represented. Seven key titles might be: Burdick and Lederer's *The Ugly American*, James Crumley's *One to Count Cadence*, William Pelfrey's *The Big V*, Charles Durden's *No Bugles, No Drums*, John Del Vecchio's *The 13th Valley*, Bernard and Marvin Kalb's *The Last Ambassador*, and Chris Mullin's *The Last Man Out of Saigon*. Teaching the war in a quasi-historical way probably means depending on a heavy dose of outside reading and leaning on novels in the realist tradition.

B. *Backhomelist:* Enlarging the focus to include the war's aftermath in the United States allows us to take in representative works about the returned veteran, like Philip Caputo's *Indian Country*, John Mulligan's *Shopping Cart Soldiers*, or Larry Brown's *Dirty Work*, and constructs that consider the continuing presence of the war on the country's psyche—works like Wayne Karlin's *Lost Armies*, Bobbie Ann Mason's *In Country*, and Madison Smartt Bell's *Soldier's Joy*. (To see the war in the context of other twentieth-century American involvements, Evan Hunter's *Sons* is a possibility. Other enlargements might open up the Vietnamese foreground, perhaps reaching back to André Malraux's *The Royal Way*, a novel of 1930, or Anthony Grey's contemporary work, *Saigon*, with its fifty-year sweep of Southeast Asian history. We might even explore Van Wyck Mason's *Saigon Singer* for a Euro-American view of Indochina in the 1940s. Teaching the war as an episode in the history of Vietnam demands making available writings by Vietnamese.)

C. *Subspecialties:* All kinds of "special topics" lists can support courses that have one or another thing to say or to examine. We could derive an ample list of literary works from any of the acts in Pratt's chronodrama. We might want to devote a major unit of a course to a *Noncombatlist* that would include works focused on officialdom, espionage, REMF, and even alternative service matters, placing Ward Just's *Stringer*, Nicholas Proffitt's *The Embassy House*, David Willson's *REMF Diary*, and the poems of John Balaban on the list. We have numerous literary efforts, too, about the combat medic, the nurse, and the prisoner of war. And don't forget that there are many books about reporting the war.

D. *Ethnolist:* This pays attention to works by and about minorities. It, more obviously than the other course lists, has an agenda that goes far beyond traditional esthetic considerations. A. R. Flowers's *DeMojo Blues*, George Davis's *Coming Home*, John A. Williams's *Captain Blackman*, plays by Luis Valdez and Adrienne Kennedy, and Larry Lee's *American Eagle* become part of the reading of Vietnam War literature as a reading of American culture. Thus we can place some of these works on the following list.

E. *Kulturlist:* Here, too, we want to consider the melting-pot military unit as etched in James Webb's *Fields of Fire* or William Turner Huggett's *Body Count*. These works and others, like Larry Heinemann's *Close Quarters*, help us examine the sexist, as well as the racist dynamics at work in American society. Other national diseases infect the plots and characters of Robert Stone's *Dog Soldiers*, John Balaban's *Coming Down Again*, and David Rabe's Vietnam trilogy of plays. Mailer's *Why Are We in Vietnam?* and Joan Didion's *Democracy*, novels that face away from the war while examining the society that conducts it, have a proper place here, as does Arthur Kopit's dramatic allegory, *Indians*.

F. *Perspectiveslist:* Most of the works mentioned above can't help but project attitudes toward the war, toward the military establishment, and toward national leadership. There is a fine and perhaps unimportant line between teaching the war and teaching (through the literature) about attitudes towards the war. However, to put these attitudes in sharper focus, we would have to place Robin Moore's *The Green Berets*, Ed Dodge's *Dau*, Lucian K. Truscott IV's *Army Blue*, and (once again) David Halberstam's *One Very Hot Day* on our *Perspectiveslist*. Lowell Jaeger's poems collected in *War on War* would work here, too. Mailer's *The Armies of the Night* would be mandatory.

To trace attitudes historically, we would need to organize titles by the time period in which they were written. Rearranging many of the titles already mentioned, we can create the "leadership" sequence (this would go over very well with my students and even support some of their other coursework), the "women" sequence, the "enemy" sequence, the "war-at-home" sequence, and the "crazedvet" sequence. There is no end to this.

From using the literature to survey attitudes, it is not a big jump to asking how literature conveys these attitudes; that is, how does it work? Unwittingly, we have stumbled into the English teacher's traditional domain. We see ourselves as teaching the literature of the war.

II. TEACHING THE LITERATURE OF THE WAR

A. *Genrelist:* Develop a spectrum of literary "kinds." Since all the major genres are well represented, there is no shortage of material for a survey that asks how and how well the various literary types serve to express the experience of the Vietnam War. In such a course, we can follow and test the arguments advanced by such critics as Don Ringnalda and Lorrie Smith regarding the limitations of the "master narrative" and the expressive dynamics of drama and poetry. We can also take up the issue of difference—or lack thereof—between fiction and nonfiction narratives of the war. W. D. Ehrhart's *Vietnam-Perkasie*—a novelistic memoir—would be a key title for this discussion. The arguments here go back at least to Paul Fussell's examination of World War I literature and would include the self-conscious discussion of that issue in Tim O'Brien's *The Things They Carried*.

   1. *Fictypeslist:* Fiction buffs may choose to build a course around types of fiction. The *Fictypeslist* might include popular forms like the adventure novel, the picaresque novel, the thriller, the detective story, the romance, the psychological novel, the lyrical novel, science fiction, realism, naturalism, and so forth. Suddenly we have reason to explore Christie Dickason's *Indochine*, Danielle Steel's *Message from Nam* (both romantic novels), Richard Currey's *Fatal Light* (lyrical), Joe Haldeman's *The Forever War* (sci-fi), Joanna C. Scott's *Charlie and the Children* (which combines lyricism and fantasy), T. Jefferson Parker's *Little Saigon* (thriller), Franklin Allen Leib's *The Fire Dream* (epic realism), and Larry Heinemann's *Close Quarters* (naturalism). We might lighten the mood in this course (or any other) with the gentle absurdism of Loyd Little's *Parthian Shot*. We might reread *The Quiet American* to emphasize its connection to the existentialist novel.

   2. *Techniqueslist:* Teaching the elements of fiction would require us to exemplify and trace the ramifications of fundamental artistic decisions regarding point of view, point of attack, methods and intervals of subdivision (creating chapters), episodic versus progressive or causal plot structures, methods of characterization, evocations of place and mood, and that tricky thing called style. There's hardly time, when these matters are under careful scrutiny, to pay attention to war. To get down to specifics, we might want to question the ways in which the three relatively self-contained parts of Hasford's *The Short-Timers* interact or examine his use of the present tense (with occasional minglings of past tense). Why does Webb grab his "Prologue" from a relatively late portion of the *Fields of Fire* chronology? How does the catastrophic scene function as the point of attack even in nonfiction narratives like Kovic's *Born on the Fourth the July* and Ehrhart's *Vietnam-Perkasie*? To what end is the alternating point of view in Wright's *Meditations in Green*? What is the impact of the ghost-narrator of Heinemann's *Paco's Story*?

   B. *Warlitgenre:* Is there such a thing? Is there an American version of it? Crane, Dos Passos, Hemingway, Mailer, and Jones should help us find out. With or without such contexts, we might observe the recurrence of initiation motifs. In fact, we could go about this whole course planning business with *Motiflists*.

C. *Highlitlist:* Here we field-test canon fodder. We advance candidates for the contemporary American literary pantheon. We invoke standards of excellence against which to judge O'Brien's *Going after Cacciato*, Jack Fuller's *Fragments* (one of the few Vietnam War novels with a plot and detailed character development), Bruce Weigl's *Song of Napalm*, and so forth. This approach might work best by setting up pairings: a fairly well established contemporary masterwork outside of the Vietnam literature category with a candidate from within.

D. *Litissuelist*: Here one builds a course to examine one or more specific literary issues:

- Limits of realism
- Discontinuity
- Fact versus truth.

Somewhere in here you put William Eastlake's *The Bamboo Bed*, John Clark Pratt's *The Laotian Fragments*, Michael Herr's *Dispatches*, and at least the combat portion of Susan Fromberg Schaeffer's *Buffalo Afternoon*. Once again, O'Brien's *The Things They Carried* would be the most likely anchor work.

E. *Transtruthlist:* How does the literature of the war formulate insights about human nature (or maybe western humanity) that transcend the particulars? This is a "humanities course" approach that steers away from "teaching the war." We can accept Tim O'Brien's position; his works are about imagination. He "just so happens" to set his narratives in Vietnam during the American war there.

Whatever approach one takes, our lists will have the good or bad fortune of overlapping more than we might like. This is because we are all driven by the *Whatsinprintlist*, which keeps offering more and more memoirs and oral histories. Still, the same lists, or very similar lists, can be the basis for very different kinds of courses.

Again, the reading list and the business in the classroom need to find their place on the continuum between a Vietnam War course that makes its points about the war through literary texts, or a literature course that establishes interest, focus, and contexts for esthetic discrimination by approaching a thematically coherent body of literature. I'm admitting, this late in the discussion, that we are likely to muddle these two distinct possibilities. It is the business of the instructor to find his or her proper place, educative role, and to make it explicit from day one. And to make it explicit again if and when the game changes.

There is a danger in the materials we teach that grows, in part, out of our passionate concern for them and in part out of our various agendas for fostering the better world that we hope our students can build. That danger is to begin with conclusions, to cut off the possibilities for genuine inquiry, to bully the students into attitudinal submission, either through the very slant of the reading list or through our approach to the literature. This danger is always present in literature classes, but it is more ominous when the literature addresses, or is used to address, our moral or political concerns. "Learning lessons" is one reason for looking backward and allowing ourselves to be moderators in the battle for the national memory that the various literary works about the war participate in. But helping our students learn how to read the works (that is, how the writings operate *as writings*)—and how to question them—may be our essential task.

It is difficult to keep the discussion of the Vietnam War open-ended, but it is a violation of the trust placed in us as educators to use the classroom as a platform for our own views or to *assess* our students by political litmus tests. (The best novel isn't necessarily the one with the liberal vision.) If we can teach them to read carefully and cautiously; if we can teach them to question, if we can help each of them find the voice to articulate their discoveries—we will have done something worthwhile.

When President Bush announced that our victory over Iraq in the Persian Gulf War (the favored euphemism) had put an end to the "Vietnam Syndrome," his unfortunate words seemed to suggest that our latest engagement was being justified as the remedy to a disease of introspection, self-doubt and wimpishness (though this is probably not quite what he meant). Watching our leader on CNN, my students—some of them, at least—were ready to join in the countrywide sigh of relief. Once I heard that bit of foolishness, I knew that we'd better fight harder than ever to establish the literature of the Vietnam War in the canon and in the classroom. Perhaps not to "teach the war," and certainly not to revive a syndrome, but to keep ourselves and our students properly humbled and shocked and alerted by the rich understandings—the wondrous constructions of language and form—concerning those human frailties, individual and national, of which we (teachers, students) are forever capable.

Representations of
War in Ethics Education

—It is never right to kill another person.
—People should never compromise their ideals or beliefs.
— "My country right or wrong" is not just a slogan—it is every citizen's patriotic duty.[1]

As target statements for instruction in ethics, propositions like these can lead to profitable discussions, discussions that will tend to be either anecdotal or abstract. A sharable, vivid presentation of ethical issues can be based on the analysis of carefully selected literature. As a student of war literature, particularly that of the Vietnam War, I am constantly surprised at what a convenient vehicle such literature is for the exploration of ethical issues. High art or men's action potboiler, the literature of war—whether poetry, fiction, or drama—is filled with heightened cases of ethical dilemmas. Students are attracted by the vividness of the stories and the ordeals of the protagonists, all of which create an interest level that can be exploited for the rich ethical content.

Within the body of war literature, leadership skills and styles are often under scrutiny, a scrutiny in which ethical action and effective action are often found to be one and the same. Preparedness, courage, and fairness are no longer abstract issues but come fleshed and uniformed in characters like James Webb's Lt. Hodges from *Fields of Fire*. Hodges, at first an uncritical heir to a noble warrior tradition, must adapt himself to unromantic and unglorious (perhaps inglorious) circumstances. He must weigh commitment to principle against commitment to the men with whom he serves. Portrayed as an effective leader, Hodges puts his men first. However, this is not an inevitable choice. Moreover, he must find ways to rally troops who are well aware of the fact that their government can neither fight the war effectively nor stop fighting the war. Faced with an ethically ambiguous duty, they have difficulty finding a basis for loyalty that goes beyond the fighting unit. They are aware, as well, of the American public's indifference.[2]

In Tim O'Brien's *Going after Cacciato*, the contrast between Lieutenant Sidney Martin, who is fragged by his men, and the older lieutenant, Corson, whom they attempt to carry to safety at great personal risk, is an explicit measuring of leaders like Corson who value life against those, like Martin, who value only rules and careers.

One of the best leadership portraits is that of Lt. Brooks in John Del Vecchio's *The 13th Valley*. Rufus Brooks is a black intellectual who is torn between his duty to his wife, his duty to his men and his country, and his deep concern for the human condition. Something of an ethical philosopher, Brooks is in part revealed by his thesis draft entitled "An Inquiry into Personal, Racial and International Conflict." Like George Orwell, Brooks is concerned with the ways in which language is used to mask otherwise unacceptable actions, cloaking it in ethically neutral or positive terms like *pacification*. Observes Brooks about America's adventure in Vietnam: "our altruism has corrupted itself until we can only be satisfied with annihilation" (562). Through the character of Brooks, Del Vecchio asks us to examine how this happened. But the novel is not an extended piece of ethical or psychological speculation; rather, it is a hard-edged series of actions in which choices and circumstances are fashioned within the realist tradition.

Within the larger body of war literature that considers leadership, a canon that goes back to Homer's epics, there is a significant portion whose focus is the development of the green lieutenant, a *bildungsroman* movement from innocence to experience, from the authority of rank to the earned authority of performance. Each step along the way, steps that include making assignments, issuing rewards and reprimands, responding to the orders of superiors, is a step taken under pressure in a context of complex and conflicting ethical demands. Does one reward intention or accomplishment? How does one protect the individual without compromising the group (and vice versa)? How many lives should be sacrificed to hazy and shifting objectives? When is it necessary to defy orders? Must one be callous in order to avoid showing favoritism? Is even-handedness the same thing as fairness? There are no easy answers to questions like these, questions that have meaning in all lives, but have heightened consequences in times of personal and collective crisis.

William Turner Huggett's *Body Count* is such a piece, as is Webb's novel mentioned above. Huggett's Lt. Hawkins arrives as a green officer intimidated by his veteran sergeant and eyed skeptically by his men through the various ordeals that prove him worthy of their respect. Dealing with race relations is a special responsibility with which Hawkins learns to cope. He also takes on the responsibility of clearly and convincingly explaining the rationale behind orders, not resting solely on his or his superiors' authority to lead his men. At each step, Hawkins's journey raises questions for class discussion. How severely can you reprimand people for improper behavior when you need to rely on their loyalty the next day? How much time can you take up with the rhetoric of logical persuasion when time is not on your side?

Of course, not all of the ethical struggles portrayed in war literature involve the development of officer-leaders. Enlisted personnel have plenty of opportunities to be tested, and the tests are of varying orders of magnitude. Several fictional treatments raise questions about whether all is fair in war. In one such work, *The Man Who Won the Medal of Honor* by Len Giovanitti, a soldier finds himself obsessed with the maniacal, war-inspired atrocities committed by his peers and leaders. His solution is to kill them before they do further damage. Though his winning the Medal of Honor is an error, the author no doubt wonders for the reader whether there is some ironic appropriateness in this distinction. By killing American soldiers, the title character has minimized additional war crimes, crimes against the enemy, crimes against civilians, as well as crimes against the powerless in American uniforms. As you can imagine, such a formulation can provide for the observation and exploration of significant ethical issues. After all, aren't many wars fought to lessen the possibility of later wars? Isn't the logic of the domino theory similar to that of Giovanitti's protagonist?

Less dramatically, Jesse T. McLeod, in *Crew Chief*, examines the ethical dimension of meeting one's basic responsibilities. He stresses the overlapping moral and practical consequences of dedication to duty for those tasked with maintaining equipment (helicopters, in this case) as well as the specter of drug use as it affects those whose lives depend upon a pilot's or technician's alertness and thoroughness. Clearly, in such situations, drug and alcohol use are not victimless indulgences. McLeod has as a secondary theme the obsessive, vengeful taskmaster who is out to break someone over a personal grudge. He explores the consequences of this personal motive on the effective functioning of a military unit.

Much literature of the Korean and Vietnam wars concerns itself with America's problems of race, a continuing ethical crisis in our nation's cultural heritage. The issue is presented on two fronts. Within the fighting unit, crippled race relations between whites and minorities compromise unit effectiveness just as they trouble American culture. Prejudice undermines cohesiveness—a merely practical concern? External to the American fighting unit, racial prejudice also hampers effectiveness. In these wars, our allies and enemies were racially identical. Prejudice against Asians both prompted the killing instinct and thwarted our sense of purpose. Who were these people to whose aid we had supposedly come? William Turner Huggett's *Body Count* is one of many novels of the Vietnam War in which the ethical disease of racial prejudice is dramatized in passing as American soldiers fight among themselves or joke crudely about the racial features of Asian women working in servicemen's clubs.

In *Bridge Fall Down*, a grotesque comic novel of unspecified locale filled with echoes of Vietnam, author Nicholas Rinaldi has his special task force refer to the different-looking enemy as monkeys, an obvious satire on the connection between dehumanizing and killing. In Wilbert L. Walker's *Stalemate at Panmunjon*, a Black 2nd lieutenant finds himself fighting not only the enemy, but also the bigotry of superior officers. Holding on to his integrity in the face of this complex of pressures is Charlie Brooks's challenge. Walker provides a unique view of the early tests and strains of racially integrated American fighting forces.

While problems of racism abound, problems of sexism receive even more attention in the literature of our recent wars. Indeed, Vietnam War literature has proven to be a rich resource for examining the psyche of the American male with regard to the very meaning of his masculinity. The constant equation of sexual aggression and killing runs through such key titles as Gustav Hasford's *The Short-Timers* and Larry Heinemann's *Close Quarters*. In the former, the very method of military indoctrination is portrayed as learning to hate (and kill) the woman in one's self. The "F" word levels female and enemy. The properly trained soldier can and should "f---" both. It is hard to imagine an ethically cleansed culture in which men are conditioned to fear and hate women.

The victimization of women, especially Asian women, is the story of the war and of our culture writ small. It is the subtheme of Heinemann's novel, in which a Vietnamese prostitute is threatened at gunpoint to perform acts she had never imagined on a large number of American soldiers. The popular literature of war exposes, sometimes unintentionally, the ethical quagmire of sexual difference and human rights.[3]

At its most sensitive, the literature of war argues for cultural awareness and respect. More often, it describes the absence of such qualities, qualities that are among the springs of ethical behavior. In the literature, the customs and traditions of enemy or odd ally are quaint, humorous, monstrous, or proof of inferiority. Asian family and village life, as well as Asian religions and folkways, are targets for abuse. Intolerance and misunderstanding, as well as the pride of ignorance, are well captured in the coarseness of speech and action through which American soldiers are rendered. Once again, the circumstance of war intensifies and magnifies these traits, but upon examination the suspicion arises that these very traits bring us to war in the first place. James Hickey's *Chrysanthemum in the Snow* orchestrates the theme of cultural arrogance by presenting the insights and wounded pride of two South Korean soldiers assigned to an American squad. William Crawford's *Gresham's War* and Thomas Anderson's *Your Own Beloved Sons* also examine the "Gook syndrome" in the Korean theater of war. With these works, it is difficult to separate racial biases from cultural ones.

Military training and military life, especially during wartime, are governed by regulations, codes, and traditions. These codes are sometimes in alignment and sometimes at odds with ethical formulations (like the Ten Commandments). There is a convenience, often an efficiency, in adhering to lists headed "always" and "never." Literary portraits of people at war question such absolutist checklists. Just as often, however, the appeal to particular circumstances and relativist judgment is shown to be impractical and dangerous—sometimes a slide into indecision. In life and death matters, the absolutist/relativist dichotomy can receive productive scrutiny through the safe distance of literary representation. In the literature, we see people bending the rules, hiding behind the rules, questioning the rules, and even putting the rules to good use. Among the areas of interest in Rob Riggan's *Free Fire Zone* is the conflict between enlisted men and "lifers" whose insistence on military formalities and appearance seems demoralizing, pointless, and finally a means of humiliation and intimidation rather than purposeful discipline. How does one decide which regulations and courtesies can be dismissed, and under what circumstances?

Much of the recent literature of war portrays behavior that is unethical by design. This is the literature that details intelligence operations, a specialty in which deceit is mandatory and suspicion is inevitable. To spy is to win and betray confidences, in the name of national interest of course. John Cassidy's *A Station in the Delta* provides a compelling look at CIA activity in Vietnam just prior to the Tet offensive. Toby Busch is a field officer with a tarnished record. Because he had embarrassed his superiors on a European assignment, his reports indicating a Tet uprising are not found credible until it is too late for effective counteraction. Thus the novel serves not only as a look at the ethical dilemmas of the intelligence community, but also brings into focus the constant tension between personal feeling and professional judgment. Busch's immediate superior, whose own career he believed was jeopardized by Busch's actions in the failed mission in Germany, sits on Busch's report out of personal pique, though the report clearly merits qualified dissemination. Moreover, Busch's romantic escapades create unneeded conflicts between mission responsibilities and personal loyalties.

A typical ethical dilemma in the intelligence sphere, one that has parallels in more strictly military operations, is that of deciding how much information to give colleagues, subordinates, and plants. Too much information risks the security of operation; too little risks lives. That is, if a subordinate knows too much, he or she can be tortured or tricked into giving away a mission. Subordinates who know too little might not be able to protect themselves or members of their unit. Toby Busch must face such a decision at the conclusion of *A Station in the Delta*.

Several war novels present characters caught between conflicting ethical systems. These include stories of captured armed forces medical doctors who must choose between ministering to those who need help and avoiding aid to the enemy. Frank Slaughter's *Sword and Scalpel* and Stephen Becker's *Dog Tags*, both novels of the Korean War, provide opportunities to explore not only ethical conflicts, but also such conflicting ethics. Does the oath of Hippocrates outweigh an oath to defend one's country against its enemies? Can "first, do no harm," have a meaningful battlefield application?

The popularity of war literature, of course, has not depended on the ethical dimensions of the situations it portrays. In fact, much of it is a vicarious call to action, a safe imaginary participation in fear, courage, bloodletting, and pain. Much older war literature glorifies war and the warrior. Recent literature tends to deglamorize war, making warriors into victims or psychos. These differences reflect changes in society that have ethical implications. A fruitful and economical way into this distinction is to have students put side by side the war poetry of Walt Whitman and Stephen Crane.[4]

Perhaps the ethical question of greatest magnitude in the literature of war is this one: Is anything worth killing for? Are abstractions like democracy worth sending armies into battle? Representations of war lead to a consideration of "isms" versus human life. Under what conditions is war an ethical choice, an ethical pursuit or means? Representations show the human cost—which when less than death is so often the disintegration of the soldier's very humanity—while they pay some attention to the cause or causes that have led to war. Conscience, country, killing—this triad, as it grips and sometimes destroys characters, can grip students as well.

In this regard, a major subset of war literature, that which examines the situation of the returned veteran, is of particular interest. The psychically and spiritually crippled protagonist of Philip Caputo's *Indian Country*, the guilt-wracked Dave Robicheaux in James Lee Burke's series of detective novels, and the voices that haunt the protagonist of Larry Heinemann's *Paco's Story* are accessible illustrations of how combat can ethically decenter its participants.

Because the consequences for the warrior are so great, ethical considerations must be at the heart of formulations of national purpose. They must also guide a nation's commitment to support those who put their lives at risk to carry it out. The literature of the Vietnam War considers the consequences to morale and mental health of perceived betrayals. When weapons don't work, when objectives are taken at great cost and then abandoned, when lies are told about the purposes and likely consequences of war, when those exposed to chemical warfare agents and psychological trauma are denied adequate care—the war effort is undermined and the debilitating trauma is aggravated. The representations that crystallize these and other issues that haunt the returned veteran include—besides several already mentioned—David Rabe's play *Sticks and Bones*, Larry Brown's *Dirty Work*, Bobbie Ann Mason's *In Country*, and Robert Bausch's *On the Way Home*. These, as well as Michael Shaara's *The Broken Land*, an undervalued novel rooted in the Korean conflict, measure the consequences of the war on its participants, their families, and their friends. The vividness and concreteness of these literary and dramatic representations assure interest, a pool of common—if vicarious—experience, and an available resource from which to select evidence.

The relationship between character and ethics, and between wartime trauma and both, is brilliantly investigated in Jonathan Shay's *Achilles in Vietnam*, a work that is a key study of the relationship between ethical issues and warfare. Shay makes it clear that the circumstances of war threaten the foundations of character. What people are asked to do and experience in war, however principled the cause, undermines character by poisoning ethical judgment. Shay illustrates this point through his trailblazing examination of the *Iliad* as well as through references to his experience as a counselor to Vietnam War veterans. He also raises questions about the ethical responsibilities of a nation's leaders and citizens toward those they send to war.

The corruption of character discussed by Shay, who shows how Achilles becomes a berserker and suffers from post-traumatic stress syndrome, was clearly understood by Robert Graves, whose poems of World War I are among the finest we have. In "Hate Not, Fear Not," he argues for what may be an impossible purity on the field of battle:

> Kill if you must, but never hate:
>   Man is but grass and hate is blight,

The sun will scorch you soon or late,
  Die wholesome then, since you must fight.

Hate is a fear, and fear is rot
  That cankers root and fruit alike,
Fight cleanly then, hate not, fear not,
  Strike with no madness when you strike.

Fever and fear distract the world,
  But calm be you though madmen shout,
Through blazing fires of battle hurled,
  Hate not, strike, fear not, stare Death out!

The ability to kill without hating is perhaps the business of the professional soldier, but for the conscript hating is the shortcut to killing and thus—along with fear—the basic mechanism of indoctrination. But what if the killing cannot be stopped? What if the soldiers become berserkers, as in this poem by Doug Anderson:

INFANTRY ASSAULT

The way he made the corpse dance
by emptying one magazine after another into it
and the way the corpse's face began to peel off
like a mask because the skull had been shattered, brains
spilled out, but he couldn't stop killing that corpse,
wanted to make damn sure, I thought maybe
he was killing all the ones he'd missed, and

the way they dragged that guy out of the stream,
cut him to pieces, the stream running red
with all the bodies in it, and the way the captain
didn't try to stop them, his silence saying *No Prisoners* and

the way when all the Cong were dead, lined up in rows,
thirty-nine in all, our boys went to work on all the pigs
and chickens in the village until
there was no place that was not red, and

finally, how the thatch was lit, the village burned
and how afterwards we were quiet riding back
on the tracks, watching the ancestral serpent rise
over the village in black coils, and
how our bones knew what we'd done.

How does this happen? Who is responsible? Ask your students this.[5]

NOTES

1. These statements are part of a sample "opinionnaire" found in Larry R. Johannessen's *Illumination Rounds: Teaching the Literature of the Vietnam War* (147). This useful text for teachers provides paper topics and lesson plans that bring a wide range of issues, including ethical issues, to the discussion table. Before and after discussing the war literature, Johannessen suggests handing out "Opinionnaire" sheets on which students are asked to agree or disagree with a series of statements and then be prepared to explain their positions.

2. Johannessen provides a very useful lesson plan for examining the changing values of three characters in Webb's *Fields of Fire*. With this model, characters and narrators in other works can be explored in terms of values. Such an exploration depends upon careful attention to the text: all assertions must be supported by quotations. He also provides structured approaches to several other key Vietnam War texts.

3. For elaboration of these issues, see chapter 2.

4. An excellent resource for teaching the poetry of the Vietnam War is the Fall 1993 issue of the *Journal of American Culture*. This special issue, "Poetry and the War," is edited by Vince Gotera and Theresa L. Brown. The essays by Brown, Stephen P. Hidalgo, and Lorrie Smith are particularly useful, as is the section on protest poetry.

5. Another fine text for teachers designing literature-based ethics units or courses is Marc Jason Gilbert's *The Vietnam War: Teaching Approaches and Resources.*

Works Cited

Aichinger, Peter. *The American Soldier in Fiction. 1880–1963*: A *History of Attitudes toward Warfare and the Military Establishment*. Ames: Iowa State UP, 1975.

Alter, Nora M. *Vietnam Protest Theatre*: *The Television War on Stage*. Bloomington: Indiana UP, 1996.

Anderson, Doug. "Infantry Assault." *The Moon Reflected Fire*. Farmington, Maine: Alice James Books, 1994.

Anderson, Kent. "Pouring on the Gore." *Washington Post Book World*, July 16, 1989, p. 9.

Anderson, Thomas. *Your Own Beloved Sons*. New York: Random House, 1956.

Anisfield, Nancy, ed. *Vietnam Anthology: American War Literature*. Bowling Green, Ohio: Popular Press, 1987.

Axelsson, Arne. *Restrained Response: American Novels of the Cold War and Korea, 1945–1962*. New York: Greenwood Press, 1990.

Balaban, John. *Words for My Daughter*. Port Townsend, Wash.: Copper Canyon Press, 1991.

_____. *Remembering Heaven's Face: A Moral Witness in Vietnam*. New York: Poseidon Press, 1991.

_____. *Locusts at the Edge of Summer: New and Selected Poems*. Port Townsend, Wash.: Copper Canyon Press, 1997.

Balaban, John, and Nguyen Qui Duc, eds. *Vietnam: A Traveler's Literary Companion*. San Francisco: Whereabouts Press, 1996.

Baritz, Loren. *Backfire*. New York: Morrow, 1984.

Bass, Thomas A. *Vietnamerica: The War Comes Home*. New York: Soho, 1996.

Bates, Milton J. *The Wars We Took to Vietnam: Cultural Conflict and Storytelling*. Berkeley: U of California Press, 1996.

Baugh, Bruce. "Authenticity Revisited." *Journal of Aesthetics and Art Criticism*, 46 (Summer 1988): 477–87.

Bausch, Robert. *On the Way Home*. New York: St. Martin's, 1982.

Becker, Elizabeth. "Meat in the Tiger's Mouth." *Los Angeles Times*, June 11, 1989, p. 1.

Becker, Stephen. *Dog Tags*. New York: Random House, 1973.

Beidler, Philip D. *American Literature and the Experience of Vietnam*. Athens: U of Georgia P, 1982.

167

_____. *Re-Writing America: Vietnam Authors in Their Generation*. Athens: U of Georgia P, 1991.

Bell, Madison Smartt. *Soldier's Joy*. New York: Ticknor and Fields, 1990.

Bibby, Michael. *Hearts and Minds: Bodies, Poetry, and Resistance in the Vietnam Era*. New Brunswick, N.J.: Rutgers UP, 1996.

Bowen, Kevin. *Playing Basketball with the Viet Cong*. Willimantic, Conn.: Curbstone Press, 1994.

Bowen, Kevin, and Bruce Weigl, eds. *Writing Between the Lines: An Anthology on War and Its Social Consequences*. Amherst: U of Massachusetts P, 1997.

Bowen, Kevin, Nguyen Ba Chung, and Bruce Weigl, eds. *Mountain River: Vietnamese Poetry from the War 1948–1993*. Amherst: U of Massachusetts P, 1998.

Brier, A. et al. "Controllable and Uncontrollable Stress in Humans: Alterations in Mood and Neuroendocrine and Psychophysiological Function," *American Journal of Psychiatry* 144.11 (1987): 1419–25.

Brittan, Arthur. *Masculinity and Power*. Oxford: Blackwell, 1989.

Brosnahan, John. Rev. of *Buffalo Afternoon*. *Booklist*. March 15, 1989, p. 1219.

Brown, Larry. *Dirty Work*. Chapel Hill, N.C.: Algonquin Books, 1989.

Burke, James Lee. *The Neon Rain*. New York: Henry Holt, 1987; Pocket Books, 1988.

_____. *Heaven's Prisoners*. New York: Henry Holt, 1988; Pocket Books, 1989.

_____. *Black Cherry Blues*. Boston: Little, Brown, 1989; Avon Books, 1990.

_____. *A Morning for Flamingos*. Boston: Little, Brown, 1990; Avon Books, 1991.

_____. *A Stained White Radiance*. New York: Avon Books, 1993.

_____. *In the Electric Mist with Confederate Dead*. New York: Hyperion, 1993; New York: Avon Books, 1994.

_____. *Dixie City Jam*. New York: Hyperion, 1994.

_____. *Burning Angel*. New York: Hyperion, 1995.

_____. *Cadillac Jukebox*. New York: Hyperion, 1996; rpt. New York: Warner Books, 1997.

_____. *Sunset Limited*. New York: Doubleday, 1998.

Butler, Deborah A. *American Woman Writers on Vietnam: Unheard Voices—Selected, Annotated Bibliography*. New York: Garland, 1989.

Butler, Robert Olen. *The Deep Green Sea*. New York: Henry Holt, 1997.

_____. *The Deuce*. New York: Simon and Schuster, 1989.

_____. *A Good Scent from a Strange Mountain*. New York: Henry Holt, 1992.

_____. *On Distant Ground*. New York: Knopf, 1985.

_____. *Sun Dogs*. New York: Horizon Press, 1982.

Camp, Norman M. et al. *Stress, Strain, and Vietnam: An Annotated Bibliography of Two Decades of Psychiatric and Social Sciences Literature Reflecting the Effect of the War on the American Soldier*. New York: Greenwood Press, 1988.

Caputo, Philip. *Indian Country*. Toronto: Bantam, 1987.

_____. *A Rumor of War*. New York: Holt, 1977

Carter, N. L. "Heart-Rate and Blood-Pressure Response in Medium-Artillery Gun Crews," *Medical Journal of Australia* 149.4 (1988): 185–89.

Cassidy, John. *A Station in the Delta*. New York: Scribners, 1979.

Cheung, King-Kok, and Stan Yogi. *Asian-American Literature: An Annotated Bibliography*. New York: MLA, 1988.

Christopher, Renny. "*Blue Dragon, White Tiger:* The Bicultural Stance of Vietnamese-American Literature." In *Reading the Literatures of Asian America*. See Lim, below.

_____. *The Viet Nam War / The American War: Images and Representations of Euro-American and Vietnamese Exile Narratives*. Amherst: U of Massachusetts P, 1995.

Clark, Gregory R. *Words of the Vietnam War*. Jefferson, N.C.: McFarland, 1990.
Connelly, Michael. *Black Echo*. Boston: Little, Brown, 1992; rpt. New York: St. Martin's, 1993.
_____. *Black Ice*. Boston: Little, Brown, 1993; rpt. New York: St. Martin's, 1994.
_____. *The Concrete Blond*. Boston: Little, Brown, 1994; rpt. New York: St. Martin's 1995.
_____. *The Last Coyote*. Boston: Little, Brown, 1995; rpt. New York: St. Martin's, 1996.
_____. *Trunk Music*. Boston: Little, Brown, 1997; rpt. New York: St. Martin's, 1998.
_____. *Angels Flight*. Boston: Little, Brown, 1998.
Coon, Gene L. *Meanwhile, Back at the Front*. New York: Crown, 1961; rpt. New York: Bantam, 1962.
Cooper, Helen M., Adrienne Auslander Munich, and Susan Merrill Squier, eds. *Arms and the Woman: War, Gender, and Representation*. Chapel Hill: U of North Carolina P, 1989.
Crawford, William. *Give Me Tomorrow*. New York: Putnam, 1962; rpt. New York: Bantam, 1966.
_____. *Gresham's War*. Greenwich, Conn.: Fawcett, 1968.
Crumley, James. *Bordersnakes*. New York: Mysterious Press, 1996.
_____. *The Last Good Kiss*. New York: Random House, 1978.
_____. *The Mexican Tree Duck*. New York: Mysterious Press, 1993.
_____. *One to Count Cadence*. New York: Random House, 1969.
Currey, Richard. *Fatal Light*. New York: Dutton, 1988.
Davis, George. *Coming Home*. New York: Random House, 1971.
Del Vecchio, John M. *The 13th Valley*. New York: Bantam Books, 1982.
Dickason, Christie. *Indochine*. New York: Villard Books, 1987.
Didion, Joan. *Democracy*. New York: Simon and Schuster, 1984.
Dodge, Ed. *Dau*. New York: Macmillan, 1984.
Durden, Charles. *No Bugles, No Drums*. New York: Avon, 1984.
_____. *The Fifth Law of Hawkins*. New York: St. Martin's Press, 1990.
Eastlake, William. *The Bamboo Bed*. New York: Simon and Schuster, 1970.
Ehrhart, W. D. *Going Back: An Ex-Marine Returns to Vietnam*. Jefferson, N.C.: McFarland, 1987.
_____. *Just for Laughs*. Silver Spring, Md.: Vietnam Generation, Inc. and Burning Cities Press, 1990.
_____. *Vietnam-Perkasie*. 1983. New York: Zebra, 1987.
Ehrhart, W. D., ed. *Carrying the Darkness: American Indochina—The Poetry of the Vietnam War*. New York: Avon, 1985.
Ehrhart, W. D., and Philip K. Jason, eds. *Retrieving Bones: Stories and Poems of the Korean War*. New Brunswick, N.J.: Rutgers UP, 1999.
Flowers, A. R. *Demojo Blues*. New York: Dutton, 1985.
Flynn, Joseph. *Digger*. New York: Bantam, 1997.
Frank, Pat. *Hold Back the Night*. Philadelphia: J. B. Lippincott, 1952; rpt. New York: Bantam, 1953.
Franklin, H. Bruce. "The Vietnam War as American Science Fiction and Fantasy." *Science Fiction Studies* 17 (1990): 341–59.
Franklin, H. Bruce, ed. *The Vietnam War in American Stories, Songs, and Poems*. Boston: Bedford Books, 1996.
Freeman, James M. *Hearts of Sorrow: Vietnamese-American Lives*. Stanford: Stanford UP, 1989.

French, Albert. *Patches of Fire: A Story of War and Redemption*. New York: Doubleday, 1997.

Fuller, Jack. *Fragments*. New York: Morrow, 1984.

Fussell, Paul. *The Great War and Modern Memory*. New York: Oxford UP, 1975.

Gatlin, Jesse C., Jr. *The U.S. Air Force in Fiction: The First Twenty-Five Years*. Research Report 73-3. [Colorado Springs]: Col.: U.S. Air Force Academy, 1973.

Gerzon, Mark. *A Choice of Heroes: The Changing Faces of American Manhood*. Boston: Houghton, 1982.

Gibson, James William. *Warrior Dreams: Violence and Manhood in Post-Vietnam America*. New York: Hill and Wang, 1994.

Gilbert, Marc Jason. *The Vietnam War: Teaching Approaches and Resources*. New York: Greenwood Press, 1991.

Gilman, Owen W., Jr. *Vietnam and the Southern Imagination*. Jackson: UP of Mississippi, 1992.

Gilman, Owen W., Jr., and Lorrie Smith, eds. *America Rediscovered: Critical Essays on Literature and Film of the Vietnam War*. New York: Garland, 1990.

Giovanitti, Len. *The Man Who Won the Medal of Honor*. New York: Random House, 1973.

Gold, Jerome. *Sergeant Dickinson*. New York: Soho Press, 1999.

Gotera, Vince. *Radical Visions: Poetry by Vietnam Veterans*. Athens: U of Georgia P, 1994.

Graves, Robert. "Hate Not, Fear Not." In *Poems About War*. Mount Kisco, N.Y.: Moyer Bell, 1990.

Greene, Graham. *The Quiet American*. New York: Viking, 1956.

Grey, Anthony. *Saigon*. Boston: Little, Brown, 1982.

Groom, Winston. *Better Times Than These*. New York: Summit, 1978.

_____. *Forrest Gump*. Garden City, N.Y.: Doubleday, 1986.

_____. *Gone the Sun*. New York: Doubleday, 1988.

Halberstam, David. *One Very Hot Day*. Boston: Houghton Mifflin, 1967; rpt. New York: Warner Books, 1984.

_____ *The Fifties*. New York: Villard Books, 1993.

Haldeman, Joe. *1968*. New York: Morrow, 1995.

_____. "Counterpoints." In *Infinite Dreams*. New York: St. Martin's, 1978; rpt. New York: Avon, 1979. First published in *Orbit* 11, 1972.

_____. "DX." *In the Field of Fire*. Edited by Jeanne Van Buren Dann and Jack Dann. New York: TOR, 1987.

_____. *The Forever War*. New York: St. Martin's, 1974; rpt. Ballantine/Del Rey, 1976.

_____. *The Hemingway Hoax*. New York: Morrow, 1990; rpt. Avon, 1991.

_____. *Tools of the Trade*. New York: Morrow, 1987; rpt. Avon, 1988.

_____. *War Year*. New York: Holt, Rinehart and Winston, 1972; Pocket, 1977; Avon, 1984.

_____. "You Can Never Go Back." *Dealing in Futures*. New York: Viking/Penguin, 1985; rpt. ROC, 1993. originally published in *Amazing* (Nov.1975).

Hall, H. Palmer. "The Helicopter and the Punji Stick: Central Symbols of the Vietnam War." *America Rediscovered: Critical Essays on Literature and Film of the Vietnam War*. Ed. Owen W. Gilman, Jr., and Lorrie Smith. New York: Garland, 1990.

Hanley, Lynne. *Writing War: Fiction. Gender & Memory*. Amherst: U of Massachusetts P, 1991.

Hasford, Gustav. *The Short-Timers*. New York: Harper and Row, 1979.

_____. *The Phantom Blooper*. New York: Bantam, 1990.

_____. *A Gypsy Good Time*. New York: Washington Square Books, 1992.

Hayslip, Le Ly, with Jay Wurts. *When Heaven and Earth Changed Places*. New York: Penguin, 1989.

Heinemann, Larry. *Close Quarters*. New York: Farrar, Straus, Giroux, 1977.

———. *Paco's Story*. New York: Farrar, Straus, Giroux, 1986.

Hellmann, John. *American Myth and the Legacy of Vietnam*. New York: Columbia UP, 1986.

Hemingway, Ernest. *The Sun Also Rises*. New York: Scribner's, 1926.

Hendricks, G. C. *The Second War*. New York: Viking, 1990.

Herzog, Tobey C. *Vietnam War Stories: Innocence Lost*. New York: Routledge, 1992.

Hickey, James. *Chrysanthemum in the Snow: The Novel of the Korean War*. New York: Crown, 1990.

Hillstrom, Kevin, and Laurie Collier Hillstrom. *The Vietnam Experience: A Concise Encyclopedia of American Literature, Songs, and Films*. Westport, Conn.: Greenwood, 1998.

Hinojosa, Rolando. *The Useless Servants*. Houston: Arte Publico Press, 1992.

Hoffert, Barbara. Rev. of *Buffalo Afternoon*. *Library Journal*. April 1, 1989, p. 115.

Huggett, William Turner. *Body Count*. New York: Putnam, 1973.

Hunter, Evan. *Sons*. Garden City, N.Y.: Doubleday, 1969.

Jaeger, Lowell. *War on War*. Logan: Utah State UP, 1988.

Jason, Philip K. *The Vietnam War in Literature: An Annotated Bibliography of Criticism*. Pasadena, Calif.: Salem Press, 1992.

Jason, Philip K., ed. *Fourteen Landing Zones: Approaches to Vietnam War Literature*. Iowa City: U of Iowa P, 1991.

Jeffords, Susan. *The Remasculinization of America: Gender and the Vietnam War*. Bloomington: Indiana UP, 1989.

Johannessen, Larry R. *Illumination Rounds: Teaching the Literature of the Vietnam War*. Urbana, Ill.: NCTE, 1992.

Just, Ward. *The American Blues*. New York: Viking Press, 1984.

———. *Stringer*. Boston: Little, Brown, 1974.

Kakutani, Michiko. "Novelists and Vietnam: The War Goes On." *New York Times Book Review*, April 15, 1984, pp. 1, 39–40.

Kalb, Bernard, and Marvin Kalb. *The Last Ambassador*. Boston: Little, Brown, 1981.

Karlin, Wayne. *Lost Armies*. New York: Henry Holt, 1988.

———. *Prisoners*. Willimantic, Conn.: Curbstone Press, 1998.

———. *Rumors and Stones: A Journey*. Willimantic, Conn.: Curbstone Press, 1996.

Karlin, Wayne, et al., eds. *Free Fire Zone: Short Stories by Vietnam Veterans*. New York: First Casualty Press, 1973.

Karlin, Wayne, Le Minh Khue, and Truong Vu, eds. *The Other Side of Heaven: Post-War Fiction by Vietnamese and American Writers*. Willimantic, Conn.: Curbstone Press, 1995.

Kelleher, Brian. *The Gathering Storm*. New York: Signet/NAL, 1989.

Kinney, Katherine. "'Humping the Boonies': Sex, Combat, and the Female in Bobbie Ann Mason's *In Country*." *Fourteen Landing Zones*, ed. Philip K. Jason.

Kopit, Arthur. *Indians*. New York: Hill and Wange, 1969.

Kovic, Ron. *Born on the Fourth of July*. New York: McGraw Hill, 1976.

Laskowsky, Henry J. "*Alamo Bay* and the Gook Syndrome." *Vietnam Generation* 1.2 (1989): 130–39.

Lawson, Jacqueline E. "'She's a pretty woman . . . for a gook': The Misogyny of the Vietnam War." *Journal of American Culture* 12.3 (1989): 55–65. Rpt. in *Fourteen Landing Zones*, ed. Philip K. Jason.

Lederer, William, and Eugene Burdick. *The Ugly American*. New York: Norton, 1958.

Lee, Larry [pen name for Larry Rottman]. *American Eagle*. Madrid, N.Mex.: Packrat Press, 1977.

Leepson, Marc. Review of O'Nan's *The Names of the Dead*. *Washington Post Book World*, April 21, 1996.

Leib, Franklin Allen. *The Fire Dream*. Novato, Calif.: Presidio, 1989.

Lewis, Lloyd B. *The Tainted War: Culture and Identity in Vietnam War Narratives*. Westport, Conn.: Greenwood, 1985.

Lifton, Robert Jay. *Home from the War: Vietnam Veterans. Neither Victims nor Executioners*. 1973. New York: Basic, 1985.

Lim, Shirley, and Amy Ling. *Reading the Literatures of Asian America*. Philadelphia: Temple UP, 1992.

Little, Loyd. *Parthian Shot*. New York: Ballantine, 1973.

Lockridge, Ernest. *Prince Elmo's Fire*. New York: Stein and Day, 1974.

Lomperis, Timothy J., and John Clark Pratt. *"Reading the Wind": The Literature of the Vietnam War*. Durham, N.C.: Duke UP, 1987.

Louvre, Alf, and Jeffrey Walsh, eds. *Tell Me Lies about Vietnam: Cultural Battles for the Meaning of the War*. Philadelphia: Open University Press, 1988.

Lynch, Michael. *An American Soldier*. Boston: Little, Brown, 1969.

MacKinnon, Catharine A. "Feminism, Marxism, Method, and the State: Toward Feminist Jurisprudence." *Contemporary Critical Theory*. Ed. Dan Latimer. San Diego: Harcourt, 1989. 604–33.

Mailer, Norman. *The Armies of the Night*. New York: New American Library, 1968.

———. *Why Are We in Vietnam?* New York: Putnam, 1967.

Malraux, André. *The Royal Way*. 1930. Trans. Stuart Gilbert. London: Methuen, 1935.

Martin, Andrew. *Receptions of War: Vietnam in American Culture*. Norman: U of Oklahoma P, 1993.

Mason, Bobbie Ann. *In Country*. New York: Harper and Row, 1985.

Mason, Van Wyck. *Saigon Singer*. Garden City, N.Y.: Doubleday, 1946.

McAleer, John, and Billy Dickson. *Unit Pride*. Garden City, N.Y.: Doubleday, 1981; rpt. London: Granada, 1982.

McDade, Charlie. *The Gulf*. San Diego: Harcourt Brace Jovanovich, 1986.

McDonald, Walter. *After the Noise of Saigon*. Amherst: U of Massachusetts P, 1988.

McGee, Celia. "A Soldier's Tale." *New York*, May 22, 1989, p. 26.

McKenna, Lindsay. *Dawn of Valor*. New York: Silhouette, 1991.

McLeod, Jesse T. *Crew Chief*. Canton, Ohio: Daring Books, 1988; New York: Dell, 1990.

Meador, D. J. *Unforgotten: A Novel of the Korean War*. Gretna, La.: Pelican, 1999.

Melling, Philip H. *Vietnam in American Literary Culture*. Boston: Twayne, 1990.

Michener, James. *The Bridges of Toko-Ri*. New York: Random House, 1953; rpt. New York: Fawcett, 1973.

Miller, Wayne Charles. *An Armed America: Its Face in Fiction. A History of the American Military Novel*. New York: New York UP, 1970.

Montero, Darrel. *Vietnamese Americans: Patterns of Resettlement and Socioeconomic Adaptation in the United States*. Boulder, Colo.: Westview Press, 1979.

Moore, Robin. *The Green Berets*. New York: Crown, 1965.

Mullin, Chris. *The Last Man Out of Saigon*. New York: Bantam, 1989.

Mulligan, John. *Shopping Cart Soldiers*. Willimantic, Conn.: Curbstone Press, 1997.

Myers, Thomas. *Walking Point: American Narratives of Vietnam*. New York: Oxford UP, 1988.

Neilson, Jim. *Warring Fictions: American Literary Culture and the Vietnam War Narrative*. Jackson: UP of Mississippi, 1998.

Newman, John. *Vietnam War Literature: An Annotated Bibliography of Imaginative Works about Americans Fighting in Vietnam.* 2d ed., Metuchen, N.J.: Scarecrow Press, 1988. 3d ed., with David A. Willson, David J. DeRose, Stephen P. Hidalgo, and Nancy J. Kendall. Lanham, Md.: Scarecrow Press, 1996.

O'Brien, Tim. *Going after Cacciato.* New York: Delacorte Press, 1978.

———. *In the Lake of the Woods.* Boston: Houghton Mifflin, 1994.

———. *The Things They Carried.* Boston: Houghton Mifflin, 1990.

O'Nan, Stewart. *The Names of the Dead.* New York: Doubleday, 1996; rpt. New York: Penguin, 1997.

Parker, T. Jefferson. *Little Saigon.* New York: St. Martin's, 1988.

Pary, R., et al. "Post-traumatic Stress Disorder in Vietnam Veterans," *American Family Physician* 37.2 (1988): 145–50.

Pelfry, William. *The Big V.* New York: Liveright, 1972.

Pitman, R. K., et al. "Psychophysiologic Responses to Combat Imagery of Vietnam Veterans with Posttraumatic Stress Disorder versus Other Anxiety Disorders," *Journal of Abnormal Psychology* 99:1 (1990): 49–54.

Potok, Chaim. *I Am the Clay.* New York: Knopf, 1992.

Pratt, John Clark. "Bibliographic Commentary: 'From the Fiction, Some Truths.'" In Timothy J. Lomperis, *"Reading the Wind": The Literature of the Vietnam War.* Durham, N.C.: Duke UP, 1987.

———. *The Laotian Fragments.* New York: Viking, 1974.

Pratt, John Clark, ed. *The Quiet American: Text and Criticism.* New York: Viking Penguin, 1995.

Proffitt, Nicholas. *Embassy House.* New York: Bantam, 1986.

———. *Gardens of Stone.* New York: Caroll and Graff, 1983.

———. "Pete Bravado's War and Peace." *New York Times Book Review*, May 21, 1989, p. 7.

Qui-Phiet Tran. "From Isolation to Integration: Vietnamese Americans in Tran Dieu Hang's Fiction." In *Reading the Literatures of Asian America.* See Lim, above.

Rabe, David. *The Basic Training of Pavlo Hummel* and *Sticks and Bones.* New York: Penguin, 1978.

Rank, Otto. "Feminine Psychology and Masculine Ideology." *Beyond Psychology*, 1941. New York: Dover, 1958. 235–70.

Riggan, Rob. *Free Fire Zone.* New York: Norton, 1984.

Rinaldi, Nicholas. *Bridge Fall Down.* New York: St. Martin's, 1985.

Ringnalda, Donald. *Fighting and Writing the Vietnam War.* Jackson: UP of Mississippi, 1994.

Roberts, John Maddox. *A Typical America Town.* New York: St. Martin's, 1994.

———. *The Ghosts of Saigon.* New York: St. Martin's, 1996.

Roskey, William. *Muffled Shots: A Year on the DMZ.* New York: Dell, 1988.

Roth, Robert. *Sand in the Wind.* Boston: Atlantic Monthly/Little, Brown, 1973.

Rowe, John Carlos, and Rick Berg, ed. *The Vietnam War and American Culture.* New York: Columbia UP, 1991.

Ruggero, Ed. *38 North Yankee.* New York: Pocket Books, 1990.

Rutledge, Paul James. *The Vietnamese Experience in America.* Bloomington: Indiana UP, 1992.

Schaeffer, Susan Fromberg. *Buffalo Afternoon.* New York: Knopf, 1989.

Scott, Joanna C. *Charlie and the Children.* Seattle: Black Heron Press, 1997.

Searle, William J., ed. *Search and Clear: Critical Responses to Selected Literature and Films of the Vietnam War.* Bowling Green, Ohio: Popular Press, 1978.

Sellers, Con. *Brothers in Battle*. New York: Pocket Books, 1989.

Shaara, Michael. *The Broken Land*. New York, 1968.

Shay, Jonathan. *Achilles in Vietnam*. New York: Atheneum, 1994.

Sheldon, Walt. *Troubling of a Star*. Philadelphia: Lippincott, 1953; rpt. New York: Bantam, 1954.

Slaughter, Frank C. *Sword and Scalpel*. Garden City, N.Y.: Doubleday, 1957; rpt. New York: Permabooks, 1958.

Slotkin, Richard. *Gunfighter Nation: The Myth of the Frontier in Twentieth-Century America*. New York: Atheneum, 1992; rpt. New York: HarperPerennial, 1993.

Smith, Lorrie. "Disarming the War Story." *America Rediscovered*. Eds. Owen W. Gilman, Jr., and Lorrie Smith. See Gilman, above.

Smith, Steven Phillip. *American Boys*. New York: Putnam, 1975.

Southeast Asian-American Communities. Vietnam Generation 2.3 (1990).

Spark, Alasdair. "Flight Controls: The Social History of the Helicopter as a Symbol of Vietnam." *Vietnam Images: War and Representation*, ed. Jeffrey Walsh and James Aulich. New York: St. Martin's, 1989.

Steel, Danielle. *Message from Nam*. New York: Delacorte, 1990.

Steinberg, David I. "Tenuous Impressions: Images of Korea in Western Literature." *Korea Journal* 22.9 (September 1982): 4–10.

Steltzer, Ulli. *The New Americans: Immigrant Life in Southern California*. Pasadena, Calif.: NewSage Press, 1988.

Stockholm International Peace Research Institute. *Incendiary Weapons*. Cambridge, Mass.: MIT Press, 1975.

Stone, Robert. *Dog Soldiers*. Boston: Houghton Mifflin, 1973.

Tal, Kali. "The Mind at War: Images of Women in Vietnam War Novels by Combat Veterans." *Contemporary Literature* 31.1 (1990): 76–96.

_____. Untitled Review. *Viet Nam Generation* 4.3–4 (Summer-Fall 1992): 140–43. Also available online at http://lists.village.virginia.edu/sixties/HTML_docs/Texts/Reviews/Tal_Detective.html. as "Contemporary Detective Fiction and the Vietnam War".

_____. *Worlds of Hurt: Reading the Literatures of Trauma*. New York: Cambridge UP, 1996.

Tavris, Carol and Carole Offir. *The Longest War: Sexual Differences in Perspective*. New York: Harcourt, 1977.

Tran Van Dinh. *Blue Dragon. White Tiger: A Tet Story*. Philadelphia: TriAm Press, 1983.

Truscott, Lucien K., IV. *Army Blue*. New York: Crown, 1989.

Van Devanter, Lynda, and Christopher Morgan. *Home Before Morning: The Story of an Army Nurse in Vietnam*. New York: Beaufort, 1983.

Vietnam Generation 1.3–4 (1989).

Vo Phien. *Intact*. Trans. James Banerian. Victoria, Australia: Vietnamese Language and Culture Publications, 1990.

Walby, Sylvia. *Patriarchy at Work: Patriarchal and Capitalist Relations in Employment*. Minneapolis: U of Minnesota P, 1986.

Walker, Wilbert L. *Stalemate at Panmunjon*. Baltimore: Heritage Press, 1980.

Walsh, Jeffrey. *American War Literature 1914 to Vietnam*. New York: St. Martin's, 1982.

Walsh, Jeffrey, and James Aulich, eds. *Vietnam Images: War and Representation*. New York: St. Martin's, 1989.

Webb, James. *Fields of Fire*. New York: Prentice-Hall, 1978.

Weigl, Bruce. *The Monkey Wars*. Athens: U of Georgia P, 1985.

_____. *Song of Napalm*. New York: Atlantic Monthly Press, 1988.

Weigl, Bruce, and Thanh T. Nguyen, eds. and trans. *Poems from Captured Documents.* Amherst: U of Massachusetts P, 1994.

West, Diana. "Does 'Born on the Fourth of July' Lie?" *Washington Times.* February 23, 1990, E1+.

Williams, John A. *Captain Blackman.* Garden City, N.Y.: Doubleday, 1972.

Willson, David. *REMF Diary.* Seattle: Black Heron, 1988.

Wilson, James C. *Vietnam in Prose and Film.* Jefferson, N.C.: McFarland, 1982.

Wittman, Sandra M. *Writing about Vietnam: A Bibliography of the Literature of the Vietnam Conflict.* Boston: G. K. Hall, 1989.

Wright, Stephen. *Meditations in Green.* New York: Scribner's, 1983.

Young, Marilyn B. *The Vietnam Wars: 1945–1990.* New York: Harper-Collins, 1991.

INDEX

About the Author

Philip K. Jason is professor of English at the United States Naval Academy. His fifteen books include other studies and anthologies of war literature: *Fourteen Landing Zones: Approaches to Vietnam War Literature* (1991), *The Vietnam War in Literature: An Annotated Bibliography of Criticism* (1992), and (with W. D. Ehrhart) *Retrieving Bones: Stories and Poems of the Korean War* (1999). Co-editor of the forthcoming *Encyclopedia of American War Literature*, Jason has also published studies of Anaïs Nin, three volumes of his own poetry, several poetry anthologies and reference works on poetry, and (with Allan B. Lefcowitz) the popular *Creative Writer's Handbook*.